51352

An Int...

York St John Co... JOHN
CAMPUS

...Roger T...

ED

D0280755

2411

An Introduction to Applied Linguistics

Approaches and Methods in Language Teaching

Roger T. Bell

Batsford Academic and Educational Ltd

© ROGER T. BELL 1981
First published 1981

All rights reserved. No part of this publication
may be reproduced, in any form or by any means,
without permission from the Publisher

Typeset by Hope Services, Abingdon, Oxon.
and printed in Great Britain by
Billing & Son Ltd
Worcester
for the publishers
Batsford Academic and Educational Ltd
an imprint of B.T. Batsford Ltd
4 Fitzhardinge Street
London W1H 0AH

British Library Cataloguing in Publication Data

ISBN 0 7134 3683 2 (cased)
ISBN 0 7134 3684 0 (limp)

This book
is dedicated to the memory of
PAUL ROBERTS (1917 – 1967)
who first taught me the rudiments
of applied linguistics

Contents

Contents

List of figures

Acknowledgements

I should like to thank a number of people for different kinds of help which they have given me in producing this book and, naturally, to exonerate them from any responsibility for the bad parts of it.

First of all, I have to thank the students of the MA in Linguistics for English Language Teaching at the University of Lancaster who put up with my struggling through the tangled thickets of Applied Linguistics over many years.

In addition, I would like to thank the students of St Martins College of Education in Lancaster on whom I tried out much of this book over a period of four years and the staff of the Language Project Centre in Singapore on whom I inflicted an earlier draft in late 1978.

Evengelos Afendras and David Richards at RELC in Singapore have also provided stern criticism of parts of this book as has my colleague at the Civil Service Institute in Singapore, Miss Teo Hee Lian.

I wish to thank them personally.

As ever library staff have put themselves out to chase up references; most helpful have been the staffs of the library of the University of Lancaster and that of the Regional Language Centre in Singapore.

Finally, I must acknowledge the support my wife Caroline has given me during the trying weeks of putting this manuscript together, the least of which was the onerous task of reading through the typescript and reaching a balance between my normal extremes of no punctuation at all or too much!

The following extracts have been reproduced by kind permission of the copyright holders:

'Stages in Language Counselor–Client Relationship from Dependency to Independence' (p. 65) and 'Counseling Foreing Language Research: Design of Different Positions' (p. 67), taken from *Counseling–Learning in Second Languages* – p. 29 and p. 53 – by C.A. Curran (1976) and published by the Apple River Press, Apple River, Illinois 61001.

Definition of training (p. 37), 'Ten steps in the design of training programmes' (p. 50), the algorithm 'Dealing with a complaint' (p. 162) and the table 'Faults Analysis' (p. 163) taken from *A Guide to Job Analysis* – p. 23 and p. 26 by T.H. Boydell (1970) and published by the British Association for Commercial and Industrial Education, 16 Park Cresent, London W1N 4AP.

'Speaking: General Assessment' (p. 213), 'Writing: General Assessment' (p. 214) and 'Reading: General Assessment' (p. 215) taken from *Approaches to self-assessment in foreign languages* by M. Oskarsson (1977) and published by the council of Europe, Strasbourg.

Unit on 'Obligation' (p. 249f), unit on 'Permission' (p. 251f) and the introduction 'To the teacher' (pp. 253–55) taken from *Survival English* by J.F. de Freitas (1978) and published by Macmillan, London.

Acknowledgements

A selection on 'subordinators' (p. 108f) and on 'modals' (pp. 228–31) taken from *Modern English: a textbook for foreign students* – pp. 407–11 and pp. 23–25 – by W.E. Rutherford (1965) and published by Harcourt Brace Jovanovich, Inc. New York.

'Proficiency levels' (p. 209f) 'supplementary scales' (p. 210f.) 'weighting table' and 'conversion table' (p. 212) taken from the *Foreign Service Institute Oral Interview* and published by the Foreign Service Institute, Department of State, Washington D.C. 20520.

'The ballistic system' (p. 185), 'the guided system' (p. 186), 'the adaptive system' (p. 187), 'four levels of evaluation in an adaptive system' (p. 188) and 'levels and questions' (p. 189) taken from 'Evaluating Training' by K.S. Brethower and G.A. Rummler (1979) published in the *Indian Journal of Training & Development*, New Delhi.

Unit 41 on 'can' (pp. 235–39) and unit 42 on 'must' (pp. 240–44) taken from *Situational English: Students' Book 2* – pp. 1–9 – published (1965) by the Department of Immigration and Ethnic Affairs, Canberra.

Extracts from Fries' preface (p. 97f), from Lesson XXIII (p. 98), from Lesson XI on 'modals' (pp. 219–26) taken from *English Sentence Patterns* by C.C. Fries and R. Lado (1958) – p. xvii, p. 225, p.p. 95–98 – and from the *Michigan Test of Aural Comprehension of English* (p. 204f) both published by the University of Michigan Press, Ann Arbor.

The example of 'Novish' (pp. 201–3) taken from 'Programmed Instruction' by A. Howatt – pp. 235–37 of *The Edinburgh Course in Applied Linguistics*, vol. 3: Techniques in Applies Linguistics – Oxford University Press.

Fig. 45 Illustration C 'A four-theme, three-year cyclic syllabus' (p. 69) taken from *Introducing Applied Linguistics* – p. 319 – by S. Pit Corder (1973) and published by the Penguin Press, Harmondsworth.

The 'vocabulary test' (p. 207) created by C. Robinson of the Oxford College of Technology.

The 'scrambled sentences' (p. 203f) created by E. Winter of the Hatfield Polytechnic.

11

TABLE OF SYMBOLS AND NOTATIONAL CONVENTIONS

*   Ungrammatical form e.g. *midnight killed him*

( )   Optional item e.g. *the letter was written (by him)*

       Choice of item e.g. tense $\longrightarrow$ $\begin{Bmatrix} present \\ past \end{Bmatrix}$

$\longrightarrow$ Is rewritten as e.g. x $\longrightarrow$ y i.e. x is rewritten as y.

/ /   Phonemic transcription e.g. /r/ i.e. the 'r' phoneme.

[ ]   Phonetic transcription e.g. [r] i.e. trilled 'r'.

Introduction

Most people don't read introductions but you are obviously an exception and I thank you for it because there are a small number of points which I want to make at the outset which may get missed later:

a) What this book is about.

b) Why this book was written.

c) How this book is organized.

It may well be possible to deduce the answers to these questions by reading the book — indeed, I hope it will be — but that is likely to be heavier going than to read it here; thank you.

What this book is about
This book is about applied linguistics. In particular, it is about some ideas in applied linguistics which have influenced or may influence in the future the teaching and learning of English as a Foreign Language.

What this book is *not* is either a textbook on linguistics or psychology or a handbook crammed with practical hints for classroom teaching. It is neither wholly theoretical nor wholly practical: it falls between the two extremes. Perhaps a word on applied linguistics is in order here.

The applied linguist stands in relation to the theoretical linguist and to the practical teacher of languages much as the engineer does to the academic physicist and the workers on the site. His role is that of the middleman, deriving information about what can be done, and how, from the theoretician, and passing that on, in a more readily useable form, to the practitioners from whom he derives feedback, for the theoretician, about the feasibility of applications of his theory.

The linguist and the teacher have different goals, methods and attitudes and it is the task of the applied linguist to attempt to bridge the gap between them.

The goal of the linguist is nothing less than the creation of a universal theory which will explain the phenomenon of language. The goal of the teacher is to help learners to master language — whatever it is — and in this the teacher may, rightly, look to the linguist for descriptions of specific languages on which he can draw in creating his syllabus.

The methods of the linguist are formal and abstract — we have already said that his goal is the creation of a theory — while that of the teacher is an essentially functional and practical one.

The attitudes of linguistics and teachers towards language are also in

13

contrast. The linguist sees language as a system — either of forms or of knowledge — but the teacher sees language as a set of skills.

It is to act as a channel of communication between the linguist (and, as we shall see, the psychologist) and the teacher that applied linguistics has grown up seeking practical applications for the theories and models of language provided by the linguist and asking teachers to weigh the insights of the academics in order to choose from among them those which seem most revealing and useful.

Why this book was written

The main motivation behind the writing of this book was a feeling of dissatisfaction with most 'introductions to applied linguistics' which often turned out to be either introductions to linguistics with a chapter or two near the end about *what* to teach or else handbooks for teachers of particular languages — more often than not, the language was English — which gave valuable suggestions on *how* to teach but skated over the reasons for selecting one particular approach rather than another.

What was needed, or so it seemed to me, was a book which discussed not only *what* might be taught — as the linguistically oriented books did — but also *how* it might be taught; as the handbooks did.

The need, as I saw it, was for a book which would answer two key questions or, at least, would raise them and suggest some possible answers:

a) What is language?

b) How do people learn languages?

Without answers to those two questions we cannot reasonably go on to ask the question that we really want answered:

c) How can we help people to learn languages?

How this book is organized

The organization of this book hinges on the questions we have just raised. In *Part I* — the first three chapters — we consider the implications of the questions for our *present* needs as syllabus designers and language teachers. In *Part II* — the next four chapters — we continue to examine the key issues which we believe underlie the enterprise of language teaching but from a *historical* point of view. We try to trace a path through the controversies of the last 100 years from the turn of the century to the present day. Finally, there are four appendices. Each takes up a topic which has been touched upon in the body of the book but not dealt with in detail there.

PART ONE

SYLLABUS DESIGN: THE KEY ISSUES

In the first three chapters of this book we shall attempt to define the problems which face the designer of training materials in general and language training materials in particular.

To begin with, we shall ask questions about the nature of language and the process of language learning which will preoccupy us throughout the book. We shall also suggest, in outline, some alternative answers to the key questions and present the elements which go together to create an *approach* in applied linguistics i.e. the inputs from linguistics and psychology, in particular, which lead us to accept a particular linguistic theory and a particular theory of learning and which take us on to the design of our syllabus, the selection of our method and the production of our materials.

Next, we ask ourselves how we can help those who wish to learn languages and build up, step-by-step, a procedure for designing training programmes, beginning with the client's request and proposed trainee group and ending with the evaluation of the programme and the provision of feedback to all concerned.

Finally, we look at three types of language syllabus — grammatical, situational and notional — which have been influential in language teaching during the last hundred years and expand on the problem of grading and of organizing the syllabus; both issues which came up in Chapter 2 but were not treated in sufficient detail there.

That will round off our *synchronic* overview of what seem to us to be the key issues facing the syllabus designer today and will have laid the foundations for a *diachronic* review of the kinds of answers teachers and linguists have given to these key questions during the last 100 years.

1 A few questions and several answers

Before even listing the questions, I feel obliged to try to justify asking them at all. This is a book about applied linguistics and, in particular, about some crucial issues in the study of language and its use as a vehicle of communication which I believe should be raised and discussed. My right to raise these issues derives not from a mere seven years of teaching English as a foreign language or thirteen more studying and teaching linguistics but from my role as one of the many different kinds of people involved in some way with the complex enterprise of language teaching and learning. Some of them are politicians and educational planners whose responsibility it is to decide who shall be taught what. Others are educational administrators faced by the task of putting into practice the political decisions of the government and balancing scarce resources and amenities as they do so. Yet others work in the linguistic and human sciences and wish to pass on what they have learned about language to a wider public. Others are practical language teachers faced by the day-to-day task of getting across the facts of the new language and giving learners the opportunity to develop skill in using it. And, finally, the largest group of all, for whom all the effort is being made, the learners, each with his own needs and interests, aptitudes and difficulties. Everyone of us has interesting experiences to relate and some of those experiences may well turn out to be helpful to others. I know something about the problems of facing a class, of struggling with inadequate textbooks, of the fearful embarrassment of knowing that something cannot be said or written but being unable to explain why. But it is not that that I wish to write about. There are many thousands of teachers with far more experience who could do that better. I wish to limit myself to three questions (my apologies to the brave souls who read the introduction and now find that I am about to repeat myself!) which seem to me to be crucial to any principled decision on the choice of an approach to language teaching:

1. What do we believe language is?
2. How do we believe people learn languages?

And, if we can come up with satisfying answers to these two questions, we can make a stab at the one we really want to ask:

3. How can we help people to learn languages?

1.1 WHAT IS LANGUAGE?

We must start with this question. Until we have decided what we think

18

language is, we cannot make a sensible decision on what we should be teaching. That much is, presumably, self-evident, but the answer to the question, unfortunately, is not. There are two answers, at least.

1.1.1. A linguistic answer

If one looks at language as a linguist, one sees it as a *code*; a set of elements which can or cannot occur and which can or cannot combine in various appropriate ways.

Language, for the linguist, is *form*; sounds, letters, their combinations into larger units such as words, sentences and so forth. Such a set of forms would also be expected to have meaning and the elements and sequences, by virtue of having meaning, would naturally be expected to be used for communication between individuals who shared the same rules.

Typically, the linguist sees language as a *closed system* — like those of mathematics, chemistry, symbolic logic — internally consistent but insulated from the environment in which it occurs. The numbers of mathematics, for example, have no external meaning. They mean the same whether they refer to atoms, human beings, stars or whatever.

Most linguists find it convenient to subdivide the system into three interrelated subsystems:

i) *Syntax:* the rules for listing elements and specifying their permitted combinations.

ii) *Semantics:* the rules for assigning meaning to units permitted by the syntax.

iii) *Pragmatics:* the rules for relating permitted units of language to social behaviour.

The British traffic-light system might provide a useful illustration:

i) *Syntax:* a) only the colours *red, amber, green* permitted to occur singly.

  b) only *red + amber* may occur in combination

  c) the only sequence permitted is:

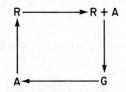

  d) this sequence is infinitely recursive.

ii) *Semantics:* a) *red* = 'stop'

  b) *amber* = 'prepare to stop'

c) *green* = 'go'

d) *red* + *amber* = 'prepare to go'

iii) *Pragmatics:* 'stop' = (for a motorist) decelerate, check in mirror for vehicles behind, optionally give a 'slowing down' hand signal, foot gently on brake and depress, prepare to declutch and change to a lower gear, etc.

There are three or four points which are worth making here:

a) The existence of a particular element in either system is *arbitrary*. We could have chosen in the traffic light system *blue* rather than *red*. In English, we could have 'chosen' to make use of the Italian 'gl' sound, /ʎ/ as in *figlio*; 'son', but we haven't.

b) Combinations are equally arbitrary. We could have *red* + *green* in the traffic light system or (as in Singapore) have forbidden the *red* + *amber* combination. In English, we have three sounds /k/, /æ/ and /t/ available and permit the combinations /kæt/, /ækt/ and (tæk/ — *cat, act, tack* — but not (the asterisk* marks an unattested form) */ktæ/, */tkæ/ or* /ætk/.

The same is true if we take words as our elements:

1) He speaks English often.
2) *He speaks often English.
3) He often speaks English.
4) Often he speaks English.

c) Meanings are just as arbitrary. *Red* = 'stop' because of danger, we might argue. Why is *red* dangerous? Blood? Fire? But without blood we are dead and without fire would have advanced little in civilization. Even odder is *red* = 'stop' and *amber* = 'prepare to stop', which together mean 'prepare to go'.

d) The enormous complexity of pragmatics has led to that level of linguistic description being only touched upon by linguists proper. Though, as we shall see, it is the essential point of the social scientist and an area in which psycho- and socio-linguists also work.

For the linguist, then, the definition of language with which he is happiest to work would be something like

A system of signals conforming to the rules which constitute its grammar, (Greenberg 1957).

A rough linguistic model, albeit a little conservative, since many contemporary linguists would prefer to begin with semantics, would look like this:

Figure 1.1
A simplified linguistic model

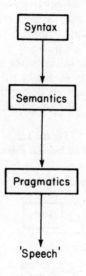

We shall see later that there is a further dichotomy within the linguistic camp between those who view *form* as *substance* — the physical manifestations of the language in speech and writing — and those who, conversely, locate form in the *mind* of the user of the language and stress that the language is not so much what the user *does* as what he *knows* i.e. a clash between an *empiricist* and a *rationalist* view of the nature of language. Since both views have had considerable influence on language teaching, we shall not pursue them here but raise the issue again when we discuss structuralism and transformational-generative linguistics in Chapter 5.

1.1.2. A human science answer
If, by way of contrast, one looks at language as a human scientist — an anthropologist, sociologist, social psychologist, psychologist, etc. — one's starting point is the direct converse of that of the linguist. One asks the

same question 'what is language?' but actually seeks an answer to the rather different question 'what is language *for?*' or 'what do people *do* with language?' i.e. a *functional* rather than a *formal* orientation. That language is a code is, for a human scientist, a 'given'. He accepts that there are elements which may or may not combine and that combinations have meaning and that there is arbitrariness in the system. What intrigues him is not so much the code itself but the people whose infinitely flexible artifact it is.

Typically, the human scientist sees language as an *open system* interacting with, changed by, and changing, its environment. He will see language as part of the culture of the group, perhaps even its most distinctive defining characteristic but, wherever he places it in relation to other aspects of human behaviour, his emphasis will be on the human-ness of human language and its place in human society as one of the most necessary and complex of all social skills. He will begin his description at the very point at which the linguist intends to stop — the pragmatics — arguing that language is a

Figure 1.2.
A simplified human science model

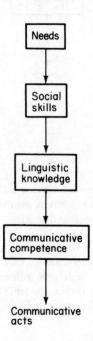

social skill which exists in order to satisfy individual and group needs. His view of language will be broader than that of the linguist, since he will want to include in his description of 'language' not only linguistic knowledge (the knowledge of the grammatical rule-system) but knowledge of, and ability to use, linguistic and social knowledge to create communicative acts which are not only *grammatically correct* but also *socially appropriate*.

The human scientist might well prefer a definition of language of the type:

A set of culturally transmitted behaviour patterns shared by a group of individuals. (Greenberg *ibid*.).

A rough human sciences model will probably look rather like Figure 1.2.

We have already commented on the divergence of opinion in linguistics on scientific method — the choice of an empiricist or rationalist approach — and should add here than an identical split exists in the human sciences. In anthropology, for example, and in sociology recent developments have been towards a rationalist approach — the cognitive anthropology of Frake (1969) or the cognitive sociology of Cicourel (1973) are clear examples — which contrast with earlier empiricism just as TG does in linguistics with the earlier structuralist tradition (see Bell 1976 218–222 for further discussion).

However, the issue though recognized by psycho- and sociolinguists has yet to reach the level of importance that it has reached in the other disciplines; a point which we shall take up again in the introduction to Part II.

1.2. HOW DO PEOPLE LEARN LANGUAGES?

Even if we had decided on a definition of language which satisfied us — and we have not — we are still left with the second question. Assuming we are agreed on *what* to teach, we cannot get any further on deciding *how* to help the learner until we come out openly and state how we believe people learn languages.

As before, we wish to take the opportunity in this chapter to outline the major views on language learning and pick them up later in greater detail.

1.2.1. A behaviourist answer
One answer to the general question 'how do people learn?' which was generally accepted for some 40 years — 1920s to 1960s — and, as we shall see in Chapter 5, linked directly to language teaching, was 'by stimulus and response'. We shall show later how, in practice, this view of learning in general became applied to language learning in particular but will limit ourselves here to listing, without comment, the major characteristics and axioms of behaviourist psychology:

a) Having postulated a mechanistic view of Man and hence disposed of such notions as mind, the psychologist, in attempting to explain human learning, was necessarily forced into a strongly empiricist position, what was observable was to be explained, that which was unobservable could neither be explained nor form part of an explanation. (See further discussion in 5.1.3.).

b) Learning consists of acquiring habits, initially by imitation e.g. parrots do this rather well and Minah Birds embarassingly better!

c) Next, the 'good' response elicits a reward of some kind; my Minah Bird is going to get the opposite treatment but doesn't know it yet!

d) Finally, the habit is reinforced by having the stimulus recur so often that the response becomes automatic e.g. the Minah Bird now greets me, to my horror, every day with 'Hello Darling' in *my* voice! (Hence my threat in the comment above).

So, we learn by imitation, mimicry, constant practice and, in the end, our new language habits become as fixed as those of our mother tongue.

1.2.2. A cognitive answer

In strong reaction against the behaviourism of the late 1950s, Chomsky (1959), already the leader of the new school of transformational–generative linguists, attacked Skinner's (1957) theories and denied virtually all of the previously accepted axioms of language learning.

Once again, we wish to leave more detailed discussion until later (5.2.3.) and limit ourselves to the barest outline here:

a) Having accepted a mentalistic view of man and thereby re-established the notion of mind, cognitive psychologists denied the tenability of an empiricist position and insisted that it was the activities of the mind, the ways it processed, stored and retrieved knowledge that were of interest not any trivial physical manifestation of that knowledge.

b) Learning, it was argued, was a matter of 'making sense' of the data which the brain received through the senses.

c) What was important was the ability of the individual to respond to new situations for which stimulus–response habits alone could not possibly have prepared him.

d) Learning, they asserted, was a mental process not a physical one; better to know and be unable to say, than to say without understanding!

1.3. HOW CAN WE HELP?

What we can do to help others to learn foreign languages depends on who we are or, rather, *where* we are in the power structure on which educational planning rests.

There are at least four levels of responsibility and influence each with relatively well-defined problems to face and solutions to propose. In Figure 1.3, we list these levels, the agencies which represent them, the issues they face and the types of output they typically produce. The table is arranged hierarchically — from most to least *powerful*; not from most to least important — and so runs from those whose sole function is to plan in very general terms, to those who often have, sadly, the sole function of carrying out, with little personal freedom, instructions imposed from above. That this is a far from satisfactory state of affairs is self-evident but it is not the purpose of this book to search for solutions to problems of educational and political organization.

Figure 1.3
Language planning: levels, agencies and issues

Level	Agency	Issues	Output
1. Political	Government	Whether, what language and whom to teach	Reports, etc. on education
2. Linguistic	a) Pure Linguist	What models of language there are	Scientific grammars
	b) Applied Linguist	Which model(s) to choose. What, when, how much to teach	Pedagogic grammars
	c) Sociolinguist	What groups have what language needs	Sociolinguistic surveys
3. Psychological	a) Psychologist	What models of learning there are	Theories of learning
	b) Psycholinguist	Which model(s) of learning to choose. How to reflect such models in the syllabus	Surveys of learning styles
4. Pedagogical	a) Professional Educationist	How to combine or balance all the above	Syllabuses, programmes, textbooks, etc.
	b) Classroom Teacher	How to teach	Modifications of textbook materials/personal or group-made materials

1.3.1. The political level

Decisions on language planning — as on other types of planning — are made by politicians i.e. by government. Cabinet or its equivalent may or may not seek 'expert' advice and may or may not take note of such advice before arriving at its decision on which language(s) should be taught, to what category of learner, for how long a period, drawing on what proportion of the available national resources, etc. The 'policy' which is handed down will inevitably be couched in political terms which may make excellent political slogans but will need a great deal of reformulating before they can form the basis of a set of goals for the teaching of the language e.g. 'we must have clean, clear, correct, concise written English'. It is always one of the tasks of those in the lower levels to make this type of policy statement plain, unambiguous and really operational.

1.3.2. The linguistic level
The linguistic level subdivides into three secondary levels:

a) *The pure linguist* — the descriptive linguist — whose interest is in the description and explanation of the phenomenon of language, rather than the problems involved in the learning or teaching of specific languages. He may, of course, find that some of the insights of psycholinguists in particular help him in his work. Conversely, his descriptions may provide insights into the structure of language which are helpful to the applied linguist and language teacher but the descriptive linguist, as such, would see information transfer of this kind as, at best, an unlooked for bonus or, at worst, a potentially dangerous trivialization of his efforts.

b) *The applied linguist* — like the engineer whose knowledge of physics and mathematics must be as up-to-date as possible, the applied linguist has the responsibility of keeping up with the theoretical work of the descriptive linguist and being constantly on the look-out for insights and models which he can use and re-present in a form which is more palatable to language learners (and language teachers!) i.e. he is constantly trying to bridge the gap between the theoretical preoccupations of the descriptive linguist — presented in the form of highly abstract models — and the practical needs of the classroom, with, for example, a *pedagogical grammar* which, without misrepresenting the ideas expressed by the theoretician, can be used as a source of data about the language by the teacher (for a fuller discussion of the distinction between descriptive and pedagogical grammars see Note, p.30).

c) *The Sociolinguist* is interested in who speaks what to whom and when and where and why i.e. in the social contexts of language use. He may adopt a theoretical stance towards language teaching and learning and concentrate on building abstract models of language use but his commitment to the social aspects of language makes it very likely that he will become involved, at some level, in the creation of language training programmes. At the very least, he will be able to offer advice on ways of discovering needs and of delineating groups; advice which ought to be made available to the politician as he makes his general plans and to the educational administrator and teacher as they attempt to actualize those plans in the classroom.

1.3.3. The psychological level
The psychological level divides into two secondary levels:

a) *The psychologist.* The 'pure' psychologist sees his role as discovering and explaining the structure of the human mind and is, of necessity, interested in how people learn. But, like the descriptive linguist, his theories and models are unlikely to have direct application to the problems faced by the language teacher. Like the ideas of the 'pure' linguist, those of the 'pure' psychologist need a middleman to put them across in a form which the practitioner can comprehend; this is the role of the psycholinguist.

b) *The psycholinguist,* like the sociolinguist, is interested in the process of language learning — often he is as much involved in the study of L1 (Mother Tongue) Acquisition in pre-school children as in L2 (Foreign or Second Language) learning by children or adults — and has unique information on theories of learning to offer the practical teacher. His relationship with the 'pure' psychologist should be essentially the same as that of the sociolinguist to the 'pure' linguist — keeping up-to-date and passing on interesting ideas about the learning process to the teacher.

1.3.4. The Pedagogical Level
Like the psychological, this level also subdivides into two sub-levels:

a) *The Professional Educationist* has the difficult task of mediating between the political level and the practical level of actual teaching and, at the same time, attempting to keep a balance between the academic and applied academic factors we have just been outlining. Typically, the professional educationist will be employed by a Ministry of Education — perhaps as a curriculum development officer or an inspector — an Examinations Board, a Teacher Training Institution, a Department of Education or a Department of (Applied) Linguistics in a University. He may even be a practising teacher — perhaps the head of a large ELT department or the teacher in charge of a group of non-centralized teachers of, for example, immigrants or migrant workers. The essential distinction between the professional educationist and the classroom teacher is one of power. The professional educationist, by virtue of his connection with political or academic influence, or both, is likely to be responsible for the design or implementation of the syllabuses under which the actual teacher is obliged to work and, perhaps, even for the production of the very textbooks he will use.

b) *The Classroom Teacher* has the final responsibility for activating the syllabus in the classroom with the learners. His sole preoccupation — as a teacher — is with methodology i.e. *how* to teach. More often than not the content of his syllabus is imposed by others and he has no say in its creation. What he can do, however, is modify the materials he is given to suit the specific needs of his own learners and, perhaps, if he is in the right environment make materials himself either alone or with colleagues.

1.3.5. Who works out the syllabus?

It is rather paradoxical that the person most directly involved in the language learning process — the classroom teacher — is the one who is most deprived of the power to influence language and educational planning. However, as we shall see throughout this book, language teaching is full of paradoxes and this is only the first of many.

1.4. CONCLUSION

This chapter has raised the two key issues around which the rest of this book will revolve and which we firmly believe must be answered before we can set about helping people to learn languages:

What do we believe language to be? The answer to this will give us our *linguistic* orientation i.e. will provide the linguistic *input* to our *approach* and provide us with a first approximation to the specification of the *content* of our course.

How do we believe languages are learned? The answer to this will give us our *psychological* orientation; the psychological input to our approach and provide us with a check on the content and, particularly, the *method* we will adopt in implementing our course.

There are, as a result of the several interested parties involved in language learning, other inputs — in particular, political and sociological — from groups whose goals and ways of evaluating the 'success' of language training differ from those of the applied linguist (we discuss this in some detail in section 2.2.9) but we shall limit our rough model of the genesis of an *approach* (see Figure 1.4. below) to the linguistic and psychological, lumping the rest together, for the moment, as 'other inputs'.

One or two comments might make this diagram clear:

a) At the theoretical level — linguistic and psychological — the input consists of the theories (or, more correctly, *models*) of the structure of language and the nature of human learning respectively (A1 and B1). This level gives us information on language, on the one hand, and on learners and learning, on the other.

b) At the next level (2) the information consists of (A2) *pedagogical grammars* in which the information derived from linguistics is represented in a pedagogically oriented way — in a form which the practical teacher can use as a source of *content* for his course and (B2) the psychological equivalent; descriptions of models of learning aimed at teachers rather than at academic psychologists.

c) The third level entails the selection of information from linguistics and psychology — and from the other sources — to create an *approach*; our statement of belief in a particular linguistic theory and a particular psychological theory, tempered by the practical, political and sociological information we also have at our disposal.

d) The syllabus, methods and materials derive, or should derive, from

Figure 1.4.
The Genesis of an Approach in Applied Linguistics

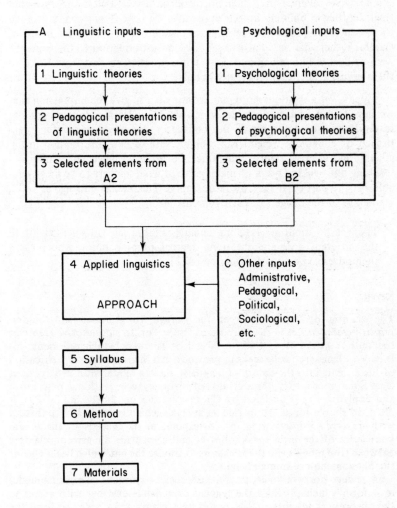

our *approach* but, just as it is unlikely that we could take a linguistic or psychological theory and apply it directly to the needs of the learner, so too the design of the syllabus, selection of method and creation of materials will never be an instant or automatic matter. We shall be concerned, particularly in the next chapter, to set out clearly the steps which we believe have to be undertaken in the design of training materials in particular.

e) Neither *approach* nor *method* have been adequately defined yet, nor have we assigned any weighting to the various inputs or asked *why* we should have taken a particular linguistic or psychological theory rather than another in building up our approach. We have intentionally avoided these issues here, since we feel that they would be better treated in a later chapter rather than in what is essentially an introduction to the issues we wish to deal with in this book. In the introduction to Part 2, we take up these points again in rather greater detail.

Finally, on a cautious note, we do not wish to give the impression that we have found a 'magic formula' which will allow learners to learn and use instantly and perfectly. We do not believe in such magic and prefer an approach of enlightened eclecticism, being aware of new information in linguistics and human sciences which has a bearing on language learning and teaching and seeking ways of making use of what appears to be most valuable for the particular task we face. George Ticknor, as long ago as 1832, warned us of the dangers of narrow-mindedness.

There is no mode of teaching languages (applicable) to persons of all the different ages and different degrees of preparation who present themselves to be taught. (Ticknor 1832)

NOTE

The essential distinction between the *pedagogical grammar* and the *descriptive grammar* lies in the purpose of the writer. In a *descriptive grammar* the author attempts to build a model of language which represents his theory of language i.e. he seeks to provide other linguists with a specification of his insights into the nature of language. Such a model must satisfy, or at least attempt to satisfy, three criteria of adequacy; observational, descriptive and explanatory (as outlined by Chomsky 1965 pp. 24–27 and 30–37). It must, in simple terms, a) provide an analysis which is minimally consistent with *observed primary data*, b) correspond in its analysis to the *innate knowledge* of the ideal speaker-hearer and c) provide a means of selecting between rival models and theories so as to choose the one which best *explains* the phenomenon of human language.

A *pedagogical grammar*, in contrast, seeks to *present* an existing model in a form which provides the teacher or syllabus designer with access to the theoretical insights of the descriptive grammar in order to form the basis of language teaching syllabuses and materials. The three criteria for adequacy which apply to the descriptive grammar are not ignored by the writer of the pedagogical grammar – they are of interest to him as criteria for selecting which descriptive grammar he will present – but are, so to speak, subordinated to the need to express the findings of the linguistic theory in a practical way. In addition, the descriptive grammar must be consistent in its choice of theory – one model-one theory – but a pedagogical grammar can be eclectic and draw on more than one theory.

A clear example of a non-eclectic pedagogical grammar would be Thomas (1965) which is based exclusively on Transformational-Generative Grammar (see 5.2.4.) while Quirk *et al.* (1972) can be taken as representative of an eclectic model drawing as it does on both systemic grammar (q.v. 6.2.1.) and TG.

SUGGESTED FURTHER READING

Bell R. T. (1976), *Sociolinguistics: Goals, Approaches and Problems*
Chapter 1 of this book is concerned with the scope, aims and problems of sociolinguistics; the sub-discipline of linguistics which attempts to bridge the gap between the 'linguistic' and 'human science' approaches to the description and explanation of language.

Bright J. A. & McGregor G. P. (1970), *Teaching English as a Second Language*
This is one of the standard 'teacher's guides' in ELT. It is aimed at suggesting answers to the pedagogical question 'what ought the classroom teacher to do?'. The level of interest is methods and materials.

Christophersen P. L. (1973), *Second Language Learning*
This book gives a short introduction to the topic of second language learning stressing the distinction between L1 acquisition and L2 learning and concentrating on the notion of bilingualism. It may be useful as a quick resume of knowledge and practice in the field up to the end of the 1960s.

Corder S. P. (1973), *Introducing Applied Linguistics*
Just as Bright and McGregor may be thought of as a 'classic' at the level of pedagogy, Corder is very much a 'classic' at the level of *approach*. Beginners should accept that it assumes a good deal of prior knowledge and start with Part I returning to the other sections as the topics they contain become relevant.

Crystal D. (1968), *What is Linguistics?*
Probably the best, and certainly the shortest, introduction to linguistics. It covers a very wide range and is written in straightforward language.

2 Designing training programmes

In the previous chapter, we considered three key questions; the nature of language, the manner in which languages are learned and the ways in which teachers might help learners.

Our answers turned out to be remarkably complex, representing alternative points of view and, in the design and implementation of language syllabuses, to involve a surprising range of interested parties.

What we shall attempt to do in this chapter is to draw on the popular analogy of the training enterprise (and language teaching and learning is part of the training enterprise) as an industrial process to list a series of steps which we believe must be followed if we are to create satisfactory training facilities — not merely *language* syllabuses. One point which we will be stressing is that there is much in common in training in general on which the language teacher can profitably draw.

In later chapters, we will be able to relate the approaches of particular periods or practitioners to our schematic training design and show where and how particular developments came in.

2.1. ON PROCESSES IN GENERAL

It is something of a commonplace to compare language teaching with an industrial production process. After all, it is argued, both have an *input* of 'raw materials', some *process* which acts upon and changes the 'raw materials' in some planned way and from which they emerge as the 'finished product'; the *output*.

The fact that our input consists of complex human beings rather than, say, simple china clay, our process a little understood series of events which alter the mental and physical abilities of the learner, rather than merely e.g. heating at a predetermined temperature for a predetermined length of time and the output for us is a group of changed individuals rather than several trays of coffee cups does not invalidate the analogy; or so we are told!

Despite the very obvious differences between making coffee cups and teaching a foreign language, the model has certain merits which we would do well to consider.

If we continue to talk in terms of 'input', 'process' and 'output', we may find that we are focusing our attention on the differences between our system and that of the production engineer, when what we ought to be doing is seeking realistic and helpful similarities. Let us, for a moment, use simpler 'commonsense' words. We have a group of potential learners,

Figure 2.1.
A simple input–output system

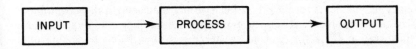

we want to do something to them and we want them to be changed when we have done it i.e. we have an input–output system.

It would be best now to try to specify the contents of each of the three boxes in our figure, since by doing that we ought to be able to see where the analogy starts to break down and what changes we need to make to the system to keep the analogy going, if it still seems useful.

2.1.1. Input

The input to the system consists not only of the minds and bodies of our students but our own minds and bodies as well. All the human beings involved in the process come into it with individual and group characteristics, attitudes to learning in general and to language learning in particular — perhaps particular strong feelings about the language we want them to learn — and we, the teachers, are by no means immune. Equally, previous knowledge and experience will form part of the input; for learner and teacher alike.

The specification of the input characteristics and the selection of individuals who match those specifications are clearly tasks that the sociolinguist ought to be happy and qualified to attempt (see Section 6.4). Often, as we suggested before (see Section 1.3.1.), the selection both of the criteria and the personnel is made at governmental level and it is left to the sociolinguist to try to make more sense — as he sees it — of the population he has been given.

To return to our coffee-cup analogy for a moment, we defined the input as 'china clay' but not all china clay is likely to be suitable; we need to select that which *prima facie* looks as though it will make good cups. We need, that is, some kind of quality-control test right at the beginning of the process. In language teaching, aptitude tests based on artificial languages or assumptions based on the earlier language learning ability of the individual have often been, and still are, used for this purpose. I clearly recollect being selected to study Latin — rather than woodwork — at school on the grounds that I appeared to be fairly good at French. Perhaps that was a

33

reasonable assumption since both are romance languages, though why my ability in French disqualified me from handling hammers, chisels and saws I have never understood!

We shall look later in some detail at the whole testing process — before, during and after the course (see Appendix C).

Teachers, naturally, are expected to be professionally qualified and experienced in the language they are teaching and, as time has gone on, the entry requirements for the profession have increased beyond all recognition. The day when mere native-speaker competence was judged to be sufficient qualification for a foreign-language teacher is now, let us hope forever, behind us!

Later, too, we shall take up another point about learners (and teachers); so far we have been considering *who* they are and, to some extent, *what* they know but *where* they are and indeed *when* they are setting about the learning of the language constitute additional variables which we need to allow for. It is probably true to say that it is only in recent years that the learner has come to prominence as one of the key factors in syllabus design, so we shall leave this issue until Chapter 6 when we can point out in a little more detail the questions involved and the kinds of answer sociolinguists in particular, can give.

2.1.2. Process

Assuming that we have specified who our learners are to be and have gathered a good deal of information about them, we are now faced by the question 'what should we teach them?'. In industry, the trainer would set about producing a thorough job analysis. With this the general comments about training needs, which are likely to have come to him from the directors of the company, are broken down into the types of knowledge and skill required for the particular job. Indeed, as we shall see later in Chapter 6 when we discuss ESP (English for Special Purposes), the language course designer needs to adopt very much the same approach.

Reduced to its simplest, the process must fill the gap between the knowledge and skills we judge the learners to already possess and those which we consider it desirable for them to have.

To design such as a process will require of us the answers to a further series of questions about our learners and our objectives:

a) What do they know?

b) What ought they to know?

c) Can we define the gap between what they know now and what is expected of them?

d) What exactly are our objectives?

e) How can we achieve those objectives?

Considered answers to these and related questions should lead us to the creation of our training process. Whether we have found the *right* answers and produced the *right* process we will not, of course, know until we have examined the *output*.

2.1.3. Output
At the end of the programme, we need to test whether, and to what degree, the objectives we set initially have been reached. Do our participants now know, and can they now do, what we felt was lacking at the beginning? In fact, we need two rather different kinds of evaluation:

a) *Internal validation* of the programme which asks 'did the programme teach what it set out to teach?'

b) *External evaluation* of the programme which asks — from the point of view of the client: the receiving system to which the learner is to return — 'was the programme worth it in terms of improved efficiency on the job?'

Both questions need to be asked, since we need both types of feedback; what we and our learners felt about the programme and what the outside world feels. The two reactions may well be different, since the criteria of success are very likely to differ internally and externally.

2.1.4. Three models of training
We have been arguing that all training schemes must, of necessity, contain an input, a process and an output and have been implying that the key element which distinguishes the sophisticated system from the unsophisticated is the extent to which *feedback* is built into the design of the system.

Three types of system defined by the degree to which each makes use of feedback have been suggested (Brethower & Rummler 1979). We shall outline them very briefly here and discuss them in much greater detail in Appendix C.

a) *Ballistic system:* in this system the input is fed into the process and passed out of it in the form of the changed output. No feedback is provided from the output back to the input and, hence, there is no mechanism for changing either the input or the process.

b) *Guided system:* in this system feedback is provided from the output to the input which allows some degree of *validation* of the course — some measurement of its *efficiency* — and therefore revisions of the input and process.

c) *Adaptive system:* in this system feedback is provided not only from the output but also from the *receiving system* to which the participants return after the course. This dual feedback allows not only some degree of *validation* to take place but also external *evaluation* of the whole enterprise. The adaptive system by being responsive to the requirements of the receiving system allows for the assessment of both the *efficiency* and *effectiveness* of the programme.

2.1.5. Summary
We have, so far, only sketched the notion of the design and implementation

of training programmes as an input-output system and have merely hinted at a few of the specific questions we shall need to ask as we build up a more comprehensive model.

The rest of this chapter will be devoted to building such a model both in general terms and with particular reference to language training. Figure 2.2. below, gives a first approximation of the model — a series of steps which need to be taken — which we may take as our starting point.

Figure 2.2.
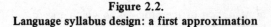
Language syllabus design: a first approximation

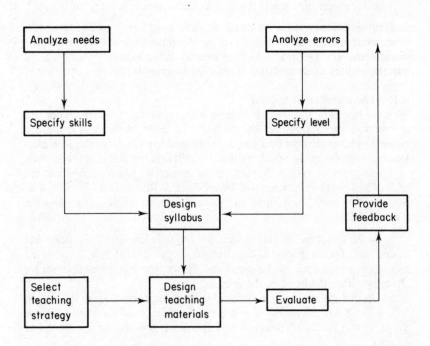

One or two points should be made about this rough outline. First, there are interconnections which, for the sake of clarity, we have left out of the diagram. For example 'select a teaching strategy' refers to our educational philosophy and of necessity influences every one of the steps we take, not just 'design teaching materials'. Secondly, the model is still relatively unsophisticated — 'evaluate' for example is extremely ambiguous as it stands here — but we feel this to be an advantage, at this point, since it forces us, in the remainder of this chapter to expand on and explain each of the steps laid out here.

A crucial part of the process is where under 'design syllabus' the needs and job skills are brought together with the language skills and welded into a coherent syllabus. In the past, most language syllabuses have tended to specify the language component but have assumed that the non-verbal skills would somehow look after themselves. Conversely, industrial training has tended to assume that, once job skills were defined — and one of them might be 'to communicate effectively' or some other vague formulation of a linguistic ability — language skills would follow naturally. What we are suggesting — in company with many language course designers, particularly those involved in ESP — is that a truly integrated syllabus can come about only as the result of a conscious attempt on the part of the designer to combine the techniques of job analysis which are already in common use in industrial and management training with the established linguistic techniques of content selection, grading and sequencing.

In the next section we shall attempt such an integration and in Appendix A offer a case study of part of a course designed for a particular job-holder.

2.2. TEN STEPS IN THE DESIGN OF TRAINING PROGRAMMES

Boydell (1970) gives us a definition of *training* which is well worth working with:

> *Planning* to give people the chance to *learn* to achieve the *results* that the *job demands* [original emphasis].

We shall take his 'ten steps' and consider them in the light of the special needs of language teaching but, already, it should be clear that there are common principles emerging, even from such a brief definition as this.

2.2.1. Step 1: identify the training needs

The first sign that there are needs at all will probably come from our clients. In the case of a private company, the suggestion will emerge from the Board Room or, possibly, from the Trades Union. In the case of an institution which forms part of the formal national education system, the directive will come from Cabinet or from some group holding delegated authority from the Government.

As we noted earlier, one of the most difficult tasks which faces the syllabus designer at this stage is to match his own perception of the need with the perception expressed by his clients. Fortunately, there are now books and articles available which give the syllabus designer who is new to the job some guidelines to follow (probably the most comprehensive at the level of context and most recent is Munby 1978).

In any case, we shall need to discover which occupations are involved and why training is needed at all e.g. to solve some current problems? (in which case some kind of 'crash programme' may have to be mounted) or perhaps to prepare for some need which is anticipated in the future? (in which case we can, perhaps, be rather more leisurely in our programme). We shall also need to know how many people will be involved, for how long and at what periods they can be released, whether the training is to take place during normal work time or outside it, at the place of work or at some training centre. We shall also need to discover the priorities. Some of what is needed may have, in the opinion of the client, top priority and must be dealt with before anything else. Can we locate the critical areas? If we clear up a particular problem, others may begin to solve themselves i.e. a careful selection of issues may speed up the whole process and give us greater and faster returns than would a piecemeal approach.

2.2.2. Step 2: relate the stated needs to the overall aims of the organization

We need to discover whether the training which has been requested really is needed or whether the effort is actually unnecessary. We might be approached for example with a suggestion that factory inspectors, whose job it is to investigate accidents and to ensure that safety regulations are being followed, need a course in interviewing techniques in English. Subsequently, by going around with inspectors and visiting factories, we may well discover that they never interview anyone in English and so we might recommend a course in interview techniques — in the languages they actually use but not interview techniques in English. Conversely, our observation of the inspector at work may throw into sharp relief a genuine need for a course in English report writing, since the face-to-face information gathering may well not be carried on in English, but all the reports of such investigations are written up in English (see Bell 1980 c for a description of the investigations involved in designing a course for factory inspectors).

In short, we cannot stress too strongly the need not only to interview the client in order to discover *his* perception of the need but also to shadow the potential student as he does his job so that we can discover what he really does. Neither must we let ourselves be deceived by the expressed needs of the potential student; he may have as little idea of his actual needs as his boss has. Finally, official 'job descriptions' make fascinating reading but rarely provide an alternative to the foot-slogging we have been advocating here (we will expand upon this in the next section).

2.2.3. Step 3: analyse the occupation(s) of the trainee(s)

We have already touched in a somewhat haphazard way on job analysis and intend to go rather further here. There appear to be, within the general task 'job analysis' three distinct stages which need to be worked through:

a) *Job Description* in which, in very general terms, the nature of the job is stated; the purpose of the job, the duties and responsibilities involved in it. By the end of this stage in the analysis, the investigator should have the job identified and should also have a rough picture of the kinds of things the job-holder can legitimately be required to do and the limits of his responsibilities.

b) *Job Specification* in which the general description is made more precise by discovering the *tasks* that are carried out by the job-holder and the *knowledge* and *skill* required in order to carry out each task satisfactorily.

i) *Task:* we have already referred to duties and responsibilities and wish here to distinguish tasks from them. Tasks, unlike duties and responsibilities, are *specific* rather than *general.* In designing our course we certainly need to know the duties and responsibilities of the participants — these, after all, define their role and status with the work group — but we particularly need information on the tasks they perform since it is in the performance of their tasks that they are likely to have signalled to our clients that there is a 'gap' between the actual and the expected; the 'gap' which our training programme will be expected to fill.

ii) *Knowledge:* in order to do the job, a person must know certain things. We, as designers, need a specification of this knowledge since our programme will need to satisfy any deficiency in the required knowledge.

iii) *Skill:* in order to do the job, a person must not only know but also carry out an act or series of acts in an appropriate manner. Skill is involved where the carrying out of the acts cannot be achieved without practice. Of course, there are many types of act — physical, social, mental — so there are different types of skill for which the programme designer will need to provide meaningful practice.

c) *Further Analysis:* in which the general listing of tasks, knowledge and skills is further subdivided into task and faults analysis:

i) *Task Analysis:* it is assumed that there is a hierarchical relationship between *duties, tasks, stages* and *steps* such that each *duty* will consist of at least one *task*, each *task* at least one *stage* and each *stage* at least one *step*. Typically, though, we should expect to find each duty involving several tasks, each task several stages and each stage several steps. To gain a clear picture of what is involved in a particular job we need to come down to this level of description.

ii) *Faults Analysis:* it is likely that we have been called in by the client to provide training because faults are occurring i.e. the staff are failing to carry out their duties satisfactorily. If faults are occurring, we shall need to *recognize* that they are, indeed, faults, *describe* their appearance, *explain* why they occur and, since our own task is training, *correct* them (in Appendix B, we shall be looking more closely at these steps in faults or, as it is normally termed in applied linguistics, 'error' analysis).

We are now at the end of Step 3. At this point we have available to us a fairly clear picture of the training need as described to us by the client and modified by our own investigations. We also have a good idea of the duties and responsibilities of the job our trainees hold, a specification of the tasks which they perform in doing the job and the knowledge and skills required to carry out the tasks adequately. In addition, through our further analysis of the tasks, we have been able to break them down into smaller units and by a faults or error analysis to discover which tasks or sub-routines of tasks are being carried out in an unsatisfactory manner.

Given the 'ideal' knowledge and skills of the 'perfect' worker – as desired by the client – and the 'actual' knowledge and skills of the 'real' job-holders, we are able to define, with some degree of precision, the training 'gap' which we are expected to fill.

However, what we have learned so far has, essentially, to do with *what* the learners need – with course *content* – rather than with *who* the learners are i.e. the composition of the learner group. It is to the characteristics of this group to which we turn in the next step.

2.2.4. Step 4: specify and select the trainees

The fourth step requires us to decide which category of job-holder is to be given the training and, from within that category, which are most in need of the training we are planning to provide. We need, that is, to specify and select and then to *appraise* those we have selected. We have already a general idea of what they are supposed to know and do and, perhaps, an equally general idea of what such job-holders actually do. What is now needed is some process which will show us the present knowledge and skills of the group we have selected and some technique for matching this with the performance expected of them.

This brings us to the complex issue of testing which we shall deal with in some detail in Appendix C. For the moment, though, we can limit our comments to the notion of 'matching' which we have just raised.

By 'matching' we mean examining the behaviour of the group as they attempt to carry out certain tasks and, having examined them, comparing their behaviour either as individuals or as a group against either each other – ranking one individual against another – or against some external criterion of behaviour (see Appendix C for the distinction between norm and criterion testing).

When we have 'matched' our potential trainees in a way which we consider to be appropriate – and we are intentionally avoiding the issue of 'appropriate' here so that we can take it up in Appendix C – we can retain those whom we judge to be in need of our training and reject those who appear unlikely – either because they are too 'good' or too 'bad' – to be much improved by it.

This done, we can move on the next step; setting the objectives of the programme.

2.2.5. Step 5: set the objectives

Our planning has so far concentrated on *what* we might include in our training programme and *who* we expect to benefit from it. Step 5 brings us to a halt with the question 'why?'. Why have we decided to include this kind of course content in a programme for this kind of trainee?

More specifically, we are now asking 'what, at the end of the training period, ought they to be able to do that they can't do now?' i.e. we are attempting to specify the terminal behaviour of the participants; *that* behaviour will be the general long-term aim of our course.

It is clear from this *ad hoc* definition of *objective* that there are two parameters involved; time and specification. Our objectives may be long or short-term and may be expressed in the form of a broad, vague statement of *aim* – and this is the way the client tends to express his objectives for the programme – or else in a narrow and very specific way.

We can arrange objectives along a scale from the single, long-term, general, *key* objective – the ultimate strategic aim of the programme – through a small number of medium-term, more precisely formulated, *critical* objectives – tactical goals to be reached along the way – to a large number of short-term, carefully defined *specific* objectives; the purposes which underlie each of the activities we plan to use (see Davies 1976 and Appendix A. step 5 for an application to an ESP course).

Having decided, in general terms what is needed by whom and why, we are in a position to move on to the next step: the design of the syllabus itself.

2.2.6. Step 6: design the syllabus

It may seem strange in a book on language teaching that we have been able to reach the halfway point in our discussion of the design of training programmes with hardly a mention of language. We feel that this should be no cause for surprise, since the steps we have been taking are, we believe, broadly applicable to the design of training programmes in general, irrespective of the knowledge or skills the programmes are to inculcate. From this point on, however, we shall be considering the selection and ordering of *content*, the creation of *materials* and their implementation in the classroom, the selection of our *educational strategy* and the *evaluation* of the programme itself; all activities which are, to a far greater extent, language specific.

In order to carry out the remaining steps – with the exception of the last – we shall be forced back again and again to the answers we gave to the two fundamental questions with which we began this book; what do we believe language to be? and how do we believe people learn languages?

Designing the syllabus involves us in the selection and ordering of the content i.e. we must decide what is to go into the syllabus; what the learners are to learn and in what order.

The view we hold of the nature of language will predispose us towards the selection of a particular type of content rather than another. If we are *formalists*, our content will consist either of the physical manifestations of the elements which combine to create the code or else the system of knowledge which allows the language user to manipulate the elements to create sequences sanctioned by the rules of the code (we shall expand on these two types of formalism and their impact on language teaching in Chapter 5). If, conversely, we are *functionalists*, our content will reflect the concept of 'language in use', either naively, by attempting to make the 'situation' primary and the language used 'in it' dependent on it (see 7.4. on 'situational' language teaching) or, in a more sophisticated way, by making 'meanings' primary and setting linguistic forms in a secondary relationship with the meanings they express (see 7.5 on 'notional' syllabuses).

To much the same extent, the ordering of the content will be crucially influenced by our view of the nature of language; we feel that certain forms or sequences or situations or notions are inherently difficult to learn because their description by the linguist is complex rather than simple. Naively, and we will be taking this point up in considerable detail in the next chapter, we are likely to equate complex description with difficulty of learning and simple description with easy to learn: a dubious correlation.

An alternative or additional way of approaching the problem of content selection and ordering would be to move away from the teacher-dominated 'top-down' approach which has been implied in our discussion so far and make use of the intended participants themselves as course designers. This may seem a radical and perhaps, to some, an impracticable idea. Radical it may be but it is far from impracticable. The motivational value of involving the learner in the design of the programme is necessarily high, since the learner can see, in what he is being exposed to, topics, knowledge and skills which he has already identified as lacking. A straightforward 'activities log' will tell us what the participants do on the job and the relative amounts of time spent on each activity and a 'self-assessment' rating scale based on the key activities will give us a tentative grading of activities ranked according to the importance of each in the eyes of the learner.

If we are serious about helping people to learn rather than just 'teaching' them – and this relates to our selection of an educational strategy (see section 2.2.8.) – we must accept that the learner should have far more influence in the creation of the syllabus, the activities which are used to assist learning and in the evaluation both of the course and his own performance than he presently has (see Bell 1980c for a description of designing a course with the participation of the learners and Appendix C for an outline of self-assessment techniques in language testing). Indeed, some educationists would argue that the learner should have total control and that the syllabus should not be devised *a priori* at all but allowed to emerge as the needs and interests of the learners change. (see Step 8 below and Section 3.6.1.).

Since Chapter 3 is concerned with the details of syllabus design – selection, sequencing and grading – and with the exemplification of the possible alternatives by presenting three types of syllabus – the grammatical, the situational and the notional – we shall leave the problems of syllabus design here and move on to the next step; the creation of materials.

2.2.7. Step 7: create the materials
In the previous steps we have been building up information on needs as perceived by the client, by us and by the potential participants, on the individuals who are to make up the class, the activities in which they engage

and the degree to which they are coping with the tasks. All this information feeds into the sixth step; the design of the syllabus i.e. the selection and arrangement of the course content.

In this step, we need to consider how learning is to be facilitated. We have already selected the content and sequenced it in some way. The next step is to create materials which will allow the points we have selected to get across to the learner – we shall consider how materials can be used in the next step (Step 8) – and which will give the learner sufficient appropriate practice in the use of the new knowledge and skills they have acquired.

When we were considering the design of the syllabus, we argued that our answer to the question 'what is language?' would greatly affect the content we would select and, though to a lesser extent, the way in which we arranged it. Now we face the converse situation. We have decided *what* is to be learned; materials production is concerned with *how* that content is to be put across and practised. It is, therefore, more crucially influenced by our answer to the second question we posed in the first chapter 'how do we believe people learn languages?'.

Rather than try to tackle the problems of writing materials head on, since we have already argued that this is the responsibility of the professional textbook writer or, when possible, the classroom teacher himself, we would like to take this opportunity to think a little about the ways people learn and draw some implications from what we know about learning for materials design.

Whenever we learn something, we have to fit it into the *system* of knowledge or skill which we already possess. Every new item of knowledge or element of skill has to be related to the existing system by means of some sort of *rule*. In order to be able to make use of the new addition to the system it is not sufficient merely to memorize it or to remember the rule which integrates it with the rest of the system; we also need *practice* in using the item in a rule-governed manner.

These three points form the basis of three essential classroom activities; presentation, illustration and practice.

In order to help others to learn, we need to create an environment in which we can:

Present the item; a unit of content which may be grammatical, situational or notional in form and may or may not, depending on our educational strategy, include the rule which links it with the system as a whole.

Illustrate the item in use; the unit needs to be shown in a range of contexts, linguistic and extralinguistic, so that its range of use can be grasped. Once again, depending on our educational strategy, the rule for the use of the unit may or may not be provided.

Practice the use of the item; giving the learner the chance to apply the newly learned knowledge or skill in genuine communication situations.

Whatever our educational philosophy, we are obliged to provide each of these activities. The order in which presentation, illustration and practice occur, the amount of each at any time, the extent to which we feel that

43

the teacher should overtly state the rules for the learner and how far we feel that the learner should deduce the rules for himself are all issues which can only be resolved by recourse to our own preferred educational strategy (the issue discussed in the next step).

The range of ways of presenting items and rules, illustrating them and providing practice is enormous (see Byrne 1976 and Mackey 1965, Chapters 8 and 9 for a fairly comprehensive listing) so we shall limit ourselves here to two comments: one on a useful distinction between two types of materials, the other on the possibility of using, with advanced adult learners especially, some of the techniques already popular in management training.

i) *Materials*; recently (Candlin *et al*. 1979) there has been a suggestion that materials should be seen as consisting of two rather different types: *content* materials which provide data and information – texts (in the broadest sense of the term) which illustrate the language in use and dictionaries, grammars, etc. which give direct access to the rules – and *process* materials which provide the learner with 'frameworks' for activities in which the data and information provided by the content materials can be applied and practised. The distinction between the two types, once made, is easily grasped but we need to keep it in mind if we are designing or selecting materials; in the past the two types have not infrequently been confused.

ii) *Techniques:* there are at least nine 'participation techniques' which can certainly be adapted for use with advanced adult learners:

1. *Lectures:* the lecture is the least participative but also the least expensive technique. It has a place when our aim is to transmit facts but the trainees must be skilled at note-taking if the content is to be remembered.

2. *Exercises:* in an exercise, the trainer provides the problem, the method of solving the problem, the criteria for success and the final evaluation. There is a degree of participation but the trainer is still very much in control. The exercise serves well as a confirmation that a particular point has been learned at a particular stage in the course.

3. *In-tray exercises:* in an in-tray (or in-basket) exercise, the trainer provides the trainee with a set of problems. The task of the trainee is to sort them into a logical order and solve them. Although the trainees work individually, there is the possibility of greater participation during the feedback stage; discussion of alternative solutions. The in-tray exercise is useful for learning how to organize work and time and for practising priority-setting, delegation and so forth. For language training, the in-tray exercise can give the learner the opportunity to practice these skills, which, if he is actually a manager, he is already using in his job, in writing and in speech.

4. *Projects & assignments:* the trainer sets a task for an individual or a group and leaves the planning and carrying out of the project to the initiative of the trainee(s). A language learning example might be the

planning of a visit to a place of interest or making the arrangements for meeting an important visitor; ideally the task should be one which arises in the daily work of the trainees. Such a project allows the practising of the skills of discussion, persuasion, explanation etc. in face-to-face inter-action and, if desirable, the committing of decisions to paper in the form of informal notes or even formal minutes of a meeting.

5. *Case Studies:* in a case study, the trainer provides details of a situ-ation and the trainees explore alternative solutions to the problem des-cribed. A strength of the case study is that it demonstrates well that there is, in management, rarely a single 'right' answer. For the language learner, the case study offers an opportunity for verbalizing his analysis of the problem and his solutions to it, in the context of an ordered discussion.

6. *Incident Process:* an incident process is similar to a case study but focuses on a single incident rather than a complex series of events. Another contrast with the case study lies in the amount of information given by the trainer to the trainees and the order in which it is given. In the case study, the information is provided *in toto* at the beginning of the exercise. In the incident process, the trainer witholds information until asked for it. In general terms, the incident process is useful as a device for following up alternative 'solutions' proposed during a case study. The language learner, too, can practise the same skills as he would in the case study but concentrating his attention on a single event rather than a series.

7. *Discussion:* the discussion can be tightly or loosely controlled and organized by the trainer. It can be used at any stage in training but, in language training, learners with poor command of the code can find the experience frustrating unless they are prepared beforehand. The value of the discussion is that it acts as a vehicle for extending the learner's *fluency* rather than *accuracy*. Its weakness lies in its misuse as a tech-nique for filling in a 'spare' period in the programme. For the language learner, except for the most advanced, discussions don't just happen; they have to be prepared for.

8. *Role plays:* in a structured role play, trainees are given roles and are expected to act them out. Normally, each role is specified on a cue card — the characteristics and attitudes of the individual role being spelled out in some detail — but much more spontaneous role play is possible in which only vague information is provided and the player has to build up the role on the basis of his existing stereotype of such a role. In the language class, the learner has often been expected to engage in role play, usually after having learned a dialogue which he is then ex-pected to 'dramatize'. We can provide more or less back up for the learner. At one extreme, we can give him the actual words he is expected to say and in the appropriate order, at the other we can just name a role and set it in a roughly specified situation. Between these two there are many degrees of control available to the trainer. One, as we demonstrate in Appendix A, is to give the role-players cue cards in which the *meanings*

they will need to express are printed but not the actual *words* they should use. For example, rather than given the cue 'I agree with you' — as one might with less proficient learners — one gives 'agree with him' and leaves it to the learner to decide what is appropriate to express that meaning.

9. *Simulations:* a simulation involves role play but within a constructed framework i.e. the 'situation' in which the interaction takes place is described in detail and changed as the simulation develops. In general training, the usefulness of the simulation is the way it demonstrates the extent to which individuals are not 'free agents'; we are all, to a considerable extent, dependent on the overall set-up. Many communication games — 'Diplomacy' is a versatile example — lend themselves to use in the language classroom, particularly, as we have been suggesting all along, with the 'advanced learner'. (Bell 1979b gives a number of suggestions which may be useful).

2.2.8. Step 8: decide on educational strategy

We have just been discussing a range of techniques which can be adapted for use in the language classroom but, in the end, the techniques we adopt — the method we select and the materials we choose to reflect that method — will depend on how we believe learners learn and how we believe we fit into the learning process. As trainers, we need to ask ourselves a very searching question indeed: what do I believe my relationship with the learners should be?

During the last 50 years there have been enormous changes in attitude on the part of teachers, changes which we should like to outline here because the choice of attitude is a choice of educational strategy and it is on that that our method will rest.

Although no particular instructional strategy has ever totally dominated training — or even language teaching — it is possible to discern a shift in focus from the teacher, to the learner and, finally, to the learning task itself. With the change of strategy has come a shift from highly authoritarian parent–child relationships (to use the terminology of Transactional Analysis popularized by Berne 1964) to co-operative, trusting adult–adult relationships in recent years. Simultaneously, we have seen dramatic changes in teacher and learner activity, beginning (in the 1930s; all dates are, of course, approximate) with highly active teachers and sullenly passive learners and ending (in the 1960s) with teachers and learners working together towards a mutually agreed goal.

The simplest way of characterizing — or rather caricaturing — this development is probably to display it diagrammatically (Figure 2.3. below).

2.2.9. Step 9: test the effectiveness of the programme

At the end of the course, we need to discover how well it worked i.e. we have to test the effectiveness of our programme in order to provide all those

Figure 2.3.
Instructional strategies 1930–1980

Type	Focus	Relationship	Teacher Activity	Learner Activity
CLASSICAL; 1930's a) Authoritarian	Teacher	Authoritarian Parent – Submissive Child Superior – Subordinate	Active Dominant. Direction of learning	Passive Submissive
b) Paternalistic	Teacher	Nurturing Parent – Child	Active. Control of learning	Passive. Co-operation on demand
ROMANTIC; 1950's a) Democratic	Group	Adult – Adult	Stimulator, Facilitator, Co-ordinator of learning	Active Participative Group-paced learning
b) Laissez-faire	Group	Child – Child	Neutrality. Withdrawal.	Competition. Lack of goal
MODERN; 1960's	Task	Equal Adults	Stimulator, Facilitator Monitor of learning. Gains acceptance from group	Trust. Permissiveness in accepting goals and methods Rotation of leadership

involved with feedback; changes may well have to be made in future courses as a result of our experiences with this one.

In Appendix C, we give a number of examples of language tests and discuss some of the problems which arise in their design and use. Here we wish to look at testing from a rather different point of view; how it fits into our programme.

As always, the simple question we wish to ask — here it is 'how did the course turn out?' — refuses to be answered simply. In view of the different interest groups involved in the language training process and the different perceptions they have of its aims, it is to be expected that there will be different criteria for judging the 'success' of a programme.

The politician, for example, will only be satisfied if the programme is a political success i.e. if it contributes to the changed future behaviour which he deems desirable. He is also virtually certain to ask financial questions; could the same result have been achieved more quickly, more cheaply, with fewer teachers, with more students, with less facilities, etc? He, by the very nature of his chosen occupation, will want *quantifiable* data — 'statistics' which will back up our claim that our programme was a success, if it was.

The employer–client will certainly ask some of the same questions as the politician — he will be just as cost-conscious — but will also think of other questions which he may term 'pragmatic'. He will want evidence that the trainees can now do their jobs better as a result of having been through our programme i.e. he will wish to see a justification of all the effort from the point of view of his own organization, the efficiency of his office-workers, receptionists, managers etc.

The linguists, psychologists and teachers are more likely to be interested in comparing scores on tests administered before — perhaps also during — and after the course and working out from them whether the selection, grading and sequencing of the content was satisfactory, whether the kind of presentation, illustration and practice used in the classroom was of an appropriate quality and quantity i.e. this group will look for testing devices which will provide feedback for the redesign of the process itself.

2.2.10. Step 10: provide feedback to all areas

Our last duty as programme designers and teachers is, since training is a continuing process, to provide feedback to all those involved and to assess the information gained during our evaluation exercises in relation to our future plans and the expected demands of our clients.

Clearly, we cannot suggest all the kinds of feedback which may become available nor the value any of it may have to any particular sector of the programme — whether a group or a process — but what we can do is often neglected by language teachers. We feel obliged to do this for two reasons: firstly, unless we are as professional in the provision of feedback as other trainers are — and, in my own experience at least, language teachers are particularly prone to feel that the end of the course *is* the end and to start concentrating on the next batch of learners, their needs and the kinds of solution we have thought of for them — we can find ourselves, literally, at a loss when the fund-providers come around again. But that is a selfish way of justifying what we propose to do. There is another reason. The level of language training which we are now called upon to organize is far higher than it was 20 or 30 years ago. Then, the demand was more often than not for courses for beginners or intermediate students. 'Advanced learners' were rare and a constant head-ache. The traditional answer was to send them off to study the literature of their chosen language. Now we are faced by 'students' with degrees in, for example, English literature who, according to our clients, still need to have their English 'improved'. To-day, the beginner and intermediate level student — however we care to define such nebulous terms — is, the world over, being taught remarkably well by local teachers and the role of the native teacher of English is increasingly to provide 'high–level' courses not in the knowledge of the *code* — that was acquired long ago by this type of student — but in the *application* of that knowledge. We are being asked to create courses which are much more *functional* in their orientation and, because so many of our clients are the leaders of trade and industry, specialized to suit a particular enterprise and, often, a particular jobholder in that enterprise. No wonder English for Special Purposes (ESP) has developed so rapidly in the last decade.

So what of the feedback? We need to keep several groups of people informed:

(a) *Our clients:* they will wish to know whether the cost of our programme has been worth it. If it has, we can hope for more orders for our product in the future. To ensure this, we will have to organize a follow-up of our trainees; observe the degree to which they are actually applying what we have taught them once they get back on the job and be on the lookout for needs which emerge precisely from their newly gained abilities. Since the motivation of our clients is political — in a broad sense — our follow-up methods must have a political aura to them too. We shall have to write reports on the 'success' of our courses and include in them recommendations for future courses. We shall have to ensure that knowledge of our 'success' is communicated throughout the client organization if only for the very practical reason that we need future trainees to welcome the thought of attending our courses and, hence, to be well-motivated towards our efforts to help them.

(b) *Our trainees:* we have touched already on ways in which we should keep in contact with those who have been through one of our programmes and perhaps need only to emphasize here that this year's trainee will in all probability be next year's supervisor who will do a far better job of convincing next year's trainee of the usefulness of our courses than we ever will.

(c) *Our trainers:* 'better' courses depend, to a very large extent, on 'improvements' made to existing courses. It follows that those involved in the

Figure 2.4.
Ten steps in the design of training programmes

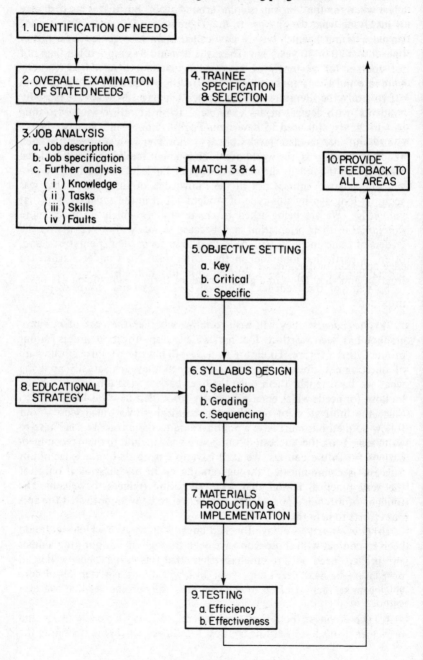

planning and implementation of programmes must be just as involved in the gathering, provision, assessment and application of feedback. We can no longer argue that we are 'only' language teachers and, for that reason, are not qualified to carry out job analyses or on-the-spot follow-up of training. The demands which are increasingly being made on us require that we develop such abilities and develop them fast.

(d) *The academics:* perhaps we have also reached a point where the academic is less keen to offer advice than he was for example 25 or 30 years ago but, as we suggested in Chapter 1, there are applied linguists, psycholinguists and sociolinguists who are interested and involved and who have a right to be informed of our results; such as they are. Just who is to inform who and how is an organizational matter and hinges more on the individuals involved in the total planning enterprise than any categorization of individuals into groups.

A final point about evaluation and feedback; evaluation is not a laboratory experiment and so we can never be absolutely certain that the changes in the behaviour of our trainees are the *result* of our training. That the changes *followed* the training is not in doubt. That the training *caused* the changes is. Even so, if we attempt a series of different measures of knowledge and skill both immediately after the course and later in the real job situation and they all — or a good number of them (a statistician will have to tell you what a 'good number' is) come up with 'improvements' and if these 'improvements' satisfy the multiple criteria of the many interest groups involved, we can be happy that we have designed and run a very satisfactory course indeed.

2.3. CONCLUSION

We have been trying in this chapter to specify the steps involved in the design of a training programme and, in doing so, we have been attempting to draw on broad principles which we believe are generally acceptable to trainers as such, rather than only applicable to those of us involved in language teaching.

The final version of the model — 'final', until we can think of ways of improving it — is given in Figure 2.4 but we feel that we ought to draw the reader's attention to three topics which we have hardly touched on; an example of the application of the model to a particular set of language needs, the place of the analysis of language errors in the programme — particularly in Step 3 and that of language testing — between Step 3 and Step 4 and as part of Step 9 — all of which we have relegated to the Appendices.

In the next chapter, we shall look at three types of syllabus — the grammatical, the situational and the notional — and take up again, within the contexts of the three syllabuses, the problem of grading and general organization which we initially raised in Step 6.

SUGGESTED FURTHER READING

Boydell T. H. (1970), *A Guide to Job Analysis*
Although not written for language teachers, this booklet has tremendous value for the course designer particularly the writer of ESP materials. It may come as something of a shock to language teachers that other trainers have been wrestling for some time and with a certain amount of success with the 'new' problems we are just beginning to face in ELT.

Byrne D. (1976), *Teaching Oral English*
This book is, in a sense, a more up-to-date Bright and McGregor. Its orientation is still pedagogic — it is particularly imaginative on the use of audio-visual aids and dialogues — but the author does also attempt to draw on insights from linguistics and, to a smaller extent, from psychology.

Davies I. K. (1976), *Objectives in Curriculum Design*
Like Boydell this book is concerned with a large issue which impinges on ELT; the design of syllabuses in general. The orientation of the book is educational rather than (applied) linguistic and seeks to clarify general problems of curriculum design. Its value for the ELT practitioner is, as it is with Boydell, that it offers us a wider perspective.

Harris D. (1969), *Testing English as a Second Language*
This is a standard introduction to the testing of language learning. The tests described are essentially tests which 'validate' what has been done in the course. The whole area of 'evaluation' of usefulness and effectiveness outside the classroom still awaits investigation in ELT.

Munby J. (1978), *Communicative Syllabus Design*
The reader should be aware of the sub-title of this book — *a sociolinguistic model for defining the content of purpose-specific language programmes* — and recognize that it covers in an exciting and novel way, only Step 6 in any detail and, indeed, concentrates on Step 6a; content selection. Even so, this is a valuable book which deserves careful reading.

3 Three types of language syllabus

In the previous chapter, we were involved in the specification of a series of steps which we argued the designer of a training programme would have to take – irrespective of the course content – in converting the request for training from a client into a coherent programme. In this chapter, by way of contrast, we intend to focus on problems which appear to be specific to the design of language training programmes; three 'approaches' to language teaching – grammatical, situational and notional (each of which will be discussed in greater detail in Chapters 5 and 7) – the grading and organization of the syllabus and the distinction between syllabuses which are designed *a posteriori* – allowed to 'evolve' in some way as the course progresses – and those which are designed *a priori* – in detail at the outset.

Initially, we are forced to face two questions:

(a) Which *forms* of language should be taught? The answer to this will suggest the course *content*.

(b) Which *order* should the chosen forms be presented in? This will suggest decisions on the *grading* and *sequencing* of the course content.

Three types of syllabus emerge from a consideration of these issues which are definable in terms of the type of item they seek to emphasize grammatical, situational and notional.

3.1 THE GRAMMATICAL SYLLABUS

The grammatical syllabus is a response to the question '*how* do users of the target language express themselves?'. Such a syllabus assumes that the learner's need is for items which can cope with, what is, after all, a grammatical demand. Most language teaching materials derive from grammatical syllabuses and accept the view that language is a grammatical system and that learning a language consists of learning that system. It matters little whether the psychological orientation of the syllabus designer is behaviourist (see 5.1. on behaviourist influences on structuralist linguistics and materials) or cognitive (see 5.2 on cognitive influences on transformational generative linguistics and materials), the items to be taught are grammatical items.

The grammatical syllabus presents several problems:

1. The 'grammar' accepted by the designer is context-free. The unit is the isolated sentence and the assumption is that the essential problem for the learner is to master *linguistic form* and only secondarily the *social meaning* and *use* of such forms.

2. A grammar is at its most efficient when it presents together forms

which are subject to the same rules e.g. it is an efficient grammar which groups *can, will, may, must* etc. under the same heading as 'modals'. However, the criterion for presentation of forms in a pedagogical grammar – in contrast with a descriptive grammar – is different, items need to be presented in a way which reflects the needs of the learner as a communicator. For example, statements are typically taught at a different stage from questions, in spite of the fact that questioning and answering are very closely linked activities in normal conversation. Indeed, the skillful use of language demands the ability to use and comprehend grammatically mixed forms.

3. The assumption that knowledge of the grammatical code equals ability to use that code is quickly seen to be false by the learner and the effect of this may well be to lower his motivation, since he is unable to see how what he is being taught corresponds to his needs.

4. The aim of teaching the whole of the grammar may well, in itself be inefficient, not only because it is a virtually unattainable goal but also because few learners will ever need the whole of the grammar in order to communicate.

In short, a purely grammatical syllabus presents linguistic items to the exclusion of other elements of the language and presents them in an inefficient way. The effect of both of these factors may be to de-motivate the learner.

3.2. THE SITUATIONAL SYLLABUS

A true situational syllabus – and none exists so far – would try to provide the learner with the knowledge and skills he would need to deal with social demands. The question would be '*when* and *where* will the learner need the target language?' and the syllabus would attempt to specify the situations. Such a syllabus would assume that language consists of *patterns of social use* (cf. the human science definition of language in 1.1.2) and that language learning implies becoming proficient in using the language in social situations. A truly situational syllabus would take the setting of the use of the language – the type of interaction involved – as primary and the linguistic forms as dependent on the situations. Linguistic items would be selected, therefore, not on the basis of their place in the grammar but on the likelihood of their occurrence in a particular social context.

The pure situational syllabus would also present problems:

1. It assumes that the syllabus designer is able to predict accurately the situations in which the learner will find himself and it is only in a very small number of cases that we can predict with any degree of certainty e.g. the flight announcer at an international airport needs only half a dozen or so 'sentence patterns' and a list of times, numbers and airport names in several languages. Consider the amount of use that can be got out of

'Announcing the arrival of *x* Airways flight number *n* from *y*'

For most learners the prediction of situational needs is an impossibility.

2. It further assumes that the components of the concept 'situation' have been exhaustively listed and their inter-relationships mapped, when the actual position is that we have, at best a number of vague taxonomies and even vaguer notions of how the elements involved influence each other (see 6.4.1. and Fig. 6.8. p. 125 ff.)

3. Another assumption is that there is some predictable relationship between the situation on the one hand and the language used in it on the other. Unfortunately, there are no strong relationships of this type, except for highly ritualized language use; prayer, greetings, leave-taking, thanking, etc. There are, however, correlations between the interaction type and the *kinds* of thing the participants might be expected to say e.g. in a telephone conversation the person called normally speaks first and says at least one of 'Hello', '345 321' 'Bloggs speaking'. The caller is also expected to identify himself and to say why he is calling. What analysis of this kind shows is that interactions have fairly clearly defined beginnings and ends but that the middles are very unpredictable.

In actual fact, those situational syllabuses which do exist are grammatical syllabuses which make use of situations to present and practise linguistic forms (see the comments on situational materials in 7.4.4.).

3.3. THE NOTIONAL SYLLABUS

In contrast with the two types of syllabus discussed above, the notional syllabus takes semantic knowledge as primary and attempts to answer the question *'what* do users of the language need to express?' This implies a belief in language as a system but a *system of meanings* rather than forms. It assumes that learning a language consists of learning how to mean. Such a syllabus would seek correlations between form and function but would define the link as being between the forms of the language available to the user and the meanings he wishes to express. Unlike the grammatical syllabus, in which the correlation is between form and form or the situational syllabus, where it is between situation and form, the notional syllabus attempts to define the communication needs of the learner and then to display the ways in which each communication need can be appropriately expressed.

The notional syllabus, too, presents problems:

1. The specification of needs may well turn out to be as global as the specification of types of situation does for the situational syllabus. Most learners will, presumably, need to express everything in the L2 which they can express in the L1. If we examine the six semantico-grammatical categories and the seven or eight categories of communicative function (listed in Section 7.5.4) we are hard pressed to decide that any one of them can be dispensed with.

2. The notions themselves tend to overlap e.g. 'tolerance' and 'approval' or to be unanalyzed e.g. the whole set 'interpersonal relations'.

3. The correlation between notion and form is extraordinarily complex, particularly since adult utterances are so frequently ambiguous — or multifunctional — and distinctions between meanings so often, in English at least, expressed by paralinguistic variations in speed of delivery, tone, stress, facial and other gestures and so forth.

3.4. SUMMARY

Perhaps the clearest way of demonstrating the difference between a grammatical and a situational-cum-notional syllabus would be to contrast two syllabuses which appeared in the same year, 1968, for Serbo-Croat and Swahili respectively (based on Banathy & Dale 1972.60).

a) *Grammatical Syllabus; Serbo-Croat*

A visitor to Yugoslavia is expected to be able, in the L2, to:
   i. Distinguish genders.
   ii. Use agreement.
   iii. Decline nouns, adjectives, pronouns correctly.
   iv. Form the present, future and past of verbs.
   v. Form the affirmative and negative statements.
   vi. Form affirmative and negative questions.

b) *Situational/Notional Syllabus; Swahili*

A visitor to coastal East Africa is expected to be able, in the L2, to:
   i. Initiate and respond to standard greetings formulae.
   ii. Tell the time to the nearest minute.
   iii. Ask a person's name.
   iv. State where he, or another person, lives.
   v. Give directions for getting to a place he knows.
   vi. Understand a price and pay a bill presented in speech.
   vii. Find out the price of an article.
   viii. Find out how far one place is from another.

We can, perhaps, also distinguish the three types of syllabus we have been considering in terms of the relationships between *form, meaning* and *use* (cf. the distinction we made in Chapter 1 between the three levels of linguistic description; syntax, semantics and pragmatics).

The grammatical syllabus moves from form, to meaning to use. The situational, if it existed in its 'pure' form, would move from use to meaning to form. The notional syllabus moves from meaning to form to use. (see Figure 3.1 below).

The need, clearly, is for a syllabus which combines the best of all three types i.e. a syllabus which gives the ideal balance between the correct production and comprehension of the linguistic forms and their appropriate use in actual communication. Such a syllabus is still eagerly awaited!

Figure 3.1.
Three types of syllabus

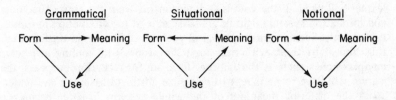

3.5. THE PROBLEM OF GRADING

If we attempt to design a syllabus *a priori* – on the basis of assumptions of what is needed by the learner, rather than on the basis of the analysis of the errors he makes – we assume not only the selection of items but the organization of those items into some rational order i.e. *grading*.

The essential problem involved in grading is to distinguish what is grammatically *simple* from what is psychologically *easy* to learn. The usual assumption has been that a syllabus moves from simple to complex and that that is identical to the movement from easy to difficult. There is little evidence to support this. For example, in the TG-based *Corso d'inglese parlato* (see 5.2.4.) the sentence *John may have been reading the paper* comes before *John isn't reading the paper*, on the grounds that transformationally, the first sentence is simpler than the second i.e. it is, essentially, a kernal sentence, while the second contains a transformation and is therefore, by definition, more complex. It seems clear, at least intuitively, that the learner would probably find the 'complex' sentence 'easier' than the 'simple' one, which would, probably, turn out to be rather 'difficult' to learn.

We shall limit the discussion in this section to the grading of items, in the sense of the order in which they are to be presented, and leave until section 3.6 the question of the way in which we might present them.

Three kinds of grading problem arise depending on the items to be graded; grammatical, situational or notional.

3.5.1. Grammatical grading

A grammatical syllabus, as we saw earlier, takes grammatical items – in the broad sense of 'code' items; sound system, syntax and lexis (vocabulary) –

to be the units to be taught and grades them from simplest to most complex.
We can look at each of the three levels of linguistic analysis in turn and
consider what problems of grading arise at each level:

a) *Phonology:* the sound system has to be learned in its entirety and,
probably, from the earliest stages. Although there are certainly some 'difficult' sounds – the English 'th' sounds /θ/ and /ð/, as in *thin* and *then*, for
example – in any language, it is impossible to avoid their use for long. The
learner will need all the vowels and consonants from the start. The stress
and intonation system might be gradable, at least for production purposes,
by only introducing a small number of patterns at first e.g. in English, limi-
ting 'tones' to those with rising or falling tones and holding in reserve
complex tones such as the fall-rise. Even so, for reception purposes, the
learner will have to be taught to recognize, distinguish among and understand the differing meanings of the whole system. In some languages,
Chinese for example, the tones need to be taught immediately, since their
function is as crucial as the vowel and consonant distinctions. There might
well also be an argument for marking word stress in English, at least until
the learner is able to manage without such markings e.g. we might mark
the noun-verb distinction between *a permit* and *to permit* with diacritical
marks *a 'permit* in contrast with *to per'mit*. Such markings were first introduced by the Alexandrian grammarians nearly two thousand years ago for
the FL learner of Greek and can already be found in many ELT dictionaries.

b) *Syntax:* while it is a relatively simple matter to decide which structures
are grammatically simple or complex and to grade on that basis, as we
pointed out earlier, the relationship between grammatically simple and psychologically easy is far from straightforward. We have, bluntly, no firm
criteria for deciding what can be easily learned and what is inherently difficult in language learning. We have criteria of usefulness however. All learners
– with the exception of those whose language can be clearly defined and
limited e.g. the airport flight announcer – will need to make statements,
negate them, question others and reply to questions, handle time reference
and so forth. But, notice that these are notional categories not grammatical.
In the end, the ability of a learner to communicate with native speakers
will depend a great deal on the goodwill of the natives; a beautiful young
woman, alone amongst monolingual speakers of the target language, will
probably find her efforts more readily accepted than those of a toothless
octogenarian man in the same circumstances! Until the distinction between
grammatical and psychological criteria is sorted out, we shall presumably
have to continue with grading on a grammatical basis, inefficient though
we recognize that to be.

c) *Lexis:* this includes not only the vocabulary of the language but the
'word-building' processes, which allow the user to derive semantically related
words from a simple base item e.g. taking the root *simple*, the learner will
need to have rules for the creation of such related words as *simply, simplify,
simplification* and spelling rules to prevent the writing of **simplelyfycateion*
in the basis of its internal structure; *simple + ly + fy + c + ate + ion*. The

degree to which the learner will find such processes a difficulty may well relate to the structure of the lexis of his L1. The world's languages differ a great deal in this respect. Chinese, for example, has a lexis which consists of un-modifiable monosyllables i.e. there are no affixes — prefixes or suffixes — in Chinese, modifications are isolated words, free morphemes in their own right. Turkish adds suffixes after the root; R + (s) + (s). In the Semitic languages, for example, Arabic and Hebrew, the root consists of three consonants before which, between which and after which affixes can be added; (p)R(i)R(i)R(s) i.e. optional prefixes, infixes and suffixes with a three part root. Not only will the learner of English need to cope with morphological rules of this type but will need to integrate them with word-stress rules, since the suffixes alter the assignment of stress in the word e.g. *'simplify* and *simplifi'cation.*

We might, again, fall back on the criterion of usefulness. If we have been able to define the needs of the learner and specify the terminal behaviour required to fulfil those needs, it should be possible to list, roughly, the items needed and grade them from short to long, assuming that shorter items are actually easier to learn than long ones. There is some evidence for this. Psychologists suggest that the optimum string — of syllables, say — will consist of 'the magic number 7, plus or minus 2' (Miller 1964).

Unfortunately, the essential words of a language, without which the learner could not hope to communicate, tend not only to be short but also irregular. If we give the learner credit for forming analogies and generalizing rules from them, what kind of rule will he assume if he has learned *be, being, been, was, were, is, am, are*? What will he expect *add*, for example, to be like?

Grammatical grading, then, presents serious problems for the syllabus designer which perhaps can only be resolved by adopting a different approach; situational or notional.

3.5.2. Situational grading

As we noted earlier, situational syllabuses are not, actually, syllabuses which list situations nor, as we shall see, are the situations graded from 'easy' to 'difficult'. The reason for this is plain; there is no way in which the syllabus designer can decide whether a situation is easy or difficult to learn or whether, in sociological terms, it is simple or complex. Indeed, the grammarian is on far safer ground, since he has strict criteria for deciding on the complexity of any sentence. He has well-articulated rules for demonstrating syntactic complexity. The social scientist is not in such a happy position. He has some rough and ready taxonomies of items involved in situations — setting, participants, etc. — but only very hazy notions of how these items interrelate. In a sense, all situations are equally complex. It is only where the actions and understanding of the participants are prescribed by ritual that a situation can be thought of as 'simple' but such situations are, of necessity, the least useful to the learner. Add to this the further complication that the language learner needs not only the appropriate non-verbal behaviour but the appropriate verbal behaviour as well and the problem becomes enormous. Once again, it is only in ritualized interaction that the language is predictable and in all other situations the language cannot be predetermined.

What can be predicted, to some degree, is what people might wish to *mean* in a particular situation; the *notions* they may wish to express.

3.5.3. Notional grading

In the past, grading has been in terms of formal structural items — Mackey (*op. cit.*) gives an exhaustive set of parameters — but recent advances in linguistics and the human sciences (see 6.1. for more detailed discussion of this) have directed our attention to the need to base our teaching on the *concepts, notions* and *functions* which are expressed by linguistic forms.

We are faced now by a double problem:

(a) How do we grade linguistic items?

(b) How do we grade concepts?

Within well-recognized limits, we know that the formal items can, albeit rather unsatisfactorily, be graded but can notions? There is some evidence to show that some concepts are easier to learn than others; at least, we can deduce that this is the case from studies of L1 acquisition. Unfortunately, this is probably irrelevant to the task of grading notions for adult learners of an L2. Such learners possess, by definition, a full battery of concepts and will, in learning another language, not be called upon to learn new concepts at all. A further complication arises with the adult learner. All, we presume, have a shared set of 'basic notions' — space, time, quantity, etc. — but the sub-concepts and sub-sub-concepts each understands will differ in relation to the degree of formal education he has had and the degree to which he needs subtle sub-divisions of concepts to play the roles he fills in his daily life. The physicist, for example, will inevitably possess a greater range of notions relating to 'space' and 'time' than does the man-in-the-street. Equally, the man-in-the-street who has studied geometry at school will perceive more conceptual distinctions in the basic notion of space than will the man who has had only an elementary education.

This begins to suggest that the teaching of any but the elemental concepts — which will not be necessary for the adult learner — is a problem of education in general rather than one specific to FL teaching.

We appear to have argued that there is no way of grading notions for FL teaching and indeed this does appear to be the case if we mean by grading the arrangement of items from easiest to learn to the most difficult and if we keep to the fundamental concepts. If we wish to expand the learner's knowledge and comprehension of the concepts he already has, we are faced by a problem of general education. If our goal is to expand the ability of the learner to express more complex notions in the L2, we are faced by the need to design a 'special purposes' course, the conceptual content of which will have to come from the specialist subject teacher who, after all, already grades the notions involved in his own discipline when designing his own syllabus. This brings us back to the sufficiently difficult issue of grading linguistic form.

However, we could approach the problem of grading from a different angle. Rather than attempt to grade from 'easy' to 'difficult', we might attempt a grading based on usefulness to the learner. This, naturally, implies a thorough investigation of *needs* as a major input to our syllabus (see 2.2. for a preliminary discussion of this, 6.5.4. for more detail and Appendix A for a case study in which needs are related to the design of the syllabus).

Apart from the difficulty we are likely to have in keeping the 'easy–difficult' and 'most useful–least useful' criteria separate in our minds as we grade, there is another question: who should do the grading? Individuals are likely to have idiosyncratic views about 'usefulness' but it might be possible to take a group of language teachers who knew the learners well and ask them to grade not only the notions but also the linguistic forms in the order in which they would present them. A consensus, if it emerged, would at least give us some insight into the intuitions shared by teachers and syllabus designers (see Bell 1980b for a small-scale experiment on these lines).

Neither Wilkins (1976) nor Munby (*op. cit.*) attempt more than a listing of notions. Wilkins' grading is of formal linguistic items alone.

3.5.4. Summary

We have, in our discussion of the problem of grading, arrived at no precise conclusion other than to state that all three types of grading – grammatical, situational and notional – present very substantial difficulties for the syllabus designer. The grammatical syllabus is difficult to grade because it is tied to linguistic units which can be ranked in order of grammatical complexity but not in order of difficulty of learning. The identical psychological problem appears with any attempt at grading situations and as we have argued above, the grading of notions may, in fact, be unnecessary.

The safest advice to the teacher may well be for him to avoid, in so far as it is in his power to do so, *a priori* syllabuses and approach the task of language teaching in an *a posteriori* way i.e. by building small-scale and short-term syllabuses on the basis of his analysis of learners' errors. The implications of this are that we capitalize on the successive pidgin-like systems which the learner creates and, by discovering the system the learner is using, provide constructive feedback which will allow him to modify his system in the direction of the norms of the target language. An attempt has been made – at the University of Poznan in Poland – to teach in just this way but the experiment has not yet been run for a sufficient length of time to allow any generalizations to be made about it. One point, however, is clear. If we were to adopt such an approach, we should need to accept, at the early stages, generalizations of the rules that would produce forms like **sheeps, *childs, *goed, *eated, *gooder*, etc. just as we do with the small child acquiring his L1 and for the excellent and sufficient reasons that such forms will communicate and are the result of the application of the powerful and productive rules which the user will need to apply to the vast majority of lexical items. The learner with a reduced system of this type will have laid the basis for later study but, even if his system fossilizes in this form, the course will still have, as Pit Corder so neatly puts it, a 'high surrender value' i.e. he will have a communication system in the L2, crude and full of error, but one which will work to some extent.

3.6. THE ORGANIZATION OF THE SYLLABUS

Irrespective of the type of item we choose as the basis of our syllabus and the grading we adopt, there is still the actual organization of the syllabus to be arranged i.e. we need to decide whether we will plan, *a priori*, the items the learner will learn, or rather, that we will teach, on a given day or whether, conversely, we will build up the syllabus as we go along, drawing on the learner's errors and designing the syllabus *a posteriori*. In addition, there is the question of the actual layout of the syllabus; will each item be presented only once or will it be returned to several times during the course? We shall discuss each of these alternatives below.

3.6.1. *A Posteriori* syllabuses

At its most extreme, syllabus design can be a refusal to design at all i.e. the advice 'go to the country and "pick up" the language there' is a sort of syllabus, the contents of which are in no way predictable or organized. In defence of such a 'syllabus', it could be pointed out that learning in that way would closely parallel the manner in which the pre-school child acquires his L1. Against such a view can be put the matter of time; the adult learner normally has not got the four or five years free to dedicate himself to the task that the child has. In any case, the teacher who advocated the sending of his students out of the country to 'pick up' the language would soon find himself without students or a job.

A less extreme approach would be the development of an organic individualized syllabus i.e. the syllabus would grow out of the needs of the learner as demonstrated by his errors. Such a syllabus would, presumably, have as its initial input the kind of items found in the first few units of *Situational English* (see 7.4. and Appendix D, Section 4); identification; the learner identifying himself and others in very simple terms e.g. 'I'm George Scott', 'He's Fred Smith', 'She's Mary Jones' etc., and location; I'm here', 'You're there' etc. Soon, the teacher ought to be introducing items which he knows the learner has an interest in, to encourage him to go beyond what he is sure of, to express what he wishes to express. This will produce ample data for error analysis but, if the learner is sophisticated and has mastered the 'avoidance techniques' of the experienced FL learner, the teacher may need to apply a diagnostic test to force the learner into using forms about which he is unsure e.g. a typical avoidance technique for English learners of French is to put nouns in the plural, thus avoiding the masculine-feminine gender problem and the obligatory selection of *le* or *la* as the definite article, by selecting the undifferentiated *les*. A syllabus of this type could be justified by pointing out that it gives the learner the opportunity to use his problem-solving skills to the full and always provides him with the data that he needs when he needs it. A number of practical problems appear evident. The 'face validity' of such a syllabus is small; educational administrators may take a great deal of persuading that the teacher intends to do anything and may feel that the lack of an *a priori* syllabus is a clear indication of incompetence and laziness on the part of the teacher. In addition, the syllabus is supposed to be individual but few teachers have the luxury of teaching one learner at a time. We teach classes, usually classes which are far too large. The question, then, is whether the learning of a group is sufficiently similar, from individual to individual, to allow the teacher to collect errors together and deal with them as though they came from a single individual. As yet, we just do not know the answer to this question, although research is going on and the first tentative conclusions suggest that such a group approach can work.

However, there are ways of helping individuals to learn in groups which recognize that the learning process involves the individual in using his existing knowledge and cognitive processes and encourages learners to learn from each other rather than be told what to learn by a teacher i.e. a process of 'self-discovery' in which the teacher plays a role more akin to that of the psychiatrist or non-directive counsellor. Two stand out as particularly well articulated: Gattegno's *Silent Way* (Gattegno 1963) and Curran's *Counseling Learning* (1972) or, more broadly, *Community Language Learning* (1976). Though in details the two approaches are different, there is sufficient common to them to allow us to list some general principles and techniques.

Both approaches recognize that the object of the exercise is *learning* and that teaching should be subordinated to this goal. As Gattegno puts it, 'the teacher must stop side tracking the learner' and let his mind 'equip itself by its own working, trial and error, deliberate experimentation, by suspending judgement and revising conclusions'. Gattegno goes so far as to call the majority of interventions by teachers 'noise' (in very much the sense we use the term in 6.4. below) which interferes with the learning process! Hence, he insists on purposive *silence* as part of the programme and for two reasons; psycholinguistic studies have shown pretty conclusively that our short-term memories last for about 20 seconds during which time the mind is able to 'process' the data it has received by inspecting it, rearranging it, even rehearsing it for future reproduction – like a tape-loop or a work-table covered with objects that need sorting out – and, learners teach themselves and each other, changing the teacher's role from that of the all-knowing, all-powerful Controlling Parent (to use Berne's 1964 terminology) to that of the understanding, all-nurturing Parent i.e. a helping resource-person.

Both approaches see the learning situation as one in which the learner begins with many child characteristics – he is ignorant of the facts of the target language (themselves parent data par excellence; externally imposed, inescapable prescriptions about how to behave), very insecure, perhaps rather self-centred and even rebellious towards, or over-dependent on, the teacher. It is all too easy for the teacher, in such circumstances, to behave in a domineering parent manner, when what is clearly needed is for both parties to develop, as quickly as possible, an adult–adult relationship. This requires of the learner a willingness to recognize his initial child status and to accept the help offered by the teacher, and of the teacher a willingness to relinquish his powerful position in favour of one which will, ultimately, make him redundant and of both to try to work together as adults to share the learning experience.

Fine words one may feel but how? Curran sees the process as consisting of two steps; *investment* during which the learner commits himself, as fully as he can, to engaging in conversation in the target language with the rest of the group and *reflection* during which he, so to speak, stands back and reviews, with the help of the teacher, what he has learned in the investment activities.

Curran suggests five stages of investment each with periods of reflection between them:

Stage 1: the learners sit in a circle and each, in order, tells the teacher what he wishes to say to the others. This can be about anything he chooses but should consist of only five or six words. At first, this will be in the L1 and the teacher will quietly tell him how to express himself in the L2. The learner will repeat this as well as he can and will record his utterance on tape. The 'turn' then passes to another learner and the teacher helps in exactly the same way. At this stage the learner is completely dependent on the teacher whose help represents maximum security for the learner.

Stage 2: as before the learners talk to each other and record their efforts. But, as their self-assurance increases, the utterances will, increasingly, be in the L2 and will be produced without assistance from the teacher. Translation will only be resorted to, at this stage, when one of the learners asks for it and, even then, it will be the responsibility of the learner, not the teacher, to provide one. Now the learner is beginning to take the first steps towards independence.

Stage 3: the same procedure continues but, as the learner grows in his knowledge of the L2, he will become annoyed by any suggested improvements made by the teacher. When this annoyance ceases the learner will have reached

Stage 4: after which his development, and that of the group as a whole, will continue so that the teacher's task will in

Stage 5: be limited to commenting on the appropriateness rather than the grammaticalness of utterances and suggesting stylistic variations which could be employed. He will intervene as little as possible.

At this stage, as Curran tersely puts it, the teacher should 'test, then get out of the way'. The five stages are illustrated in Figure 3.2. below.

Figure 3.2.
**Stages in language counsellor–client relationship from
dependency to independence**

I
Total dependence on language
counsellor. Idea said in English, then
said to group in foreign language, as
counsellor slowly and sensitively
gives each word to the client.

II
Beginning courage to make some
attempts to speak in the foreign
language as words and phrases are
picked up and retained.

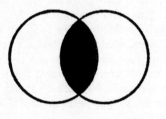

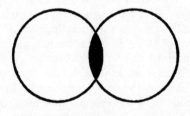

III
Growing indipendence with mistakes that are immediately corrected
by counsellor.

IV
Needing counsellor now only for
idioms and more subtle expressions
and grammar.

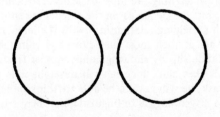

V
Independent and free communication in the foreign
language. Counsellor's *silent* presence reinforces correctness of grammar and pronunciation.

Three stages of reflection are suggested:

Stage 1: learners are encouraged to discuss what they have learned, what their problems have been and so forth. They are encouraged to approach this discussion as whole persons, exploring their experience in their cognitive, emotional and physical aspects.

Stage 2: the tape is played back and listened to without any comment from the teacher. This can be done quickly, because a recording which took perhaps 5 minutes to make can be played back in 20 or 30 seconds. The play-back should have the effect of encouraging the learners. After all, it is a record of them actually communicating about things which interest them in the target language; something which cannot be expected for a long time in a more traditional course.

Stage 3: the tape is played back but this time utterance by utterance which gives teacher and learners the opportunity to discuss, question, check, generalize, etc.

It is to be expected that each of these reflection stages will be used after each investment session but, inevitably, the amount of time given to each will change as the learners become more confident and knowledgeable and several arrangements are, of course, possible (see Figure 3.3. below).

The Silent Way, is even more revolutionary, since it makes use of ten rods, all with the same cross-section but differing from each other in length and colour, as the basic 'props' for speech production. The rods can be moved about to create models, pictures, maps, whatever the learners have imagined and wish to illustrate. There are, too, word and sound charts, drawings, worksheets, books, tapes and records which are drawn upon as and when they seem appropriate. In this approach, the teacher's speech is reduced to the absolute minimum; the learners doing as much as 90% of the speaking from the earliest stages of learning.

Both the Silent Way and Counselling Learning stress the importance of allowing the learner to find his own way through the intellectual puzzle of a new language and, in this way, both are highly cognitive in their orientation (see 5.2.3. on this). As Curran says 'In order to unify and bring together the whole person in the learning process, we have to do more than merely label it whole-person learning. We must basically restructure our approach' (Curran 1972.6). But the demands on the teacher are enormous. Not only must he establish a 'helping relationship' with the learners from the very start when they are at their most suspicious and vulnerable but he must never let this attitude slip by showing annoyance or frustration when the learner makes mistakes and, since he will never be able to predict what they will say or ask, he will have to be able to 'think on his feet' and cope with any problem, psychological or linguistic, that may arise.

3.6.2. *A priori* syllabuses

At the other extreme from the random non-predictive syllabus is the totally predictive syllabus which lays down in advance the items to be taught, the

Figure 3.3.
Counselling foreign language research:
design of the different positions in language counselling discussions

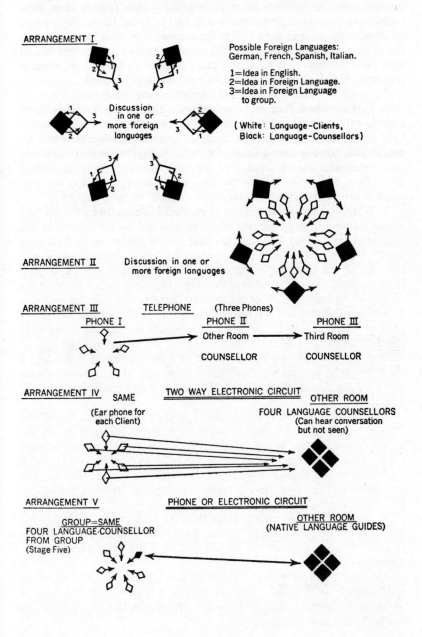

ARRANGEMENT I

Possible Foreign Languages:
German, French, Spanish, Italian.

1=Idea in English.
2=Idea in Foreign Language.
3=Idea in Foreign Language
 to group.

Discussion
in one or
more foreign
languages

(White: Language-Clients,
 Black: Language-Counsellors)

ARRANGEMENT II   Discussion in one or
more foreign languages

ARRANGEMENT III   TELEPHONE   (Three Phones)
PHONE I   PHONE II   PHONE III
Other Room   Third Room
COUNSELLOR   COUNSELLOR

ARRANGEMENT IV   SAME   TWO WAY ELECTRONIC CIRCUIT   OTHER ROOM
(Ear phone for
each Client)   FOUR LANGUAGE COUNSELLORS
(Can hear conversation
but not seen)

ARRANGEMENT V   PHONE OR ELECTRONIC CIRCUIT
GROUP=SAME   OTHER ROOM
FOUR LANGUAGE-COUNSELLOR   (NATIVE LANGUAGE GUIDES)
FROM GROUP
(Stage Five)

order of their presentation, the drills and exercises to be used (cf. the Michigan Materials 5.1.4.). This type of syllabus can be termed a *linear* syllabus. It is designed on the assumption that, since teaching is organized institutionally to follow a linear progression — class follows class, term follows term — learning must necessarily also be linear. Hence, virtually all FL textbooks are organized in a linear manner. The most linear syllabus, the single-route programmed learning syllabus, proceeds from unit to unit with no alternative pathways, and loops to clear up specific problems as they arise. Few language syllabuses are even that sophisticated.

There are two false assumptions underlying linear syllabuses:

1. That learning is linear and cumulative i.e. that human learning follows a single path and that an item cannot be learned unless those taught earlier have already been learned. Psychological experiments have shown that we can, and do, partially learn a range of items or skills, that we make advances on a broad and uneven front, that we need revision to shift the learned items from the short-term to the long-term memory and that we need practice in order to achieve mastery over the skills we have learned.

2. That the order of learning can be predicted in advance by the teacher, whose learning strategy can therefore be imposed on the learner as the only teaching strategy. We shall see later, in our discussion of the strong claim of contrastive linguistics (Appendix B) that this assumption was at the root of the structuralist materials of the 1950s and derived, in part, from the stimulus-response view of learning. Cognitive psychology, stressing as it does the individuality of the learner, suggests that learning strategies cannot be predicted and the teacher would be better employed acting as a kind of 'resource centre' to which the learner would have recourse in checking his hypotheses about the structure of the target language.

One way of mitigating the effects of an *a priori* syllabus is to adopt a spiral or cyclic approach rather than a linear one. Most linear syllabuses contain some degree of revision i.e. they are, in a very crude way, partially cyclic.

A more sophisticated spiral syllabus (we shall use the terms 'spiral' and 'cyclic' indiscriminately) would consist of items or topics to which the learner would return, at regular intervals, for more and more profound study, the depth of which would be decided upon in an *ad hoc* way, through error analysis and diagnostic testing i.e. it would be a compromise between an *a priori* and an *a posteriori* syllabus: (the notional materials reproduced in 7.5.5. are based on this approach)

A notional syllabus clearly lends itself to such an approach e.g. the notion of future time reference is first introduced with the form *going to*, returned to later with the forms *will* and *shall* and again with the form present tense + adverb.

An other alternative (Howatt and Treacher 1969) would be to take a small number of themes — four, in the example we shall give — each of which would appear in each of the years — in this case, three — of the course but with varying weightings:

Theme 1: Personal relationships; relationships between family and friends.

Theme 2: Social relationships; the activities of the community.

Theme 3: Cultural life; the habits, customs, traditions and so forth of the community.

Theme 4: Natural environment; the ecology, human geography, science, technology, etc. of the country in which the students live.

For example, within the main theme 'cultural life', there might be a sub-theme 'festivals and holidays', introduced in the first year by focusing on the major festivals and holidays in Britain assuming that our learners are learning British English and acquiring some elements of British culture — giving an outline of when they take place and how they are celebrated. In the second year, the topic can be returned to and studied historically; the origin of the festivals and the ways in which they were celebrated in the past. In the third year, the topic reappears and is studied comparatively; such events in the English-speaking world are compared with festivals in the home culture(s) of the students. The four major themes might be distributed something like this:

Figure 3.4.
A four-theme, three-year cyclic syllabus

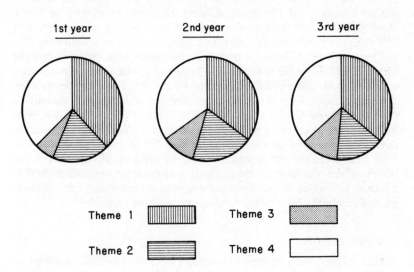

Such a cyclic progression has substantial advantages over a linear syllabus:

1. Themes can be chosen on the basis of prior research into the areas of

interest of the student and will, therefore, assist student motivation.

2. Themes can be seen to be broad areas of knowledge dealt with, initially, in a superficial way but later approached in greater detail. The learner will see that he is not only learning the language but, in an organized way, the cultural background he will need in order to use the language appropriately.

A number of courses have used or are using this kind of approach – the Poznan course (referred to earlier), the *Scope* materials for teenage immigrants in Britain (Derrick *et al* 1968) and the Kuwait secondary syllabus (Hajjaj *et al..* 1976) for example – all of which claim successes greater than those achieved by the linear syllabuses.

Summary

It seems clear that the ideal syllabus would be one based on a needs analysis in which language items were presented cyclically and, if graded at all, graded in a rather *ad hoc* way which reflected both usefulness and ease of learning.

The implications of this for traditional syllabus design are striking. For example, most courses tend to introduce language appropriate for face-to-face interaction at a very early stage but in a course for science students, for example, who would only use the language for access to written materials and for whom lectures, seminars and laboratory work would all be in the mother tongue – the typical situation of the science student in the 'developed' world – such skills would be redundant. Similarly, a science student will need the passive construction in English from the very beginning. The textbook will state *the water is then boiled* rather than *then you boil the water.* It will also make use of *should* as part of the language of instruction e.g. *the experiment should be repeated several times.* We can contrast the very early appearance of *should* in an ESP course for science students – *Nucleus; General Science* (Bates & Dudley-Evans 1977) – in unit 6, with its traditional place in a general linear syllabus – *The Study of English in India* (Ministry of Education 1967) – in unit 271 of a total of 376.

A final word on the organization of the syllabus. We need a syllabus which reflects the needs of the student, in so far as we can predict them in advance, but which is also flexible enough to permit changes as feedback, particularly in the form of learners' errors, becomes available.

3.7. CONCLUSION

In this chapter, we have been examining a number of specific problems involved in the creation of language syllabuses and considering some of the answers which have been suggested as solutions to those problems.

In particular we have been suggesting that there are three distinct types of syllabus – grammatical, situational and notional – each with its own strengths and weaknesses and for that reason have been forced to fall back on our belief in 'enlightened eclecticism'. We accept that this is, in some ways, a weak position to adopt and intend in the next three chapters to re-examine the problems of language teaching from an historical view-point in the hopes of deriving from an examination of the range of approaches which have been used during the last 100 years, a clearer picture of what appears to work best and why.

In the next chapter, we shall put the clock back to the turn of the century and examine the influence of 'traditional grammar' and that of the Early Modern Linguists on language teaching up to the early 1940s.

SUGGESTED FURTHER READING

Banathy B. H. & Dale L. L. (1972), *A Design for Foreign Language Curriculum*
The authors argue that most books on curriculum design have tended to stress *method* at the expense of *content* and state that the aim of their book is to redress this imbalance. In essence, this book covers the same area but Banathy and Dale reach the level of the design of the individual unit which we do not attempt.

Candlin C. N. *et al.* (1978), *'Study Skills in English; theoretical issues and practical problems'*. in Mackey & Mountford (eds.)
A useful survey of the issues involved in the design of an EAP (English for Academic Purposes) course. To some degree now superseded by Munby (1978).

Diller K. C. (1978), *The Language Teaching Controversy* (Newby House)
Diller argues, in this book, that the crucial distinction between approaches in FLT rests on the scientific method and philosophy of the linguists involved. This is in strong contrast with the position we adopt in the next section and, if only for that reason, worth reading.

Mackey W. F. (1965), *Language Teaching Analysis* (Longman)
The 'classic' attempt to operationalize the analysis of language teaching methodologies. The book is beginning to show its age but is still valuable for its comprehensiveness (up to 1965, that is).

Wilkins D. A. (1976), *Notional Syllabuses* (OUP)
This spells out the work done on notional syllabus design by the Council of Europe and by Wilkins in particular up to 1975. It should be supplemented by referring to the original Council of Europe publications, especially van Ek (1979).

PART TWO
A CENTURY OF CONTROVERSY IN LANGUAGE TEACHING

In Part I, we were concerned with defining the problems faced by the designer of training materials, listing the kinds of likely response to such problems by focusing attention on, what we believe to be, the key issues and specifying a step-by-step approach to syllabus design.

In Part II, we shall still be facing the same issues but our orientation to them will be different. In Part I, we were approaching the problems in a *synchronic* way i.e. asking what we should do *now* to solve particular difficulties. In Part II, our orientation will be *diachronic* i.e. surveying the ways language teachers have attempted, over the last 100 years, to solve the same problems.

Such a survey will involve us in looking at some of the *materials* produced during the period, linking them to a particular *method* and, finally, assigning them to a specific *approach*. Unless we organize our survey, all that will appear will be a disconnected series of 'methods', listed, but in no way analyzed.

Let us introduce Part II by stating what we mean by an *approach* and how it differs from a *method* (in doing this we are picking up a series of distinctions we first made at the end of Chapter 1; in 1.4).

An *approach* is an orientation to the problem of language learning which derives from an amalgam of linguistic and psychological insights into the nature of language and the nature of the learning process. Well-articulated, an *approach* is a Theory of Applied Linguistics which seeks to explain the phenomenon of language-learning in terms which will assist the learner to achieve his goal. At its root will be the answers which the particular applied linguist gives to the two key questions we raised at the beginning of this book:

(a) What is language?

(b) How do people learn languages?

A *method* is the application of the insights which constitute the *approach* to the problem of language learning. Typically, a method will have a *pedagogical grammar* − or grammars − associated with it and principles which guide the creation of such grammars, the selection of elements to be taught and of techniques for teaching them.

Materials are the texts and other aids the teacher uses to assist in the learning process. They are, necessarily, the output of the *approach* arrived at by the application of the method.

We wish to argue that the primary question on which an *approach* rests is the first; what is language? The answer to this defines the content of the

75

syllabus; *what* is to be learned. We would further argue that the answer to the second question – how is language learned? – is, by definition, one of method, since it leads us to a specification of how the content is to be learned and is, therefore, not a defining characteristic of an *approach.*

If this is accepted, we begin to see why Transformational-Generative Linguistics has had so *little* impact on Applied Linguistics. The specification of the content to be learned has not been changed by the shift from an empiricist to a rationalist view of the nature of human learning. Indeed, this leads us to understand why TG itself is revolutionary in its influence in Theoretical Linguistics – it constitutes a radical change in Scientific Method for the discipline – but has thrown up hardly anything 'new' in language teaching.

We have, it would appear, only *one approach* which contains, or would contain if they had been more clearly specified, two *methods.*

A contrasting *approach* must rest on a contrasting view of the nature of language, since it is that which will give us different content for our syllabus.

Distinct though Structuralist and Transformational-Generative Linguistics are in their selection of Scientific Method and, when drawn upon to create an Applied Linguistics *approach*, their psychology – *behaviourist* versus *cognitive* – they are in agreement on the issue of *content*; it is *form.* By our definition both theories are subsumed in the same *approach*; one which sees the goal of language learning as the mastery of a decontextualized *code.*

We realize that in asserting this we are running counter to recent explanations of the controversy which has raged over language teaching methods during this century (Diller *op. cit.* in particular leans heavily on the empiricism–rationalism dichotomy) but we believe it to be the case that the controversy has been, in our terms, over method rather than approach and that a new *approach* has only begun to emerge during the last decade.

If, rather than define language as a *code*, we take it to be *social behaviour* or a *social skill*, we are adopting a 'human science' view of the phenomenon and, to be more specific, that adopted by Sociolinguistics. (We are using the term 'sociolinguistics' in a rather general sense here to cover both *sociolinguistics* proper and the *sociology of language*. The terms are defined in Bell 1976.28.). Such a view implies a question hidden in the first question – within 'what is language?' lies the further question 'what is language for?' – and this forces the Sociolinguist into a *functionalist* rather than a *formalist* attitude to language and language learning.

However, just as there were two answers to the question 'how do people learn languages?' when we defined language in *formal* terms, so too, there must be two answers when we define it in *functional* terms. Simply put, an *empiricist linguistics* in contrast with a *rationalist linguistics* implies an *empiricist sociolinguistics* (we have labelled it Sociolinguistics 1 below) in contrast with a *rationalist sociolinguistics* (labelled Sociolinguistics 2 below).

Language is:

		Form	Function
Scientific	Empiricism	Structuralist Linguistics	Sociolinguistics 1
Method	Rationalism	Transformational–Generative Linguistics	Sociolinguistics 2

In the discussion above, we used the term 'implies' when referring to the existence of Sociolinguistics 1 and 2. Logically, the existence of the two types of Sociolinguistics is implied but their actual manifestation is, as yet, still shadowy and hinges on the attitude of the individual scholar to the *competence-performance* dichotomy and, specifically, his definition of the sociolinguistic resolution of that dichotomy: *communicative competence.*

The sociolinguistic definition of language as a social skill, and the goal of sociolinguistics as the description and explanation of that skill – the *communicative competence* of the skilled language user – clearly provide the applied linguist with a specification of the content of his syllabus which is markedly different from that offered by the linguist: the contextualized use of the code.

Just as there are empiricist and rationalist ways of looking at the *code*, so too, there are empiricist ways of looking at *communicative competence* – Labov (1966) typifies this view – or rationalist; typified by Hymes (1972). As yet, in contrast with the situation in theoretical linguistics, the clash between the opposed views has yet to become open in sociolinguistics and, therefore, in applied linguistics.

What we now have in applied linguistics are two *approaches* – one *formalist* the other *functionalist* – and a range of methods.

In Chapter 4, we shall survey the influences at work in language teaching during the first four decades of this century. In Chapter 5, we shall look at the impact of *formalism* in linguistics on language teaching before moving on, in Chapters 6 and 7, to a discussion of *functionalism* and the new *approach* it is creating.

However, before we start on our survey, one or two points of terminology ought to be cleared up. We shall be using such terms as *mechanistic* and *mentalistic, behaviourist* and *cognitive, empiricist* and *rationalist, 'traditional', structuralist* and *transformationalist* (or TG) in our descriptions of *philosophical orientation, psychology, scientific method* and *linguistic theory*, respectively.

We wish to distinguish the various elements which make up each *approach* before we begin our discussion. For example, *structuralist linguistics* (the linguistic theory) rests on an *empiricist* scientific method which, in turn, rests on a *mechanistic* philosophy. When applied to language teaching, structuralist linguistics naturally associated itself with a congenial psychology: *behaviourism*. All this, as we shall see is in direct contrast with the *rationalism, mentalism* and *cognitive psychology* associated with TG.

It is not our intention to define any of these terms here, merely to show with which discipline they belong. We shall see, however, in Chapters 4 to 7 a shift from primitive versions of rationalism, mentalism, and cognitive psychology to their converse — in the 1940s and 1950s — and back, in the years following, to a more sophisticated approach, the roots of which lie in the pre-19th-century era.

Perhaps, too, it is appropriate here to explain our selection of examples from published teaching materials. We are not attempting in this book a survey of teaching methods exemplified by 'typical' textbooks in EFL. Our focus is on the more abstract level of the *approach* and our intention to show the relationships between insights derived from linguistics, the human sciences and practical administrative considerations that come together to create an approach. Our selection of examples may seem partial and idiosyncratic — no doubt it is in some ways — but we ask the reader to recognize that the examples have been selected because they conveniently reflect a particular influence and *not* because they are, necessarily, well-known. If our purpose is kept in mind, it ought not to appear perverse that we discuss Roberts' *Corso d'inglese parlato* (1962), which was surely not widely known outside Italy, and ignore, for example, *Essential English* C. E. Eckersley (1963), *New Concept English* Alexander (1978) or *Success with English* Broughton (1978), which must rank amongst the best known and most influential of the post-war ELT textbooks.

A book which sets out to examine materials closely and thereby build up a picture of the development of ELT at the level of materials and method would be interesting and valuable but this book does not do that. We are interested in the interface between the 'parent disciplines' — linguistics, etc. — and applied linguistics and the theoretical result of attempting to combine insights from the contributing disciplines; an *approach* to language teaching.

4 The turn of the century

In this chapter, we shall examine two contrasting approaches to language teaching which derive from differing views on the nature of language, its manner of description and, in so far as it can be deduced, the way in which languages are learned. This will bring us up to the early 1940s, at which point European and American approaches diverged. The appearance of Structuralist Linguistics and, later, Transformational-Generative Linguistics, produced a new approach in North America which, as we shall see in Chapter 6, was little accepted in Europe, where the older tradition of what we have called the 'Early Modern Linguists' continued and expanded its essentially *functional* orientation; in contrast with the *formalist* orientation of the Americans.

4.1. THE WESTERN TRADITION

The study of language has, in Europe, a very ancient history stretching in an unbroken line from the Greeks, through the work of the grammarians and rhetoricians of Alexandria and Rome, to the Scholastic grammarians of the Middle Ages and the normative grammarians of the eighteenth and nineteenth centuries (one of the most accessible surveys of this long tradition is Titone 1968).

From the very beginning, there was a split between those who saw language as a system of elements to be catalogued in a logically satisfying way and those who saw it as a human artifact which had arisen from social and individual needs i.e. a dichotomy between those whose interest in language was the study of its *form* and those whose aim was to describe its *function* (Hörmann 1971 expands on this point).

Equally, there has been a division between those who seek to discover universal characteristics of language as a phenomenon – the *grammatica speculative* of the Middle Ages – and those who wished to produce definitive descriptions of individual languages: *particular grammars* as 19th-century linguists called them (see 4.2.2.).

In scientific method, too, linguistics has oscillated over the centuries between *empiricism* and *rationalism* and the choice of scientific method has always implied a belief about the nature of language learning; a leaning towards what we would today call *behaviourism* or *cognitivism*.

Although we can trace foreign language teaching back as far as Hellenistic times – and by inference, at least back to the Hittites – when, in order to help L2 learners, accents were added to Greek words for the first time, we shall take the Renaissance as our starting point and sketch in from the sixteenth century the tradition on which nineteenth and twentieth-century language teaching rests.

During the period from the Renaissance to the beginning of the nineteenth century, language teaching was seen as a practical matter; teaching people so that they could communicate face-to-face with the native speakers of the chosen language. The orientation to the task was essentially functional. This is in direct contrast with the attitude of the nineteenth-century language teacher who saw in the learning of the language a valuable mental discipline rather than the acquiring of communication skills. The nineteenth century also brought a shift in attention from the spoken to the written medium − in the Renaissance even Latin and Greek were taught to be spoken and only secondarily written − a process which reduced even French and German in Britain to the status of 'dead' language.

The use of the mother tongue in language teaching, which became essential in the nineteenth century, since most learning was through translation and the explanation of the grammar of the L2 in the L1, also marks a contrast between nineteenth-century practice and what had gone before. In the preceding centuries, a kind of 'semi-direct method' was normally used, the teacher only falling back on the L1 where an explanation could be given more efficiently in it than in the L2. Indeed, we can trace this preference for the use of the L2 − the 'target language' − and the exclusion of the L1, where feasible, to no less a source than Comenius' *Didactica Magna* − the Great Didactic − of 1568 but, by the nineteenth century, languages were no longer being taught for communication, so the L1 had to be used.

In his attitude to the learning of rules, the pre-nineteenth-century teacher assumed, as would many modern teachers the *deduction* of rules by the learner from data provided by the teacher. John Locke, the English philosopher (1632–1704), went so far as to take Aesop's *Fables* as his data and have his students deduce the rules of Latin from it. By the nineteenth century, in contrast, language teaching had become a matter of presenting rules in tables and paradigms which the learner was required to memorize by rote.

In short, far from being the 'traditional' approach to FL teaching, the nineteenth century stands out as a deviation from the mainstream of European language teaching to which, during this century, we have been returning. It is remarkable how much in agreement the contemporary and eighteenth-century language teacher would appear to be; language teaching should be geared to producing individuals who can communicate, the mother tongue should be avoided in class, if possible (the Berlitz method, first popularized at the end of the last century is, of course, adamant about this) and learners should be helped to deduce the rules of the L2 from texts rather than be given the rules and be expected to learn them.

4.2. 'TRADITIONAL' GRAMMAR

By 'Traditional' grammar, most people mean nineteenth-century grammar and its teaching. We have already argued above that there is, in fact, nothing 'traditional' about nineteenth-century attitudes to language and language learning but, for us to understand why the late nineteenth-century and early twentieth-century linguists took the stand they did and why the attitudes of many teachers to 'correctness' are as they are, we need to discuss nineteenth-century language teaching, as if it were typical of what had preceded it.

4.2.1. Nineteenth-century 'traditionalist' views on the nature of language

Science, in the nineteenth century took biology as its model and sought, in other phenomena, the open evolving-system characteristics of the living organism. Hence, the traditional linguist would answer the question 'what is language?' by comparing it to a living creature. He would study languages in terms of their evolution from some 'primitive' ancestor into the 'living' languages of the present. He would point to further analogies with living organisms: languages were 'living' or 'dead', they were 'sophisticated' or 'primitive', even 'weak' and 'strong'. There were 'mother' languages which produced (presumably through some unique parthenogenic process!) 'daughter' languages.

In contrast with the normal view of Evolution, many linguistics appeared to believe that the present day language was in some sense 'degenerate' and that the 'purest' form of, for example, English could be found in the recent past; the favourite models were usually prominent writers of the previous century i.e. seventeenth-century for eighteenth-century grammarians eighteenth-century for nineteenth-century grammarians and so forth.

The direct influence of this view of the nature of language on foreign-language teaching cannot have been very great, except in so far as some etymology might be taught to foreign learners and the model offered to them would be rather old fashioned. The indirect influences, which we shall discuss below, were far more important.

We can, perhaps, list a small number of axioms which were universally accepted:

1. *Language is an organism:* growth and change are of more interest than the static formal rules which might describe contemporary usage.

2. *Language is writing:* the written record of the language is the 'purest' form. Speech is secondary and to be distrusted since it is ephemeral and, being contemporary, degenerate. The 'best' models are the writers of earlier periods.

3. *Language is conventional:* 'Language is conventional, and not only invented, but, in its progressive advancement, varied for the purposes of practical convenience.' (Kirkham 1835)

4.2.2. Nineteenth-century 'traditionalist' views on the description of language

Kirkham, in his 1835-grammar, indicates clearly two major streams of thought in traditional linguistics: the notion of a Universal Grammar — the

'Grammatica Speculativa' of the Middle Ages – and the application of the principles of such a grammar to a particular language; a distinction which is, as we shall see, taken up again in the 1960s by transformational-generative linguists. Kirkham says: 'Grammar may be divided into two species, universal and particular. UNIVERSAL GRAMMAR explains the principles which are common to all languages. PARTICULAR GRAMMAR applies those general principles to a particular language, modifying them according to its genius, and the established practice of the best speakers and writers by whom it is used.' (Kirkham *op. cit.* 18)

However, the models for the 'universal grammar' were Latin, and, to a lesser extent, classical Greek, and the inevitable result was that any 'lack of fit' between the ideal and the actual was treated as a mistake and a further example of degeneration. Hence, speakers of English are warned that they should not 'split infinitives', end sentences with prepositions, say 'It's me', all for the apparently sufficient reason that one cannot do any of those things in Latin! The 'split infinitive' is worth a little detailed thought. It is acceptable, even to the traditional grammarian, for users of English to 'split' auxiliaries from main verbs by inserting an adverb, for example; 'can boldly go', 'is boldly going', 'has boldly gone' but not 'to boldly go'. Other than the conventions of Latin grammar, themselves, of course, arbitrary, there appears to be no motivation for such a prohibition.

When the traditional grammarian comes to the actual creation of his grammar, he produces 'rules' and 'explanations' which fail to square with the facts:

1. The rules of traditional grammar derive from logic or semantics. The 'rule' which insists that two negatives make a positive in English is excellent for mathematics or logic but untrue for the language. As a normative rule – 'two negatives ought to make a positive' – it is ideal but not as a descriptive rule i.e. no user of English *really* believes that the utterances 'I haven't no money' and 'I have some money' are equivalent in meaning.

2. The categories used for analysis are semantic and follow the traditional Latin order for Parts of Speech (first century BC). 'A verb is a doing word', 'A noun is the name of a person place or thing', etc.

3. Many of the rules and explanations are incoherent e.g. a 1968-grammar defines an 'object' as 'the term indicating the being or the object acted upon'. Thus in the sentence

John hit Mary

Mary is defined as the 'object'. However, how should *Mary* be classified in

Mary was hit by John?

A glance at a grammar of Latin, on which so much traditional grammar depended, would have shown clearly the distinction between the active sentence containing the form – *Mariam* with the – *am* object ending – and the passive – *Maria* with the – *a* subject ending – and distinguished between the logical and semantic criterion, 'sufferer' of the action, and the purely grammatical criterion, 'subject' of the verb. (we shall take up this point again in Chapter 6).

4.2.3. Nineteenth-century 'traditionalist' views on language learning
It is probably true to say that until this century linguists had no overtly stated view of how foreign languages were learned, even though the earliest surviving FL textbooks go back to the Hellenistic Period and demonstrate, in their addition of accents to stressed syllables, that the distinction between L1 and L2 learning was at least recognized. However, by the nineteenth century the distinction had been lost (see Nesfield 1898, preface III who equates the needs of L1 and L2 learners) and the actual method had evolved into 'grammar and translation' but, the 'grammar' was of necessity, inadequate since it assumed:

1. That the written code was the norm and, indeed, the written code of an earlier period.

2. The learner was already in possession of the general rules of the language and therefore required a prescription of structures and forms to be avoided rather than a description of what was permitted.

3. Where the grammar did attempt to describe, its categories were so ambiguous that the 'explanations' were often more of a confusion than an enlightenment.

4. Description emphasized morphology to the virtual exclusion of syntax i.e. the word-building mechanisms rather than the sentence-building mechanisms and so deprived the learner of the knowledge he needed to create sentences for himself.

In short, as Roulet so aptly puts it: 'in concentrating on the classification of rules and exceptions ... grammars emphasized the prescriptive and mechanical, rather than the systematic aspect of grammar ... In fact, they actively discouraged the pupils' capacities for observation and analysis.' (Roulet 1972.13)

It was just this learning of 'rules' and the final ability to 'talk *about* the language' rather than perform *in* it that, as we shall see, led to the Structuralist emphasis on *practice* and their distrust of explanation in language teaching (see 5.1.4.).

4.2.4. Normative attitudes in language teaching
In an EFL or ESL situation (see 4.2.3. for a definition of these terms) the most normative view which could be expressed would be that the learner was expected to conform to the rules of English as laid down in a nineteenth-century grammar and that his pronunciation was not to deviate in the slightest from some idealized 'BBC English' or 'Queen's English' or 'Oxford English'. Fortunately, teachers are, for the most part, too realistic to set their sights on such an unattainable goal but that does not prevent educational planners, who do not, after all, have to try to implement the policies in the classroom, from setting goals which cannot and should not be reached.

The problem which faces the teacher of a language to non-natives is a straightforward one; the teacher must be normative in the sense that there must be some criteria for deciding whether or not an utterance produced by a learner is to be encouraged in that form or modified in some way. In short, the learner needs a model. Whether that model is to be based on the conventions of one of the great L1 communities – essentially, 'American' or 'British' – or on some locally emerging standard – 'Educated West African', 'General Indian English', etc. – is the key issue.

Let us consider the pros and cons of the two possible sources of a norm for ELT, noting, first, that we are, of necessity, thinking of an ESL situation rather than an EFL situation, for the simple reason that the EFL situation is one which is defined as failing to permit a local version of English to arise through day-to-day use.

4.2.4.1. *Metropolitan models*

By a 'metropolitan' model, we mean the social and regional variety already selected by one of the mother tongue communities to act as the Official Language of the state (see 6.4.2. on this). It will be characterized by *de jure* rules of usage, which are available in grammars and dictionaries and used not only for the teaching of foreigners but also as part of the formal education of the young native.

'Network American', 'Received Pronunciation', 'Educated Australian' and the like are typical labels of such varieties. In grammar and lexis, the distinctions between the various metropolitan varieties are, in fact, very small indeed, so small that it is possible to list them; the American use of the auxiliary 'do' with 'have', as in 'do you have a match?', as against the British 'have you (got) a match?', for example. Even these differences are tending to disappear as the internationally acceptable varieties of English, through increased contact, grow closer together. In pronunciation, the differences are much more apparent; and 'a' in *bath* or the 'o' in *no* or the use of 'r' in *car* and *card* all act as indications of the regional and social provenance of the speaker. However, short vowels – as in *bit, bet, bat, pot, put, putt* – differ little from variety to variety. Nor do the conventions of stress assignment in individual words; the noun-verb contrast seen in *a 'permit* and *to per'mit*, for example, or the fundamental rules for sentence rhythm and intonation; the last lexical item which supplies 'new' rather than 'given' information tends to bear the nuclear tone, etc.

In its written form, the differences between the varieties of internationally acceptable English all but disappear; the half-a-dozen regular differences between American and British spelling conventions – *theater theatre, neighbor neighbour*, etc. are the most striking. Indeed, given the diversity of possible accents available to the user of International English, the written form, complex and seemingly irrational as the spelling system appears to be, provides the only sure means of communication between users of different varieties; if the worst comes to the worst we can, like the Chinese, always write it down.

The advantages of choosing one of the metropolitan varieties as a model are clear:

1. The existence of a codification of its norms which can be referred to when there is a question of acceptability.

2. Large numbers of L1 users whose intuition can be tapped for judgements of grammaticality and acceptability.

3. Large numbers of L1 teachers of the language.

4. Massive numbers of publications and hundreds of thousands of hours of broadcasting annually in the language.

The disadvantage is simply stated: such a model is, no matter how well-known, still *foreign*. Each of the available varieties has grown up to suit the social needs of a community which is not, by definition, the community in which our learners live and in which they will use the language.

4.2.4.2. *Local models*

By a 'local' model, we mean a variety of English which has grown up within the community in which English is being taught. To think in terms of a homogeneous variety here would be as false as to think of a monolithic international English. Language, by its very nature, is variable. It needs to be flexible in order to adapt to changing demands. The range of local Englishes worldwide is enormous; at one end of the scale of intelligibility with international English are the pidgins of Papua–New Guinea and West Africa, next come the varieties of creole found in West Africa – Liberia and Sierra Leone especially – and the Caribbean, next the vernaculars and dialects – an enormous range in themselves; American Black English, regional dialects like Lancashire, Lowland Scots, Southern States dialects, Indian Englishes, etc. – and finally, 'educated' local versions used by the English-educated elite.

The advantage of adopting a local model is the converse of the comment we made above about foreignness: a local model is local and has arisen and changed from the metropolitan standard simply because local people have found the changes necessary and convenient. A local model, then, will be attractive to the learner, if only for the reason that he hears it around him all the time and knows that he can use it without denying his cultural roots.

The disadvantage of a local model are, however, large:

1. The variety will have no *de jure* norms of usage i.e. there will be no published grammar or dictionary. If, by chance, such publications do exist, they will be in the form either of popular pamphlets which list local 'idiosyncrasies' by overtly comparing local usage with the metropolitan standard or else they will be monographs, theses or books written by and for linguists in a style unlikely to be all that clear to the general reader. Nor will such texts be in use as part of the formal education of the young of the community.

2. There may well be *de facto* norms of usage i.e. there will be rules in

85

the minds of the users, but not at a level of consciousness which permits them to be brought out into the open, as it were. The user will 'feel' that certain pronunciations, words and constructions are appropriate and others not e.g. in relaxed Singaporean English the particle — *la* can be attached to the last word of a clause but, if this rule is followed in every instance, the effect would be judged to be rather strange. Consider the extract from a telephone conversation (from Richards and Tay in Crewe 1977):

'Hey' . . . . . . How is life ah? Now jobless still. You working? . . . . . . How about our photos? See nice or not la? I at Lido la . . .'

If we add in a *la* after each clause, the effect is that the speaker is being intentionally sarcastic compared with the first version which is judged to be 'more natural'. But how to express the rule which the users obey in a formal grammar?

3. In the case of the standard metropolitan variety, there is a clearly definable community of users whose intuitive knowledge can be drawn on. In the case of the local varieties, there is no such community. It is possible, in principle, to define a community and then describe its usage but, for local varieties, this has yet to be done.

4. If we selected the speech of the elite of the country as our model, we should still be left with the problem of style. The formal, careful usage of such a group — leading politicians, senior executives, radio and television announcers for example — is likely to conform very closely, except in accent, to the worldwide standards for such a style of spoken English. Their written English will, also, be virtually unrecognizable as a local variety but what of relaxed speech? Relaxed local varieties are, after all, what the learner will hear and use most, both during his schooling and afterwards.

5. The emphasis on a metropolitan version of English as a model for *all* functions presents the learner with a dilemma. If he tries to use such a formal and alien English amongst his family and friends, it will not work. It will not work for two reasons, firstly formal English is not designed to cope with informal situations — that is why there is, in addition to formal British English an informal version (or more properly, a range of versions expressing degrees of formality and informality) — and secondly, there is, already, a relaxed local form which has proved itself through use, which the learner already controls. What is needed, in such a situation, is a recognition by teachers and planners that the local vernacular exists and has a place in the community and that an attempt to hold up a norm of formal British English for all purposes is doomed to failure i.e. the goal should be to sensitize teachers and taught to the fact of variation and the proper use of formal and informal English.

In short, there is a danger in contemporary ELT of aiming at a model which is as inappropriate for the learner as the normative model of nineteenth-century English is for the L1 student. What needs to be done in selecting a model is two-fold:

1. The available varieties need to be described.
2. The appropriate social contexts of the use of the various varieties need to be defined.

Only by doing this can the teacher become normative in an enlightened way which will permit the learner to concentrate on realistic goals.

4.3. 'EARLY MODERN LINGUISTICS'

In the previous section, we painted a rather too bleak picture of the state of linguistics and of language teaching in the nineteenth century. In fact, as the century progressed, considerable advances were made, particularly, though not exclusively, in phonetics. The International Phonetic Association — initially, and, from our point of view, very significantly, known as the Phonetic Teachers' Association — was founded in 1886 and immediately set itself the task of producing an International Phonetic Alphabet by means of which all the sounds of all the world's languages could be represented.

In applied linguistics too, advances were being made. In particular, such figures as Henry Sweet (1845-1912), Otto Jespersen (1860-1943) and Harold Palmer (1877-1949) stand out as the founders of modern language-teaching methods, giving advice and suggesting techniques which have an embarassingly 'contemporary' ring to them.

We shall not discuss in detail the contribution of each of these linguists (Titone *op. cit.* does that) nor list and describe the various methods which were in vogue in the period (Diller *op. cit.* provides such a survey), but rather try to build up a composite picture of the views and practices of linguists and language teachers in the last decades of the nineteenth century and the first quarter of this. It should be recognized, however, that our use of the term 'early modern linguists' for these scholars does not imply that they belonged, in any official sense, to some common school. They did not. What they did have in common was a series of assumptions about the nature of language, the way in which it should be described and the implications of those assumptions for language teaching. We shall outline these below and contrast them with the views of the nineteenth-century 'traditionalists'.

4.3.1. Early modern views on the nature of language
By the end of the nineteenth century, the physical sciences were beginning to assert themselves as models of scientific endeavour, stressing the closed and static-system characteristics of the physical universe rather than the open-system, evolving characteristics of the living organism. The turn of the century linguist would attempt to answer the question 'what is language?' by comparing it with physical objects. He would avoid reference in his description to earlier stages of the development of the language — the *diachronic* approach as de Saussure described it in his seminal book the *Cours de Linguistique Général* (published postumously in 1915) — and would attempt to explain language *synchronically* i.e. by reference to its present structure.

Such a view, combined with the intention of making linguistics a purely objective and descriptive science, necessarily led to an emphasis on the contemporary language and a refusal to accept that it was, in any sense, inferior to earlier forms. Jespersen (1904), for example, argues: 'The truly historical point of view leads to a recognition of the right to exist of present-day usage, however widely it may differ from the language of former periods'.

The influence of this objective and descriptive view of language had important implications for language teaching; speech was seen to be primary and phonetics was therefore taken to be the fundamental science on which language teaching should be based. Also, normative attitudes derived from an acceptance of earlier written varieties as the model at which the learner ought to aim were firmly denied and a contemporary model sought.

We can, as we did earlier, suggest three key axioms which typify the approach of the early modern linguist:

1. *Language is a system:* de Saussure's analogy with chess is the clearest statement of the nature of the system. Each element of the language has a value only in terms of the rules under which it operates and in relation to all other elements. In the game of chess, each piece is limited in the way it can move – the rook, for example, may only move along the horizontal and vertical ranks of the board – and by the positions of the other pieces – the rook, for example, cannot 'jump over' other pieces in the way the knight can.

2. *Language is speech:* the written system is no more than a crude approximation to the spoken language, secondary and derivative.

3. *Language is conventional:* language is ' . . . partly rational, partly irrational and arbitrary.' (Sweet)

We should note that in two out of the three axioms the Early Modern linguist was in direct conflict with the views of the 'traditionalists' and that in the third, his view of the conventionality of language was far more sophisticated than theirs. It would also be true to say that, in essence, these axioms, which derive from the scholarship of the latter part of the last century and the early years of this, still, to-day, form the starting point from which linguists set out to describe and explain language.

4.3.2. Early modern views on the description of language

The early modern linguist saw the task of linguistics as the attempt to describe and explain the linguistic 'facts' which constituted the system of language. Such a description was to be synchronic – reference to earlier stages was to be avoided – and objective. The present-day language was to be described in its own terms without the normative and prescriptive attitudes of earlier descriptions. Sweet (1899), for example, stated the position plainly, 'I shall confine myself to the statement and explanation of the facts'.

One effect of this commitment to objective description was, inevitably, to be a growing recognition that 'correctness' was not a concept which could be easily or arbitrarily defined, since the appropriateness of a sample of language depends very much on the context of its use. Hence, different 'styles' were recognized and a beginning was made on the description of their characteristics; a task which was to be taken up in earnest in the 1960s and 1970s with the study of *register* and the development of socio-linguistics (see 6.2 on this). An immediate effect in language teaching could be seen in the acceptance of the typical contractions and assimilations of speech as normal and correct, when judged against actual spoken usage rather than the conventions of the written language.

4.3.3. Early Modern views on language learning

Early Modern views on the nature of language and on the description of language had profound effects on language teaching.

The acceptance of the systematic nature of language led to an emphasis on the teaching of grammatical structures rather than isolated words and an attempt to grade items and structures in terms of their 'easiness' and 'usefulness' (see 3.5. for a fuller discussion of this still unresolved problem). However, the same view led to a rejection of translation as a method of teaching since, it was argued, language systems were unique and translation would serve only to confuse the two systems in the mind of the learner.

The commitment to the primacy of speech led to an emphasis on pronunciation as the foundation of learning and the use, by some teachers, of articulatory descriptions and phonetic symbols in the classroom.

The attempt to make linguistics an 'objective' science had the effect of forcing the teacher, who must in the end be normative in the sense of selecting a norm for his learners, to choose a target variety and to state the rationale behind his choice. We have already discussed this problem at some length in the context of 'local models' of English in non-mother-tongue communities (see 4.2.4.)

Palmer in his *Principles of Language Study* (1921) neatly sets out the order in which learning, in the opinion of the early modern linguists, takes place:

1. The learner becomes proficient in recognizing and producing the sounds and tones of the L2 both in isolation and in combination.

2. The learner memorizes, without analyzing them, a large number of complete sentences which have been selected by the teacher or the text-book writer.

3. The learner begins to build up, for himself, sentences — regular and irregular — into utterances.

This order, it should be realized, reverses the 'traditional' which begins with words, in their written form, and only as a final step (if at all) teaches the learner how to speak, by means of reading aloud and by so-called conversation lessons.

4.4. CONCLUSION

In our survey of attitudes to the nature of language and to its description and their impact on language teaching, we have reached the mid-1930s and can now summarize the 'state of the art' at that time.

By the mid-30s, linguists had generally accepted the need to distinguish between the present form of a language and the processes of linguistic change by which it reached that form. They had also accepted that their description of language should be as objective as possible and that value judgements should be totally outlawed from a description. Their data, from which they would deduce the system, was to be speech and not writing and their method based on that of the physical scientist. We shall see, in the next chapter, how the Structuralists applied these principles and how, ultimately, their interpretation of the principles but not, in the main, the principles themselves, was overturned by a new school of linguists: the transformationalists.

In applied linguistics, the stage reached by the practical teacher was, in the case of the best of them, hardly less sophisticated than our own present condition. Most of the principles on which we operate and many of the techniques we commonly use had already been defined and converted into forms which would serve in the classroom – the need for a rational decision on a model; the acceptance of the sentence, rather than the word, as the unit of learning; the need for the selection and grading of items to be put on a sensible footing; the preference for some kind of Direct Method, in which the L1 of the learner is avoided, even the substitution table (invented as long ago as 1914 by Palmer) had by the mid-30s all become part of the stock in trade of the well-informed teacher of languages and still are to-day.

However, there are still several issues which, though first defined with some precision by the 1930s, are not yet resolved:

How are learners to learn the rules of the language? Should they be overtly taught the rules or should they deduce them for themselves?

What is the relationship between knowing the rules and being able to apply them?

What is the status of learners' errors? What should be corrected and what ignored?

What type of practice, and how much, should learners have?

We shall be spending most of our time in the next two chapters considering these issues and the possible answers to them.

SUGGESTED FURTHER READING

Alyeshmerni M. and Taubr P. (1970), *Working with aspects of Language*
This workbook which accompanies Bolinger's *Aspects of Language* (1968) contains a number of interesting exercises. Particularly relevant to this chapter are those in their chapter on evolving approaches to language i.e. exercises 2 and 3.

Jesperson O. (1904), *How to Teach a Foreign Language*
An example of the mature views of one of the founding fathers of applied linguistics, this book should be read especially if we are suffering under the illusion that we are making significant new advances in language pedagogy; so much which we take for granted and even some of what we have recently 'discovered' is already spelled out here.

Palmer H. E. (1921), *The Principles of Language Study*
Like Jespersen and Sweet, Palmer can be properly regarded as one of the earliest applied linguists. His eclectic and practical approach to language teaching still has messages for us today.

Prator C. H. (1968), *The British Heresy in TESL*
In this paper Prator takes issue with the British view that 'local Englishes' are arising in the Commonwealth and that they can act as models for ELT in such countries. It should be read by teachers since it raises the fundamental issue: what constitutes correct English?

Sweet H. (1899 reprinted 1964), *The Practical Study of Languages*
This book, in conjunction with the two by Jespersen and Palmer, forms the historical underpinning of modern ELT methodology and contains, even after such a length of time, much that is still relevant and valuable.

5 Formalism in linguistics and its influence on language teaching

5.0 INTRODUCTION

In this chapter, we shall be considering the views and methods of two major schools of linguists whose influence on language teaching has been, and still is, very strong indeed: Structuralism and Transformational-Generative linguistics.

5.1 STRUCTURALIST LINGUISTICS

Structuralist linguistics arose in the 1930s as a result of two needs felt by the academic community in the USA. First, there was a general feeling of dissatisfaction with 'traditional' grammar (for the reasons discussed in Chapter 4) and, secondly, linguists in the Americas were faced by a severe practical problem: the description and, indeed, preservation of the native Indian languages before they literally died out. Fieldworkers soon discovered that the structures of the Amerindian languages were utterly different from those of Europe, to the extent that such familiar categories as 'word' and syntactic relationships such as 'subject', 'object', etc. failed to do justice to the data and traditional grammar was quite unable to provide the kind of analysis required.

5.1.1. Structuralist views on the nature of language

For the structuralist, language was a system of speech sounds, arbitrarily assigned to the objects, states and concepts to which they referred, used for human communication. From this, four key axioms can be derived:

1. *Language is speech* — this is in direct contrast with 'traditional' linguistics which relegated speech to a position of secondary importance, after writing. The structuralist, like the Early Modern Pioneers immediately before him, reversed the order declaring 'The speech *is* the language. The written record is but a secondary representation of the language' (Fries 1940 original emphasis).

2. *Language is a system* — for the structuralist, language was a system of *forms* — elements or items of which combined in certain regular ways to create sentences. The role of the linguist was to build up a description of this system without having recourse to meaning i.e. the analysis was to be of observable 'facts' — the sounds of the language — and was to be objective and distributional (see 3.1.2 below for an example of structuralist syntactic analysis).

3. *The Language system is arbitrary* – the dispute about the relationship between words and the 'things' they denote goes back, in the Western World, to the Greeks; was there, for example, a 'natural' link between the object adult-female-homo-sapiens and the word *woman* or was the connection merely 'conventional' i.e. had speakers of English, in some sense 'agreed' to use the sounds which make up /wʊmən/ to refer to *woman*? On this point, the structuralist, and indeed most modern students of language, came firmly down on the side of the 'conventionalists' (as had the traditionalists: see 2.1.2.). A *cat* is /kæt/ in English because native-speakers of English 'want' it to be. It could, just as easily be /aekt/ or /taek/ – though both those combinations are already in use for other referents – but not (as we saw in 1.1), because of the arbitrary combination rules of English, */ktæ/, */ætk/ or */tkæ/.

4. *Language is for communication* – this extremely promising axiom was, in actuality, never developed by the structuralists, except to the extent that they collected the 'real' data of speech from their informants. Work on longer stretches of speech – ritual greetings, story-telling, etc. – could not be pursued by the linguist, since there was an embargo on the study of meaning. However, a direct result of this self-imposed limitation was the development of anthropological linguistics and the serious study of the unwritten, and hence wrongly-termed 'primitive', languages of South and Central America, Africa and Oceania.

5.1.2 Structuralist views on the description of language
Following the prevailing notions of physical scientists, the structuralist linguist adopted a strongly empirical and inductive approach to the description of language (see Fig. 5.1. below) i.e. 'texts' – actual sound recordings or transcriptions – constituted the data which was then segmented into progressively small units. The parallel with physics is very clear: physical objects 'cut' into smaller and smaller pieces until the ultimate – the atom – is reached.

Figure 5.1.
Induction

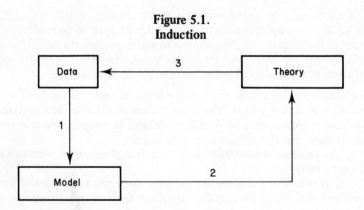

An example might be in order here:

The Germans changed money at the bank

The structuralist procedure — called *immediate constituent analysis* or *IC analysis* — is to 'cut' the components of the sentences into their *immediate constituents* — one 'cut' at a time — until the process cannot be continued and the fundamental 'building-blocks' of the sentence — the *ultimate constituents* or *morphemes* — have been reached:

```
Cut
1   The        Germans | changed    money      at    the      bank
2   The        Germans | changed    money |     at    the      bank
3   The        Germans | changed  | money      at    the      bank
4   The        Germans | changed    money      at  | the      bank
5   The        Germans | changed    money      at    the  |    bank
6   The   |    Germans | changed    money      at    the  |    bank
7   The   |    Germans | chang | ed  money      at    the  |    bank
8   The   |    German | s | chang | ed  money   at    the  |    bank
Cut        6         8  1       7   3           2    4        5
```

The process is slow and laborious but has certain strengths;

1. The analysis is a taxonomy which can show syntactic relationships in a clear way by means of 'slots' and 'fillers' of those 'slots' e.g. it is plain that *the* and any other item which can appear in the 'slot' directly before such items as *Germans, bank*, etc. need to be listed as functioning in the same way. Note that this greatly increases the class 'article' or (more correctly) 'determiner' which now includes *the, this, that, these, those, a, an, some, many* . . .

2. No appeal is made to meaning. The categories are arrived at in a purely mechanical manner. Hence 'noun', for example, is no longer defined as 'a person, place or thing' as in 'traditional' grammar but as any item which can occur in the 'slot' immediately after *the*.

3. It supplies the analyst with the notion of 'patterns' of items and relationships and strengthens the view of language as an orderly system.

It should also be noted here (the point is taken up below in section 5.1.4.) that the display appears to lend itself, with little or no modification, to use in the language teaching classroom and to provide the teacher with a rationale for his selection of teaching points. However, there are some criticisms of the analytical technique used by the structuralists:

1. Although the data is 'real', in the sense of being derived from actual speech, it is in fact, edited. The pause phenomena, incomplete sentences, overlapping speech, etc., so typical of situated language in use is omitted and the data, thereby, idealized to some degree.

2. The emphasis on recorded data — surface phenomena — has two important effects:

a. It makes the analysis incomplete, since any text or set of texts, however large, cannot be the whole language. One has only to consider the amount of speaking a single individual does in a single day and to multiply that by the millions of speakers of a lanaguage like English and the thousands of days of their lives to recognize that the 'sample' is too pitifully small to bear scrutiny by a statistician.

b. It leads the analyst into classifying sentences which are clearly different in meaning and structure as though they were the same e.g. the analysis of these two sentences suggests that the prepositional phrase has the same syntactic function but a native speaker will recognize that the 'sameness' is more apparent than real:

He was killed by midnight
He was killed by the enemy

Traditional grammar would distinguish the 'time adverbial' in the first case from the 'agent' in the second and the native knows too that we can say

The enemy killed him　　　　　but not
*Midnight killed him

3. Though structuralist grammars are strong on *morphology* – the affix system of the language; prefixes, suffixes – and in the creation of word-classes, they are weak and even, as we have just seen, misleading on syntax.

In brief, structuralist descriptions are partial and fail to reveal the infinite capacity which language has for creating new sentences. To show that we need a very different kind of grammar (see 5.2. and 6.2.).

5.1.3 Structuralist views of language learning
The structural linguist soon became involved in language teaching. The Second World War, in particular, created the urgent need for teaching methods which would bring learners up to native levels of proficiency in a short time. This was especially true of the USA, where much was learned about language teaching in classes of service men learning 'enemy languages'; German, Italian and Japanese (see Titone *op. cit.* 106)

One can be a little cynical about the high 'success' rate. After all, the motivation of the learners could hardly have been greater. It is surely a unique situation for the teacher to find himself in: if the learners fail, they will get shot! Motivation was rarely considered as an important factor in producing success or failure in language teaching at the time.

It is possible to suggest a small number of axioms on which the applications of structuralist linguistics rested:

1. The philosophical position adopted by the structuralists in relation to human learning was *mechanistic* i.e. the dichotomy between mind and body was denied and the activities of the mind were seen as no more than complex extensions of the activities of the body; different, that is, in degree not in kind. Learning, then, was an activity which needed a psychological and physiological explanation.

2. The psychology of the Behaviourist school – Pavlov, Thornedike,

Hull and latterly Skinner — provided the model of learning accepted by the Structuralists. Since language was a human activity, it was believed that learning language was achieved by building up *habits* on the basis of *stimulus-response* chains. Human behaviour and learning was seen as being like that of animals, it was as though, to be flippant, the teacher believed that inside the mind of every learner was one of Pavlov's dogs waiting for the correct stimulus to trigger off salivation, or rather, speech!

3. The way of building up these habits was to provide unremitting practice: the sentence patterns repeated and drilled, until they became as habitual and automatic as those of the mother tongue. A typical assertion of this belief comes from a text book published in 1960 (Brooks, page 46) 'The single paramount fact about language learning is that it concerns, not problem solving, but the formation and performance of habits'.

A number of critical comments need to be made about such a view of language learning, particularly since the attitudes, materials and hardware — in the form of massive investment globally in language laboratories — are still popular and widespread.

1. Habit and stimulus-response learning is an inadequate model for language learning. This is particularly true of First Language acquisition; the child's generalization of rules — such utterances as 'Daddy goed', 'I eated my dinner', etc. — clearly demonstrate that learning is also by analogy, not by stimulus alone. The foreign language learner too, in the mistakes he makes, often demonstrates that he is using a technique very like that of the small child. Indeed, his mistakes are often the same as those the child makes. This suggests that L1 and L2 acquisition both follow a very similar path (the implications of this are taken up in detail in Section 5.2.).

2. Structuralist descriptions of language, because of their partial nature and, at times, misleading analysis, do not provide an adequate basis for the input data the learner needs. Since the description is of linguistic forms as fillers of syntactic slots, the materials produced by applied linguists depending on the description inevitably stress form and the apparent overriding need to manipulate form. The assumption is that the automatic manipulation of linguistic items in differing syntactic environments leads to, or even, constitutes, the ability to communicate.

3. Language teachers accepted pretty uncritically the assumption made by the linguist that he was competent to advise the teacher on pedagogical matters. This led to the feeling that language was the only variable involved in language learning when, in fact, much more comes into play: the age, educational level, motivation of the students, individual, social and political attitudes to the target language and so forth. The linguist can properly advise on *what* can be taught — the content of the course — but, as linguist, has no special qualification to advise on how the teaching should be done. One reason for this confusion was the failure of linguists and teachers alike to recognize the essential difference between a descriptive grammar of a language — the result of the work of the linguist — and a pedagogical gram-

mar — the product of applied linguists and pedagogy — in which linguistic facts are presented in an order which, it is hoped, facilitates learning and is, almost certainly, eclectic in that it draws on several descriptive grammars.

5.1.4. Structuralist language teaching materials

Structuralist language teaching materials cover an enormous range of textbooks which are to a greater or lesser extent faithful to the tenets of structuralism we have just been outlining. In Appendix D (section 2) we shall provide an example of what we feel are the most typical of all the structuralist materials; the Ann Arbor materials issued during the 20 years between the mid-1940s and the mid-1960s by the staff of the English Language Institute of the University of Michigan led by C. C. Fries and Robert Lado.

Fries' preface to *English Sentence Patterns* (1957) stands on its own as a monument to structuralism as applied to language teaching. We can hardly do better than quote at some length Fries' admirably clear statement of belief:

'Considerable controversy has for more than a half century centered upon the usefulness of "grammar" for the practical mastery of a foreign language. Part of the difficulty in reaching agreement in such controversies arises from the fact that "grammar" means very different materials to different persons. To some it means memorizing paradigms of declensions and conjugations; to some it means recognizing and naming the "parts of speech" and diagraming sentences; to others it means learning and applying rules of "correctness" based upon "logic" or the "laws of thought". "Knowing" grammar has often meant the ability to use and respond to some fifty or sixty technical names and *to talk about sentences* in terms of these technical names. Often, one of the chief reasons offered for learning the grammar of a language is that it provides a vocabulary to facilitate explanations concerning "correct" usage.

'The materials of the English Language Institute rest upon the view that learning a foreign language consists *not* in learning *about* the language but in developing a new set of habits. One may have a great deal of information about a language without being able to use the language at all. The "grammar" lessons here set forth, therefore, consist basically of *exercises to develop habits, not* explanations or talk about the language.

'The habits to be learned consist of patterns or moulds in which the "words" must be grasped. "Grammar" from the point of view of these materials is the particular system of devices which a language uses to signal one of its various layers of meaning — structural meaning (see Charles C. Fries, *The Structure of English*, Chapters 4 and 13). "Knowing" this grammar for practical use means being able to produce and to respond to these signals of structured meaning. To develop such habits efficiently demands practice and more practice, especially oral practice. These lessons provide the exercises for a sound sequence of such practice to cover a basic minimum of production patterns in English.' (Fries & Lado *op. cit.* original emphases).

In the student's introduction we similarly find Fries advising the learner 'Remember, it isn't necessary for you to explain the grammar . . . ' and again 'Learning about the problem is not your goal. You must become so familiar with the pattern that you can use it automatically. In order to attain this goal the student must practice orally.' (Fries & Lado *op. cit*. xvii)

Perhaps a short example would be in place here. Each unit or lesson of the series is laid out following a set format (we shall discuss this in Appendix D, Section 2) the major part of which — Fries suggests 85% of the available time — consists of exercises. Here is a brief example taken from Lesson XXIII, an exercise designed to force a choice between *if* and *unless*:

The weather is nice. We have a picnic every Sunday.
    WE HAVE A PICNIC EVERY SUNDAY IF THE WEATHER IS NICE
It's raining. We have a picnic every Sunday.
    WE HAVE A PICNIC EVERY SUNDAY UNLESS ITS RAINING

The student is given 'clues' like those found in the first two sentences of each set and is expected to 'show the relationship between the ideas with IF or UNLESS, (Fries & Lado *op. cit*. 225).

Comment: mechanical though these exercises are — and we shall have a great deal more to say about them in Appendix D — they do provide practice. Whether this is the kind of practice the learner needs — practice in the manipulation of the surface forms of the language with little regard for meaning, cohesion or appropriateness (in the sociolinguistic sense of the term) — is a moot point but the materials, in their day, marked a substantial step forward not only by attempting to put to practical use the theoretical work of contemporary linguists but also by providing a step-by-step methodology for the teacher to work through.

We suggested earlier (2.2.7.) that there were three crucial elements in the organization of face-to-face instruction; *presentation, illustration* and *practice*. Structuralist methodology favours the order:

    Present the item.
    Illustrate its use.
    Practice its use.

The *rule* which governs the use of the item(s) may be given initially (or students may be encouraged to suggest what it is from the examples they are given) but, as we have just seen in Fries' comments, structuralists tended to react strongly against the earlier tradition of learning rules rather than applying them and hence to avoid precise specification of rules and to insist that any explanation of the form of a structure be kept to an absolute minimum.

We might contrast this *(rule)* → *illustration* → *practice* order with the 'traditional' *rule* → *illustration* sequence and the *rule* → *illustration* → *practice* → *rule* order of materials influenced by transformational–generative grammar (see 5.2.).

5.1.5. Summary
Structuralist linguistics from the time of de Saussure early in the century

to that of Fries and Harris in the 1950s represented a major advance in the establishment of linguistics as an independent discipline, an advance which supplied the language teacher with more precise and objective descriptions of languages than had previously been available and, when linked with behaviourist psychology, suggested a new *approach* in language teaching.

We shall see in the next section that the late 1950s saw a strong challenge not only to structuralist linguistics but also to the psychology associated with it; a challenge which reoriented linguistics towards a more mentalistic philosophy, rationalist scientific method and, when applied to language teaching, a cognitive psychology.

However, striking though the differences are between the two theories of language, we shall argue that they share a common answer to the question 'what is language?' i.e. both theories see the essential nature of language as *form* and *structure* in a *context-free closed system*. Indeed, Piaget (1971) goes so far as to state that a structure can be defined as ' . . . a system of transformations' (Piaget 1971.5.), the transformation having been seen by linguists as one of the key distinguishing features of TG which marked it off from structuralism.

Even conceding that the 'forms' of structuralism are physical and those of TG mental, we feel justified in classing both theories as formalist and, if our ranking of the question 'what is language?' higher in the creation of an *approach* in applied linguistics than the question 'how do people learn languages?' is accepted, it follows that in language teaching the distinction between structuralist and transformational-generative linguistics is one of *method* rather than *approach*. It is for this reason that we have grouped both theories together in the same chapter and contrast them with *functionalist* approaches in the next.

We shall see, in the next section, that the truly dramatic reorientation of linguistics which was brought about by TG had remarkably little impact on language teaching and it was not until the 1960s and more noticeably the 1970s that functionalism introduced a genuinely new approach in language teaching.

5.2 TRANSFORMATIONAL-GENERATIVE LINGUISTICS

Transformational-generative linguistics (or grammar), normally abbreviated to TG, was the result of a period of mounting dissatisfaction in the 1950s with structuralist linguistics. The first important publication in which the TG approach was outlined was Chomsky's *Syntactic Structures* (1957), followed by a series of books and papers the most important of which were *Aspects of the Theory of Syntax* (1965), in which Chomsky expanded the model introduced in 1957, and *Language and Mind* (1968), in which he formulated the philosophical bases of the theory. Applications to language teaching were, however, slow in coming, the earliest probably being Roberts' course for Italian Secondary Schools *Corso d'inglese parlato* (1962) and Chomsky himself in 1969 is on record as having argued that linguistics could not help the language teacher. However, what TG has provided is a new way of looking both at language and at language learning which has had important influences on the attitudes of teachers towards the issue of the nature of language and the means by which human beings acquire it.

5.2.1 Transformationalist views on the nature of language

For the transformationalist, language is a system of knowledge made manifest, it is true, in linguistic forms but innate and, in its most abstract form, universal.

Just as we were able to present some key assumptions for the Structuralists, so too, we can suggest the following as axiomatic for TG:

1. *Language is a system which relates meanings to substance:* this is in contrast with the structuralist view that language is a system of forms and that meaning is not to be emphasized in a linguistic description. The notion of language as meaning ties TG in with traditional grammar and, as such, may be seen as re-asserting a much older view of the nature of language.

2. *Language is a mental phenomenon:* this too is a reversal of the Structuralist position and a return to the 'traditionalist'. It is, however, more than a simple return to the older view, if only because of the advances in psychology which have taken place during this century.

3. *Language is innate:* the transformationalist would point to the fact that all normal children acquire their mother tongue in an amazingly short time – the average pre-school child has pretty well mastered the syntax of the language – and that it is far from unusual for individuals to operate skillfully in more than one language. The innateness of language – acquired but not inherited in the form of a specific language – suggests a genetically imparted ability for language learning. It is this ability which distinguishes man's language from animal communication systems which appear to be inherited directly from their parents.

4. *Language is universal:* for the transformationalist, language is universal in the two distinct senses. It is universal in the sense that all normal children the world over acquire a mother tongue but it is also universal in the sense that, at a highly abstract level, all languages must share key characteristics which permit us to label them as human languages. Clearly, these characteristics cannot be features of linguistic form – the surface realizations of differing languages are too far removed from each other to argue that – but systems of knowledge about language.

5.2.2. Transformationalist views on the description of language

Just as the nineteenth-century linguists had modelled themselves on the leading science of the day – biology – and linguists in the first half of this century had taken physics as their model, so the transformationalists, in the second half of the century, reoriented themselves to the 'new' physics of Einstein: relativity and, in particular, quantum mechanics. Now, the earlier static closed-system models of, for example, the atom and, indeed, physical models of any kind – the last in the physical sciences was probably the 1952 DNA molecule model – are being, or have been, discarded in favour of dynamic open-system models of phenomena, expressed in mathematical or logical terms.

The approach of the transformationalist to the task of describing or better, explaining, language was, once again, a reversal of that of the structuralist i.e. deduction and introspection (see Figure 5.2.) rather than the induction and empiricism (cf. 5.1.2. above). The linguist needs data in the physical sense of texts, only as a check against his description. He begins by building a hypothesis of how language works and checks it initially by introspection, since, he would argue, as a native speaker, he already has complete mastery of the system he is attempting to describe. All that remains to be done – not that the task is an easy one – is to 'bring out' of his mind the knowledge he already has. It might be easier to explain this by referring to the ambiguity of a statement like 'I know English'. In one sense, I do know the system by which grammatical sentences are created, since I am able to produce novel sentences myself, understand those produced by others, judge whether a sentence is grammatical or not and, if not, correct it. But in another sense, I do not know the system or rather I do not know how to *explain* it to someone else. My theory – my notion of how the system works – is perfect, but my model – the formulation of my theoretical knowledge – is very defective indeed.

Figure 5.2.
Deduction

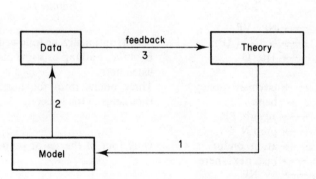

Before we move on to give an example of how TG works, it might be as well to point out that it is, in contrast with structuralist grammar, a synthetic rather than an analytic technique, although it can, of course, be used for analysis. Chomsky's definition of a grammar as 'a device which generates all the grammatical sentences of a language' makes the prime aim of TG clear; it is to be a set of overtly-stated, ordered rules by means of which we can manipulate symbols which, ultimately, through further rules, become sentences.

The traditional transformational-generative grammar (i.e. the 1957 model which is the most straightforward to understand and which has had the greatest influence on language teaching) consists of two sets of processes:

1. *The phrase structure rules* (later called the *base rules*) in which successive strings of symbols are built up until a terminal string is reached. The PS resembles in many ways the IC analysis of the structuralists but differs from it in two important respects; the output is *not* a sentence – and this is a point which we shall need to bear in mind when we look at applications of TG – but a 'string' of symbols and, in addition, these symbols are by no means all morphemes i.e. some are indicators of *'processes'* which still need to be 'carried out' e.g. *tense*.

2. *The transformational rules* by means of which the elements of the terminal string are manipulated – moved, added to, deleted – until they express, normally in a phonemic transcription, a grammatical sentence.

We are now ready to look again at the sentence we used earlier for IC Analysis; *The Germans changed money at the bank.*

We begin, however, not with the sentence – we want to generate that from more abstract and general symbols – but with the most universal symbol of all: Σ meaning 'sentence'. We shall then expand each symbol by 'rewriting' it – the symbol is an arrow → as other symbols, some of which will ultimately be words.

Rules		*Comments*
Σ	⟶ NP VP	
NP	⟶ D N (AP).	N can, optionally, be followed by AP.
D	⟶ The, ∅	D = *the*, nothing or some others not listed here.
N	⟶ German, money, bank	Three nouns from the hundreds of thousands in the lexicon.
AP	⟶ adverb, PP.	
PP	⟶ prep N	
prep	⟶ at, in, on, of . . .	Only four of the set of prepositions.
adverb	⟶ fast, next, here	
VP	⟶ V NP	
V	⟶ aux V	
aux	⟶ tense (m) (have + en) (be + ing).	
m	⟶ can, will, may, must, shall	
V	⟶ change	Just one verb out of thousands.

By successively applying those PS rules, even with the very limited vocabulary we have defined – two determiners, three nouns, four prepositions, three adverbs and only one verb – we can actually generate an infinite number of sentences. Some of them, it is true will be meaningless – *Money changed the bank at the Germans* or even *The Germans changed Germans at the Germans* – but, our output will not actually be in this form i.e. they are still only symbols not words, since we have yet to apply rules which define the syntactic and semantic features of the symbols and rules which, for example, prevent inanimates behaving like animates!

Because of the rule NP → D N (AP), we can continue to add adverbial or prepositional phrases to nouns an infinite number of times and still finish up with a grammatical sentence. The rule is *recursive* i.e. it can be applied as many times as we choose. The fact that English sentences do not have an infinite number of adverbial or prepositional phrases following each noun does not alter the fact that they *could*. We are listing rules which demonstrate the generative potentialities of the language, not rules to explain data in front of us. Recursive rules in particular help us to see, for example, why children are so fascinated by songs and rhymes like 'The House that Jack Built' or the 'Boy who put the powder on the noses of the ladies of the harem of the court of King Caractacus'.

If we choose the symbols needed to lay bare the structure of our sentence or, if we follow a particular route through the available alternatives, we arrive at terminal string of symbols:

The German + plural tense + change money at the bank

This is not a sentence but it is close to being one. What is needed next is to apply the transformational rules to the string.

There are a range of these, some obligatory – the 'affix hopping' rule which must shift affixes from the front to the back of the word they are tied to – others are optional – negation, question, passivization – and can be selected or ignored without creating an ungrammatical sentence.

We shall use only the obligatory rules here but point out one or two optional ones which could be chosen.

Tense Rule

$$\text{tense} \longrightarrow \left\{ \begin{array}{l} \text{present} \\ \text{past} \end{array} \right\} \qquad \text{the braces mean 'chose one and only one'}$$

Affix-hopping Rule

$$\text{Af} + \text{v} \longrightarrow \left\{ \begin{array}{l} \text{v} + \text{Af} \\ \text{tense} \end{array} \right.$$

$$\text{Af} \longrightarrow \left. \begin{array}{l} \text{en} \\ \text{ing} \end{array} \right\}$$

$$\text{v} \longrightarrow \left\{ \begin{array}{l} \text{V} \\ \text{m} \\ \text{have} \\ \text{be} \end{array} \right\}$$

This rule is crucial otherwise we get; *past may haven being eat;* instead of *might have been eating!*

Morphophonemic Rules: We also need rules which allow us to interpret, for example, the tense rule above, which, after all, means 'do whatever has to be done to the v to make it present or past'. In the case of most verbs, the present tense requires a distinction between NPs which consist of a singular noun or pronoun and those which do not; the 's' ending. In the past tense, too, the directive 'do whatever has to be done' may mean 'do nothing', where the verb is *cut, shut, hit,* etc. or it might mean the choice of an apparently unrelated form *go + past → went.*

Ultimately we shall arrive at our sentence. Slow and laborious like the IC analysis but far more revealing and powerful:

1. The rules proceed from the most abstract and general to the most substantial and individual i.e. beginning with the symbol Σ and ending with rules for the pronunciation of the individual word.

2. The rules are explicit; each step is governed by rule and no changes can be 'understood' or carried out without the application of a rule.

3. The rules are complete, in the sense that any sentence which is attested but cannot be explained by the existing rules, can be accommodated by an alteration of the rules; at worst, an *ad hoc* rule can be created, at best a small modification to an existing rule will probably suffice.

4. The rules, being logical and ordered, allow the linguist to trace surface structures which differ back to a common underlying set of symbols, where their meaning is the same e.g. *John hit Mary, Mary was hit by John, Hit Mary that's what John did, It was John that hit Mary,* etc. all must derive from the same 'deep structure', otherwise how would we recognize that each is no more than a 'stylistic variant' of the other; the essential *actor + action + sufferer* relationships of the semantics are shared despite the different surface syntax and the shifts of emphasis we sense (see 6.2 on this).

It should be said clearly here, that the above is by no means an adequate representation of TG. The form of the grammar we have used is inadequate and, possibly, even slightly inaccurate but, we hope, sufficiently clear to allow the reader to tackle 'the real thing' i.e. the writings of the grammarians themselves. Our example is defective for another reason; it is pretty old-fashioned. Most modern grammars begin with the semantics. But a discussion of the differing schools of TG would be quite out of place here. We need, now, to move on to language learning.

5.2.3 Transformationalist views on language learning

Unlike the structuralists, who believed that linguists could and should help language teachers, the transformationalists have been very cautious in applying their theory to actual classroom FL teaching. What applications there have been have not usually received the 'blessing' of the grammarians and have been partial applications of the theory, often mixed in an unhappy way with essentially behaviourist techniques.

In 1957 Fries was claiming: 'The most efficient teaching materials will be those which are based upon a scientific description of the language to be learned, carefully compared with a parallel description of the language of the learner' (Fries 1957). Twelve years later Chomsky was denying that any such help could be forthcoming: 'I do not believe that either linguistics or psychology have yet reached a level of sophistication which could support the kind of technology required by the language teacher.' (Chomsky 1969)

However, language teachers and applied linguists have drawn out of TG a number of assumptions which have influenced language teaching in the last decade or so. They can be listed:

1. The philosophical position adopted by the transformationalists in relation to human learning is mentalistic i.e. the dichotomy between mind and body has been reasserted and the activities of the mind are seen as different, in kind, from those of the body, not different merely in degree. Learning, then, requires a philosophical rather than a physiological or psychological explanation.

2. The psychology of cognitive theorists provides a model for the learning or acquiring of language. Since language is essentially a *thinking* process and its production as speech, only in the last resort, a bodily activity, language learning can best be explained as a process of 'problem-solving' in which the learner, exposed to the data of the language – and it matters little, in principle, whether the data is L1 or L2 – attempts to create 'cognitive maps' for himself by means of which he makes sense of the data. He acts, that is, like a scientist formulating hypotheses about the system to which he is being exposed and trying the rules he has worked out on native speakers. On the basis of their acceptance or rejection, he can move on in the knowledge that the rule is correct or else try out alternative hypotheses, until he hits on one that they will accept.

3. Far from being a matter of habit formation, learning, according to psychologists seeking to support the anti-behaviourist stance of transformational-generative linguists, could be shown to be a matter of creativity and analysis on the part of the learner. Miller (1964. 299) demonstrated rather conclusively that there is just not enough time for the L1 acquirer to learn his mother tongue by stimulus and response alone; if we take the number of possible 20-word sentences in English, we arrive at the incredible total of 10^{20}. Not only is it impossible that the learner could have practised all these sentences until they become a habit, he would not even have had the time to hear them. Miller estimates that the utterance of all these sentences would take somewhat longer than one thousand times the length of time the earth has been in existence! If this is the case, language learning is best served by the provision of data for the learner to work on and feedback so that he can check his own progress. If this approach could be used, the role of the teacher would change dramatically. For the behaviourist, the teacher plans and directs the learning; he predicts the needs of the learner at each stage and is ready with appropriate exercises. For the cognitive

psychologist, the teacher no longer directs and predicts. His role is to act as a 'resource centre' and a 'judge' for the learner as he picks his individual way through the intellectual puzzle that is a new language (see Bell 1979b)

4. The acceptance of a cognitive view of language learning forces the teacher to reconsider his traditional attitude to the mistakes made by the learner. Most teachers still accept that mistakes have to be corrected but little thought is given to what mistakes *are*. According to structuralist-behaviourist beliefs, mistakes are the result of failure on the part of the learner to develop the correct habit. They are explained in terms of *interference* from the L1 — a carry-over of L1 habits into the L2 — and ought to have been predicted by the teacher and stopped before they started. A transformationalist-cognitive approach to mistakes must be quite different: if the mistakes are the result of hypothesis-testing on the part of the learner, far from being a bad thing, they are the only indication for the teacher of the way in which the learner is trying to cope with the intellectual problem of making sense of the structure of the language to which he is being exposed. (We shall return to the topic in Appendix B under the heading of Contrastive Linguistics and Error Analysis).

As general principles the above are stimulating for the teacher but very few have actually been able to make much use of TG in the classroom. Why should this be? There appear to be a number of reasons:

1. The grammarians have done little to encourage, and have, finally declared that they cannot help, the teacher. Even so, some have not taken 'no' for an answer and materials have appeared which claim to be based on or oriented towards TG. We shall examine part of one of these textbooks below (see 5.2.4.).

2. The concepts underlying TG are clearly articulated but expressed in the language of symbolic logic which is difficult for those without a training in logic to use and comprehend. Hence, the transformational grammars which became available to teachers were expressed in a form so abstract that little direct use could be made of them.

3. What in fact happened was that teachers grasped a number of the terms and processes of TG and attempted to apply them in the classroom e.g. exercises in 'transforming sentences' appear as early as Roberts' *Corso d'inglese parlato* (1962) which begins with the shattering statement, for the learner in his first English lesson: 'Esistano in inglese come in italiano due tipi di frasi *kernal sentences* e *transformed sentences*' i.e. 'There are in English, as in Italian, two types of sentence, *kernal sentences and transformed sentences*' (my translation). Learners were taught to operate transformational rules on *sentences* e.g. *John hit Mary* is 'transformed' into, say, the passive, by the application of the passivization transformation $X + Y + Z \rightarrow Z + \text{tense} + Y + en + by + X$ i.e. *Mary was hit by John*. As we noted above (5.2.2.) the output of the phrase structure is not a sentence but a terminal string of symbols. The underlying abstract relationship is lost and to some extent trivialized.

4. The terminology of symbolic logic was equally misunderstood and misinterpreted e.g. 'generate' in logic means no more than 'define' and most readers of TG, at least in the early days, assumed that 'generate' had the meaning it has in normal everyday language i.e. to create. This misunderstanding is easy to explain, particularly in view of the emphasis in TG on the 'creativity' of the language user and the definition of the grammar as 'a device that generates . . . sentences'.

In brief, despite the intellectually exciting nature of the ideas and hypotheses embodied in TG, most applications of it to teaching have been no more than misunderstandings or trivializations. The most serious misunderstanding has been that TG is a psychological theory when it is, if anything, philosophical. A transformational grammar is a logical specification of the syntactic knowledge which the learner needs in order to produce grammatical sentences. As such, it should be thought of as being more like a computer programme for an automaton which can bring out an endless series of grammatical but communicatively disjointed sentences. For TG to be a psychological theory which modelled the processes which take place in the human brain, it would need components which ordered *social* as well as *linguistic* knowledge i.e. such a model would be a model of communicative competence (see our comments on this in chapter 1).

5.2.4. Transformationalist teaching materials
TG, in contrast with structuralism, is exemplified by a very small number of language textbooks indeed. Three stand out most strongly: Thomas's *Transformational Grammar and the Teaching of English* (1965) – an interesting example of a non-eclectic pedagogical grammar (see 1.3.2. on the notion of pedagogical grammars) – Roberts' *Corso d'inglese parlato (1962)* and Rutherford's *Modern English: a textbook for foreign learners* (1965).

We shall take a few points from Rutherford here and expand them in Appendix D (Section 3) since we feel that Rutherford's materials demonstrate very clearly the advantages and disadvantages of attempting to apply TG to classroom teaching.

In the Foreword to the book Bowen and Stockwell argue that Rutherford has produced a book which is ' . . . an excellent example of the proper kind of application (of linguistic theory to language teaching), deriving from a thorough grasp of the facts of English and from a linguistic theory capable of organizing them into a coherent body of knowledge . . . generative-transformational theory, an exciting and significant advance in the history of linguistics' (Rutherford *op. cit.* viii). They also imply that the materials will help the student to make ' . . . the most difficult transition . . . from mechanical skill in reproducing patterns acquired by repetition to the construction of novel but appropriate sentences in natural social contexts' (Rutherford *op. cit.* vii). Rutherford, they tell us, will ' . . . challenge the attention and interest of the intermediate student who wants to bridge the gap between the manipulative activities of a beginning class and the skills necessary for meaningful and nonpredictable communication in a social situation' (*op. cit.* viii).

Rutherford himself affirms his acceptance of TG as the 'linguistic orientation' of the book and goes on to expand on the 'prime assumption' of TG in relation to language acquisition ' . . . a person's verbal behaviour is the result not of reinforced habit but of the "internalization" of an intricate set of abstract rules, which enable him to fashion an infinite number of novel sentences'. He admits that TG does not tell us how languages are learned but insists that the theory does reveal 'the extent to which they (languages) have underlying regularity, deep and surface structure differences, and universal similarity — discoveries which do have great relevance for language teaching' and claims that his book ' . . . organizes in an informal way many of these regularities and develops through drill work the student's ability to distinguish forms having similar surface structure but different underlying deep structure' (Rutherford *op. cit.* ix).

We should expect, then, from these materials a reflection of the linguistic assumptions of TG — the contrast between deep and surface structure, the notion of language universals, etc. — and also of the cognitive psychology which, in applied TG, often goes with it: the notions of creativity and nonpredictability, for example. We should further expect them to contrast very strongly with the materials designed by structuralist linguists; drill, 'mim-mem', active, dominating teachers and passive reacting learners should not find any place here.

It comes as something of a shock therefore to discover that the materials look rather like those of the Michigan School of the mid-1950s; each unit introduced by a dialogue containing the grammatical points to be studied, a pronunciation exercise to practice utterance discrimination, a passage for memorizing and a list of the new phrases which the student will meet in the unit. After this come a number of grammar sections in which a grammatical point is presented, drilled — initially only by means of a simple replacement drill — explained and 'verified' by means of 'a wide variety of oral drills'.

In order to show the kind of exercise Rutherford uses, we shall give a short example here (taken from section 88; subordinators 407–411) and more extensive illustration in Appendix D (in Section 3 where we shall deal once again with modals).

Rutherford includes *if* and *unless* in his section on subordinators — *if, unless, since, because, although, even though, whether, so* (*that*) — and provides a number of drills ranging from the mechanical simple replacement exercise to the 'free reply':

Simple Replacement
> He'll do it if *he has to.*
> > *it's necessary.* etc.
> He won't do it unless *he has to.*
> > *it's necessary.* etc.

Completion

    I won't let them have the story if ——
    I won't let them have the story unless ——
                    etc
    If you don't want the story made public ——
    Unless they call a strike ——
                    etc

Free Reply

    Do you usually have time to read it? (unless)
    What do you do if you don't like the editorial? (if)

Comment: at first reading, the exercises appear to differ little from those of the structuralist materials which preceded them; the exercises are drills and the activity of the learner consists of manipulating forms just as it did in the earlier materials.

However, this judgement is far from fair. The drills are by no means solely the mechanical manipulation of linguistic forms. The very first in each section — simple replacement — is, but its role is to fix the word order of the item in the learner's mind as a prior condition to working with it. The other exercises require manipulation, not merely of form, but of the logical and semantic correlates of the forms; the sentence completion exercise, for example, requires of the learner the ability to comprehend the first part of the sentence and create spontaneously an appropriate second part. The 'free reply' demands even more of the learner; in contrast with the completion exercise where he might be able to remember appropriate answers, in the 'free reply' he is on his own.

Although our example is too short to show this, there is some attempt at providing the learner with sentences which form a coherent text but it is inconsistently followed through in the book: some sets of sentences hold together rather well, others not at all. We can trace this rather cavalier treatment of cohesion to the commitment of transformational grammarians to the description of *sentences* and their *internal* structures rather than the inter-relationships between sentences which bind sentences together to make rhetorically satisfactory texts (we take this point up again in 7.2. when we discuss the issue of authenticity and the creation of dialogues for language teaching materials).

Another critical comment we might make is that the exercises do encourage the learner to express meanings which arise naturally from the sentence cues he is given but the emphasis of the activities is still essentially syntactic rather than semantic. A real commitment to 'creativity' would imply a course organized on semantic or notional principles (see 7.5. below).

5.2.5 Summary

We have seen in this section that TG represented for descriptive linguistics a major advance on the structuralism which preceded it. The underlying philosophy of the discipline shifted from mechanism to mentalism, the scientific method from empiricism to rationalism and the focus of investigation from the physical manifestations of the language system to the structure of the knowledge of the system which permits the creation of such physical manifestations. At the same time linguists shifted their attention from the features which marked languages off from one another to those which were common to human language as a universal phenomenon. This reorientation necessitated an increase in the level of abstraction found in descriptions of language and of the idealization of the data which manifested the system and idealization of the language user.

The effect on applied linguistics and, in particular, on language teaching was in part to make the insights of the academic linguist less accessible to the teacher — thus providing further motivation of the development of an *applied* linguistics which could act as a mediator between theory and practice — but also to make teachers more aware of the intellectual processes involved in language learning; from this new awareness came not only more cognitively oriented methods but a reassessment of the nature of learner's errors (see Appendix B on this).

5.3. CONCLUSION

This chapter has been concerned with two extremely influential linguistic theories — structuralist linguistics and transformational-generative linguistics — and their impact on language teaching.

We have put the two theories together in this chapter not out of a sense of perversity — they are, indeed radically different linguistic theories — but because we believe that the implications of TG have not been followed up in applied linguistics — the approach of Fries' Ann Arbor materials (1943-1964) and that of Roberts' *Corso d'inglese parlato* (1962), for example, is essentially the same — since both theories are *formalist* in their orientation to the question 'what is language?'.

The way forward for applied linguistics in the 1960s and, much more clearly in the 1970s, was to be through a new answer to the question 'what is language?'. From this would emerge a new *approach* which, as we shall see in the next two chapters, was *functionalist* in its orientation rather than formalist i.e. it emphasized the learning of contextualized language in use.

Initially, in the early 1960s, the *situation* and the language which co-occurred with it, became the focus of attention — particularly in the materials *English for Newcomers to Australia* — and, in the 1970s the focus shifted from the situation in which learner might need to communicate the kinds of *meanings* he might wish to express; *notional syllabuses* have been the product of this.

In the next chapter, we shall outline the influences which have come together to create the functional approach and then go on, in the last chapter of this book to examine some situational materials and some notional and discuss their strengths and weaknesses.

SUGGESTED FURTHER READING

Floyd A. (1976), *Cognitive Styles*
This set of materials from the Open University course on Educational Studies usefully summarizes what is known about strategies employed in learning and provides the teacher with a range of views which he needs to consider as he selects his 'approach'.

Fries C. C. (1947), *Teaching and Learning English as a Foreign Language*
This book sets out the fundamental assumption of structuralist linguists involved in EFL in the 1940s and 1950s. On it rests the structuralist methodology and materials exemplified, in particular, by the textbooks issued by the English Language Institute at the University of Michigan.

Greene J. (1975), *Thinking and Language*
An excellent introduction to psychology in relation to language acquisition, learning and use which surveys and evaluates the major approaches to the problem. It forms part of the useful *Essential Psychology* series edited by Herriot.

Lado R. (1957), *Linguistics across Cultures*
A development of the views of Fries, significantly subtitled 'Applied Linguistics for Language Teachers'. This book is still worth reading not only because it restates the fundamental doctrines of structuralist applied linguistics but also because it stresses the need for comparative and contrastive studies between the L1 and the L2 (see Appendix B on this).

Lyons J. (1970), *Chomsky*
An eminently readable introduction to the work of Chomsky and to TG.

6 Functionalism in linguistics and its influence on language teaching

We argued in the introduction to Part II of this book that, in the creation of an *approach* to applied linguistics, the answer to the question 'what is language?' takes precedence over the answer to the question 'how is language learned?' which, we suggested, primarily influences *method* i.e. how the *approach* is implemented.

If this is so, a new *approach* must derive from a new view of the nature of language. In the previous chapter, we looked at two extremely influential theories of language — structuralist linguistics and transformational-generative linguistics — and their impact on language teaching. We put the two theories in the same chapter, since we consider both to be *formalist* in their attitude to the nature of language; despite the fact that the philosophical stance they adopt, scientific method they employ for the description of language and, when involved in the consideration of L1 acquisition or L2 learning, the psychology normally associated with them could hardly be more different. Now we wish to contrast them with the *functionalist* approach in this chapter.

6.1. FUNCTIONALISM

By 'functionalism' we mean a view of language as a dynamic, open system by means of which members of a community exchange information. This is in contrast with the static, closed-system view of language which has been, until recently, the commonly accepted orientation since de Saussure (1915), seeing language as a code made up of elements and their relationships with each other.

Clearly, a functionalist view of language requires of the linguist a different answer to the question 'what is language?' and raises several new questions; 'how does language work?', 'what is language for?' i.e. questions which lie in the borderland between linguistics and the human sciences; psychology, social-psychology and sociology in particular. We shall see that the pressure to find answers to questions like these led to the growth of two 'inter-disciplines'; psycholinguistics and sociolinguistics and that both of these have important contributions to make to applied linguistics in general and to language teaching in particular.

However, during the 1960s and 1970s descriptive linguists themselves were evolving models of language which concentrated more and more on *semantics* and this led them to accept that part of the meaning of a word or a sentence lies in the situation in which it is used i.e. that semantics overlaps to some degree with *pragmatics*.

Simultaneously, the philosophers were turning their attention towards the analysis of 'ordinary language', a process which had begun in the 1920s with the work of Wittgenstein but only began to have a substantial impact on linguistics in the 1960s with the appearance of Austin's *How to do things with words* (1962) and Searle's *Speech Acts* (1969, see 6.3.)

We shall examine these influences and then move on to describe the kinds of change they caused in applied linguistics; particularly the growth of the *notional* or *communicative* approach to language teaching.

Figure 6.1. below shows the inputs to the new approach in diagrammatic form:

Figure 6.1.
Inputs to functional language teaching

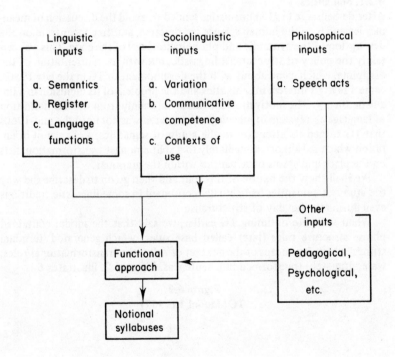

6.2. LINGUISTIC INPUTS

Although, as Chomsky stated in 1969, the mainstream of linguistic scholarship has during this century concentrated on the description of language as a homogeneous code without reference to its social context or, from the point of view of 'classical' structuralist linguistics, even its meaning, the study of variation and of semantics had continued and, for reasons we shall see in a moment, re-emerged as important issues in the 1960s.

In this section, we shall consider three key problems which have important implications for linguistics proper as well as for applied linguistics: the place of *semantics* in the grammar, the relationship of *variation* to the model and the problem of the *functions* of language. In section 6.4. we shall take up the same issues and look at them from a sociolinguistic rather than a purely linguistic viewpoint but it should be understood that the distinction between the linguistic and sociolinguistic approaches is very much a matter of degree and attitude rather than a clear-cut division and so our placing of a particular approach to these issues under the linguistic or sociolinguistic heading is somewhat arbitrary.

6.2.1. Semantics

After de Saussure (1915) linguistics tended to avoid the discussion of meaning, leaving it to the human sciences to describe, and to concentrate on the description of the syntactic and phonological level of the code. This was certainly the policy of structuralist linguistics but with the reorientation of the discipline, which came about with the development of TG in the late 1950s, came a revived interest in semantics and the problem of its inclusion in a linguistic theory. The motivation for this arose mainly from the TG definition of language as a system of *meanings*. However, it was not until the mid-1960s that TG turned its attention to the study of semantics; a change of orientation which led almost immediately to a split amongst transformationalists on the place and status of semantics within the grammar.

We shall show the nature of this split and then go on to describe the way the study of semantics had actually continued in some linguistic traditions even during the heyday of structuralism.

When we were outlining TG earlier, we said that the model contained phrase structure rules (later called base rules) which generated 'terminal strings' which, by means of the next set of rules, the transformational rules, were ultimately transformed into sentences. Figure 6.2. illustrates this.

Figure 6.2.
TG: Model 1 (1957)

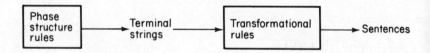

114

Notice that this model makes no mention of semantics at all. By 1965, discussion amongst transformationalists had led to the acceptance of the need for some way of representing meaning; a formal, logical, orderly set of rules similar to those already in use for the specification of the syntax. Figure 6.3. below is a rough outline of Chomsky's proposal set out in *Aspects of the Theory of Syntax.*

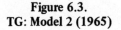

Figure 6.3.
TG: Model 2 (1965)

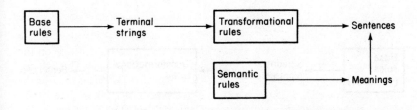

Notice that the semantic rules only operate after the transformations have taken place and that meanings are 'mapped' onto the sentence forms. The exact method by which this 'mapping' takes place is none too clear but relates to the form of the semantic rules – they specify the meaning, grammatical and semantic, of each lexical item in the lexicon – as definers of meaning on the one hand and controllers of appropriate collocation on the other e.g. the lexical item MAN would be glossed in this way:

$$MAN \longrightarrow \begin{bmatrix} + \text{ Noun} \\ + \text{ Countable} \\ + \text{ Animate} \\ + \text{ Human} \\ + \text{ Male} \\ + \text{ Adult} \end{bmatrix}$$

in contrast with *woman* which would, clearly, have an identical specification except for the entry (-male) rather than (+ male). Equally, *child* would be the same as *man* or *woman* except for the entries (+ adult) which would be (-adult) and the sex marker which would need, in English, to be ambiguous i.e. (± male).

This type of rule not only prevents 'mass' nouns from being pluralized – *money*, for example, cannot be counted; we cannot talk, except in legal terms, of **monies* – but also prevents such anomalies as inanimate nouns becoming the subjects of verbs of action e.g. we can have the Germans changing money but not the money changing Germans — except in a highly figurative sense which is only striking *because* it breaks the rule.

However, a number of grammarians were not satisfied with Chomsky's proposals and suggested a different model in which, far from being a system running, so to speak, parallel with the syntax, semantics should be the base element in the whole grammar. A simplified schema might look like this (fig. 6.4.).

Figure 6.4.
TG: Model 3

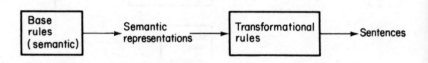

In order to see, in a little more detail, what this proposal implies, we need to look at the work of two British linguists (neither of them would ,however, claim to be transformationalists): Halliday and Wilkins, the first a grammarian, the second an applied linguist (see below and 7.5. respectively).

While mainstream linguistics, particularly in American, was concentrating on language as a system of formal items and arrangements, a tradition rooted in a more sociologically oriented linguistics continued in Europe and especially in Britain through the work of Firth and his students.

J. R. Firth, in the 1930s working in a strongly anthropologically-oriented tradition, much influenced by the anthropologist Malinowski, evolved a theory of language which provided '. . . techniques for the statement of meanings' (Firth 1964. 183) and recognized the complexity of semantics as a multi-level phenomenon the description of which '. . . cannot be achieved by one analysis, at one level, in one fell swoop' (Firth *ibid*). Indeed, Firth's 'contextual theory of language' with its aim 'to link language studies with social human nature' (Firth *op. cit*. 186) locates him not only as the founder of an alternative linguistic theory but also as one of the founders of modern sociolinguistics.

However, it is Firth's influence on many present-day British linguists — in particular Halliday who would describe himself as a 'neo-Firthian' — which is most important to us here, since it is through them that we can trace the development of systemic linguistics and the attempt by applied linguists to create semantically-based language syllabuses; particularly the Notional Approach of Wilkins (see 7.5. below).

Since the early 1970s Halliday, working in the tradition, has been elaborating a series of grammars beginning with a model which, superficially, resembled structuralist (IC) grammar; *systemic* or *scale-and-category grammar* (see Berry 1977 for a comprehensive description) and arriving in the mid-1970s at a grammar which, like Fillmore's (one of those who support the third TG model described above; 1968) sees as its foundations the *logical* rather than the *syntactic* relations between elements in sentences.

Specifically this type of grammar, often called a *case grammar*, would distinguish *roles* from *processes* — participants and circumstances on the one hand, from the states and actions on the other — subdivide them. Figure 6.5. might make this clear:

Figure 6.5.
Elements in a Case Grammar

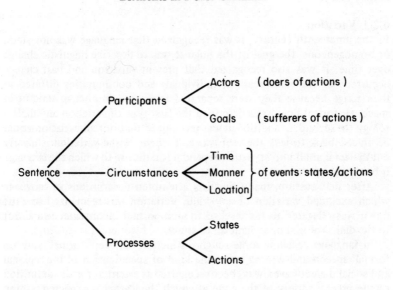

A few examples might also help at this point. Let us take again the sentence *The Germans changed money at the bank* which we have already used as an example of IC and TG description.

The case, or logical structure, of this sentence looks very like a normal syntactic analysis, except, that is, for the changed terminology:

Agent (or 'doer') + *Process* + *Goal* (or 'sufferer') + *Location*

Syntactically, we get essentially the same 'slots' filled by the same items:

Subject + *Predicator* + *Object* + *Adjunct*

However, if we apply a passive transformation to the underlying form we get, in place of *The Germans changed money at the bank, The money was changed at the bank by the Germans*; the grammatical subject is now the logical 'sufferer' and the logical agent or actor has become a 'circumstance'.

There are two crucial points here; agent, goal, etc. are *logical* concepts which, at times, co-occur with the grammatical concepts 'subject' and 'object' but, as we see above, by no means always. Secondly, a grammar which begins with meaning must, of necessity, contain a base structure or a set of base rules which are logical rather than syntactic in nature.

The next problem, is how to get from such logical relationships to the syntax and finally to the sentence, which is what all the effort is about. For an answer to this question, we need to look at the work of Wilkins and Munby (7.5).

6.2.2. Variation

In the nineteenth century, it was recognized that language was not static or homogeneous; the goal of the linguist was to describe linguistic change over time. It was also recognized that present variation and past change occurred for the same reasons: individuals and communities differed in their usage because they were separated from one another in time or in space. Historical linguistics described the first type of variation and dialectology the second. In addition, it was recognized that not all variation could be traced back to *who* the user was and *where*. Some variation is clearly not dialectal at all but 'stylistic', depending on the *use* to which the language is being put by the user.

After de Saussure, many linguists attempted descriptions of language which excluded variation of any kind. Variation was recognized to exist but it was relegated to the level of an unimportant inconvenience and left to the dialectologist or stylistician to study.

In language teaching some rough distinction between 'formal' and 'informal' speech and writing and some kind of specification of the regional and social dialect have always been recognized as essential for the definition of the precise variety of the code at which the learner is expected to aim; the dialect and style which is to act as his model (see our comments on Early Modern views on variation in 4.3.2.)

The dialectologists who produced the *Linguistic Atlas of the USA and Canada* during the 1930s recognized — as Wyld had years earlier — the existence of social as well as regional dialects (see Kurath 1939) and more sophisticated views of 'style' emerged over the years, in particular Joos' influential *Five Clocks* (Joos 1969) in which the simplistic dichotomy between 'formal' and 'informal' was divided into five levels of formality running from *frozen* through *formal, consultative* and *casual* to *intimate*.

However, within mainstream linguistics, it was not until the 1960s that interest in variation began to revive and particularly in Britain with the work of Gregory (1967), who took Firth's 'context of situation' further in an attempt to specify the relationships between code and choice and the structure of the situation. From this grew substantial work on 'register' (particularly Crystal & Davy 1969), which showed how different varieties of a language were a product of the 'situational constraints' under which they were used: addressee relationship, purpose, time, place, etc. (see our comments on this notion under Figure 6.8. p. 125).

This is not the place for a long discussion of the notion of 'register' (see Bell 1976. 26.76f & 114) but before moving on to the functions of language, we wish to contrast register study with the sociolinguistic approaches to the description of variation which we will look at in 6.4.

A 'register' was seen as a kind of 'sub-language' or 'limited language' — indeed the *whole* language was thought of as made up of a collection of registers — which was described by correlating the linguistic forms in appropriate texts with situational variables. The language forms were 'given' and their grouping in the same register achieved by explaining them in terms of their extralinguistic context. The analysis moved from *form* to *function* and thus contrasted very clearly with the *function* to *form* approach of the majority of sociolinguists, as we shall see in a moment. In applied terms, the study of registers suggested as Spencer (1973) neatly put it 'teaching (new) rules' rather than the 'learning roles' of a functional approach (see 7.5. on this).

One major contribution from the study of register was the rehabilitation of the notion of 'appropriateness' or 'acceptability' in a discipline which had for so long excluded them in favour of 'grammaticalness'.

Even to raise the issue of acceptability leads the linguist into the social context of language use and for the applied linguist that is a considerable step forward.

6.2.3. Functions

If we inquire into the function of a piece of language, we are asking the question 'what is language *for*?'

Traditionally, the answer to this has been something along the lines of 'to convey information'. True though this certainly is, it is worthwhile considering just what information is or can be conveyed by language.

First of all, language conveys 'ideas'. We think and attempt, through language, to share our thoughts with others. Primarily, then, language has a *cognitive* function, focusing on the context in which the message is transmitted, referring to objects and concepts.

Secondly, language has the ability to convey information about the speaker; his age, sex, social class, level of education, his attitude to the topic and to the other participants. This function has been termed *indexical* (Abercrombie 1967) and is far less under the conscious control of the speaker than is the cognitive information he transmits. Whether he likes it or not, the speaker cannot easily prevent a kind of 'leakage' of information about himself as he speaks.

Thirdly, language conveys our participation in the process of communication. By this we mean that language is used to refer to the interaction, the point that has been reached, our desire to gain or concede the floor or our willingness to bring the conversation to a close. Speakers constantly produce utterances such as 'as I told you earlier', 'I'm not sure if this is relevant but . . .', 'better be going now; my dinner's ready', etc. Or with eye-contact or pausing, we show that we wish someone else to take over the role of speaker e.g. '. . . and . . . er . . . well . . . that was . . . er . . . that, you know.' This function can be termed *interaction management*. Like the indexical function this, too, is not under the conscious control of the speaker but as hearers, we are all quickly aware of the speaker who is unable to follow the conventions. We will soon label him 'inarticulate' or 'rude' or 'opinionated', depending on which of the techniques he is unable to control.

A more sophisticated view of language functions (Jakobson 1960) suggests six functions which derive from the particular aspect of the communicative event which is being focused upon e.g. when the speaker focuses on himself, the function of the language is to express his emotions. When the focus is on the code, as in a book or lecture on linguistics, the function is metalinguistic: language used to talk about language and so on. (see Figure 6.6.)

Figure 6.6.
Speech Functions

Aspect	Function
Addresser	Emotive, expressive, affective.
Addressee	Directive, conative.
Context	Cognitive, referential.
Message	Poetic.
Contact	Interaction Management, phatic
Code	Metalinguistic.

For the teacher, the problem is to decide which functions the learner needs and in what order. An additional problem is the fact that many messages transmitted by adults are multifunctional — or ambiguous — and the hearer has to discover which meaning is intended.

This model, however, does not cover the ground completely, since it defines neatly the *content* of the six functions — it tells us what emotive language or referential language are *about* — but does not tell us what people are doing when they use emotive or referential language. What we must now ask is not 'what is language for?', since that gives us partial answers of the type suggested above but rather 'what do people do with language when they want to express a particular concept from a particular point of view?'. How, to be precise, do we go about promising, threatening, thanking and so forth? (se shall take this up in 6.3. below).

6.3. PHILOSOPHICAL INPUTS

We made the point earlier (see 6.1.) that philosophy has, during this century, become progressively more interested in the nature of language and, hence, has provided insights which are of value to the linguist, if only because they come at the problem of explaining the phenomenon of language from a different angle.

Philosophers have, of course, tended to ask what appear to be linguistic questions from the very beginnings of Western Philosophy; 'what is Justice?', 'what is Truth?' etc. But the Greek philosopher who posed this apparently semantic question was actually investigating the nature of the concept rather than the relationship between the concept and the word that expresses it. A truly semantic question would seek to discover the components of meaning which built up into the linguistic item 'justice', the collocations which tended to co-occur with the word – 'absolute justice', 'even-handed justice', 'blind justice', 'Justice of the Peace', etc. – and the linguistic mechanisms which allow us to relate the meanings of *justice, just, justify* and so on to each other. It was not until the work of Wittegenstein in the 1920s and 1930s that philosophers became seriously concerned with an explanation of 'ordinary language' which brought their own interests closer to those of the linguist and, from the mid-1950s moved away from purely referential uses of language to the study of the social uses to which language is put; an interest which relates closely to that of sociolinguistics.

Austin in 1958 and, more recently, Searle (1969) have raised the question, 'what has to be done, for example, for a "promise" to *count as* a "promise"?'. In answer, Searle has suggested that promising, and the like, constitute *speech acts* which are created and comprehended in accordance with rules which define their form and regulate their use and that, without such rules, communication in language would be impossible.

Each speech act is thought of as consisting of two elements (a) the *propositional content* – what is being referred to, what it is about – and (b) the *illocutionary force*; the meaning the act is intended to convey or the emphasis given to it by the speaker. In simple terms, a speech act consists of its content + the orientation of the speaker to that content and these together give the speech act its social meaning. For example, I can refer, in a completely neutral way, to a past action of my own and say 'I burned the toast this morning'. This, as a speech act, is one of simple reference: the content is the burning of the toast and my attitude to that event is merely that of a reporter. However, I could take the same content and say 'I'm sorry I burned the toast this morning'. This, clearly, is more than neutral reporting of the event. The user of English instantly recognizes it, despite the shared content, as something else: an apology. What, then, are the rules which we all follow to make speech acts different from each other, even if, as can be the case, the actual words are identical? Let us take the speech act 'threatening' and suggest some rules:

A preliminary rule would state 'normal input and output conditions prevail' i.e. both speaker (S) and hearer (H) speak the same language, can hear each other, are serious, etc.

The prepositional content is a future act (A) of the speaker.

In order for the speech act to work, both of these initial conditions need to be fulfilled e.g. if I write here 'vengo darti una botta', there is no threat unless, of course, you happen to be able to read Italian and I know where to find you! Equally, I cannot threaten anyone by referring to a past or present action of mine, e.g. 'I hit you last week' and 'I'm hitting you now' are not threats but reports of earlier or contemporaneous acts.

The following rules are also required if the content is to be given a 'threatening' social meaning:

1. S believes that A will be detrimental to H.
2. S believes that he can carry out A.
3. H believes that S can carry out A.
4. H believes that S will carry out A.
5. It is not obvious to S and H that A will happen in the normal course of events.

If I threaten someone else — 'I'll go and hit my brother on the head' — there is no threat to the hearer, unless I am being obtuse and H is my brother or if you happen to be particularly fond of him, i.e. you would be 'hurt' if I hurt him. Equally, if I 'threaten' you by saying 'I'll buy you a present', there is no threat in stating that I intend to do something which will be to your good.

If I know that I cannot carry out the action, the threat is a hollow one.

The threat is also hollow if the hearer knows that I cannot or will not carry it out. For example, 'I'll shoot the next person who speaks' rings very hollow unless I have a gun and am holding the hearers hostage.

Finally, I cannot threaten to do what I would do normally anyway. I can, for example, hardly 'threaten' to be home by 5.30 this evening, since that is the normal time for me to arrive home.

If these rules are followed the speech act which emerges will 'count as' a *threat*. Notice, however, that the change of a single rule can change the 'meaning'. If, in rule 1, we have 'S believes A will be beneficial to H', we have the makings of a promise rather than a threat. If we change the content to 'future act (A) of hearer (H)', we begin to get a warning, and so on.

This may all seem rather 'philosophical' and so it is, until one realizes that the rules for the production of speech acts and the kinds of language regularly associated with them may well differ a good deal from culture to culture. The learner will need to learn these conventions, just as he will need to master the grammar, sound system and the meanings of the words in the language he is trying to learn. This is far from being a simple matter, particularly since many speech acts differ, as we saw just now, only in the form of one of their rules.

We shall see in Chapter 7 (specifically in Section 7.2. and 7.5.) that speech acts can be used as the basis for some very imaginative teaching especially to adults and are far from being the dry academic topic they might seem.

6.4. SOCIOLINGUISTIC INPUTS

As we have just seen (in 6.2.) recent work in linguistics has raised the problems of the description of meaning, the inclusion of variation within a model of language and the functions of varieties of a language. Each of these issues, seen from the point of view of linguistics, can be reduced to the question 'how can semantics, variation and language functions be included in a closed-system model of language?'. The sociolinguist adopts the reverse approach. He is interested in these questions, it is true, but only in so far as they illuminate for him the social working of language.

The sociolinguist asks 'how does language work?' rather than 'what is language?'.

6.4.1. How does language work?

A first approximation to an answer to this question was given by work in information theory in the late 1940s (Shannon & Weaver 1949); a *message* is transmitted from a *source* along a *channel* (where interference — noise — distorts part of the message) at the end of which it is received by a *receiver*. Figure 6.7. below illustrates this.

Figure 6.7.
Communication: information theory model

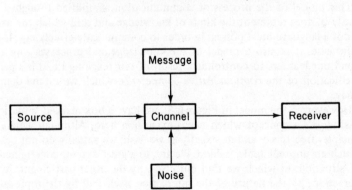

This model is, however, rather too crude for human language. The source and receiver are individuals whose experiences and perceptions differ and for whom the very meaning of the words spoken or written varies. Meanings are, after all, not inherent in the words themselves but in the people who use them.

The channel, for human language, is far more complex than the telephone wire depicted in the information-theory model where speech is being transmitted, there is a multiple channel, audio and visual, which carries the code itself; non-verbal gestures — facial expressions, hand and arm movements, body movements, posture — and, more integrated with the code, the manner of articulation, i.e. the speed of delivery, rhythm, stress, tone; the 'tune' to which the words are put (see Bell *op. cit.* 1976 for more detailed discussion).

The fact that the communicators involved are distinct individuals who can rarely be certain that they share meanings and the fact that face-to-face communication takes place in a social context which permits conflicting messages to be transmitted and received through the range of channels in use — consider the way the actual words can have their meanings reversed by a change in intonation or gesture or facial expression — makes the 'noise' which occurs severe and complex. The sender and the receiver are both sources of 'noise', so are the various channels and so is the social context in which the message is being sent and received.

We need a more sophisticated model which recognizes the two-way nature of human communication — that speakers become hearers and that hearers provide feedback — and the paramount importance of the situational constraints under which communicators operate.

In Figure 6.8. we give a social-psychological model of face-to-face communication which illustrates the steps in the process from the speaker's 'intended message' through its transmission and reception to the hearer's understanding of the message and his feedback on it to the speaker.

This model of the process of communication, simplified though it obviously is, does represent the kinds of knowledge and skill which the native user of a language must possess in order to communicate effectively. If this is the case, it is also a model of the knowledge and processes which we intend our learners to control as a result of our teaching i.e. it is a partial specification of the *communicative competence* which we intend them to achieve.

However, in the model in Figure 6.8., we have a box marked 'situational constraints', a concept which needs expansion here. Although we are, in principle, free to say and do exactly as we wish, we actually do not behave in such an unpredictable fashion. We are, to a great extent, constrained by the 'situation' in which we find ourselves, by the other participants in the interaction, by the nature of the interaction itself and by the topic about which we are speaking. The skilled communicator takes the situational constraints into account as he speaks or writes, listens or reads, revising his assessment of the constraints and the weightings he assigns to each as he receives feedback from the other participants.

Figure 6.8.
A social-psychological model of communication

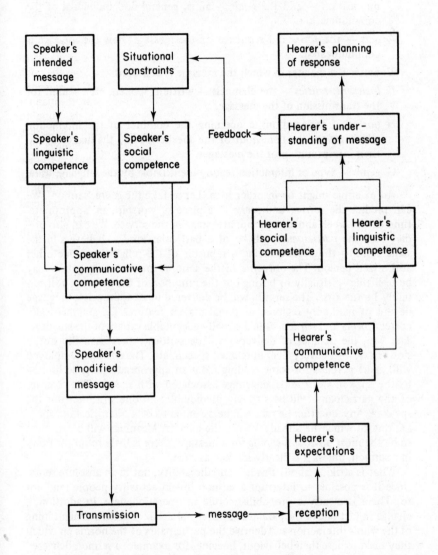

A neat acronym — SPEAKING — has been suggested (Hymes 1972) as a listing for the constraints:

S *setting* — time and place — and *scene* — the cultural definition of the interaction.

P *participants* – the sender(s) and receiver(s) of the message(s).

E *ends* – the *outcomes* – results, intended or otherwise, of the communication – and the *goals* – aims, general and individual of the communication.

A *acts* – the *form* and *sequence* of the message; how the message is communicated.

K *key* – the manner in which the message is delivered.

I *instrumentalities* – the channels – written, spoken, etc. – used for the transmission of the message.

N *norms* – expectations concerning the conduct of the interaction which govern the behaviour of the speaker(s) and the hearer(s) and their interpretation of the messages.

G *genre* – type of interaction readily identifiable by the language used.

An example might be in order here. Let us take the *genre* 'sermon'. We can predict the *setting* and *scene* – a place of worship, an 'appropriate' time of the week and an 'appropriate' stage in the service. We can also predict that the *participants* will be of a particular kind – believers in the same faith – the speaker being a minister of the religion or some other authorized person. The *outcome* of the sermon for the congregation may be uplifting spiritually or boring but the *intention* of the preacher will certainly be the first. The sermon will be delivered in an appropriate language devoid of markedly regional or social dialect features i.e. grammatically correct *forms* and *sequences* in a socially acceptable variety of the language. The *key*, the manner of delivery, will be serious rather than flippant, a slower rate of delivery than in relaxed speech, etc. The *channels* employed will, apart perhaps for some reading from an appropriate text, be limited to the spoken and the paralanguage associated with speech. The *conduct* of the participants will be strongly predictable: no one will interrupt the speaker. Any question he asks will be assumed to be a 'rhetorical question' i.e. one to which he already knows the answer. Meanings will be assumed to be the most obvious meaning for a message; there is little room for irony in a sermon, unless it is clearly marked as such.

What is striking about this is its predictability, not in an absolute sense, since it *is* possible to interrupt a sermon but in actuality people tend not to. There is clearly a probabilistic rule in operation here. In addition, a change in just one of the parameters can signal a change in the social meaning of the whole interaction and deprive the participants of the norms on which they need to base their behaviour. Imagine, for example, a sermon delivered at 3.00 a.m. or in a bar or by the lead guitarist of a pop-group; people would find any one of these changes difficult to reconcile with their notion of a 'sermon' and feel embarrassed by the whole event.

6.4.2. What is the range of contexts in which language operates?

We have been considering the social working of language from a social-psychological perspective – taking the individual as our locus of investigation and considering the problems he faces as a social individual interacting with others – so it is now important to redress the balance by considering the factors which influence language use from a more sociological viewpoint i.e. asking questions about the sociological, political and educational milieu in which languages are used and learned.

From the Applied Linguistic point of view, it is as important to plan language courses with an eye to the social and political constraints under which the learning will take place as to select, grade and teach appropriate language items. *Who* the learners are, and *where* they are, crucially influences their motivation (see 6.5.) and, as any teacher knows, strong motivation will go a long way to repairing the efforts of poor facilities and materials but poor motivation will be impervious to all our efforts. No one can be forced to learn but the individual who truly wishes to learn will learn somehow.

In this section, we shall examine three factors which affect the design and implementation of language training programmes:

(a) The sociolinguistic profile of the society in which the learners are living.

(b) The language and educational planning policies of the state.

(c) The social functions of the L2, e.g. is it a *foreign* or a *second* language for the learners?

6.4.2.1. Sociolinguistic profiles

It is possible, with the backing of sufficient research, to create a profile of the language situation in which our learners are operating. Several variables are involved all of which have implications for educational planning and hence for language education.

Three features stand out as paramount; the degree of linguistic heterogeneity of the state, the legal status of each represented language and the functions each has assigned to it (see Figure 6.9. below for a tabular presentation of the situation in Singapore, Bell 1979c for information on the linguistic profile of the EEC and Bell 1976 for a more general treatment).

I. *Linguistic heterogeneity* relates to three key factors:

a) The total number of languages found in the state, e.g. Iceland is virtually monolingual in contrast with highland New Guinea where scores of languages are spoken.
b) The ratio of L1 users of each language to the total population. One might contrast the position of English in the United Kingdom with its position in South Africa.
c) The demographic characteristics of each language, e.g. a language may be widespread or confined to a small area, the language of a single tribe or group or of many. We might contrast Welsh and English or Basque and Spanish in this respect.

Figure 6.9.
An example of a sociolinguistic profile
Singapore

Language	Genetic Relationship	Mother Tongue Speakers (1957) Population – 1,445,929 N (thousands) %		Status	Type	Function
Malay	Malaya-Polynesian (Western)	167	13.2	Major	Standard	Official, Wider communication
English	Indo-European (Germanic)	27	1.8	Major	Standard	Official, Wider communication, International communication
Mandarin	Sinitic (Chinese)	1	0.1	Major	Standard	Official, International communication
Tamil	Dravidian	76	5.2	Major	Standard	Official
Hokkien	Sinitic (Chinese)	434	30.0	Major	Vernacular	Group communication
Teochew	Sinitic (Chinese)	246	17.0	Minor	Vernacular	Group communication
Cantonese	Sinitic (Chinese)	218	15.1	Minor	Vernacular	Group communication
Hainanese	Sinitic (Chinese)	74	5.2	Minor	Vernacular	Group communication

Sources: 1957 data based on State of Singapore: Report on the Census of Population, 1957, by S. C. Chua, Department of Statistics, Singapore, Government Printing Office, 1964, Table 39–43, pp. 155–161. 1972 data based on National Reports on a Comparative Study of Husband-Wife Communication and Practice of Family Planning (Report I: Singapore), by Peter S. J. Chen, Bangkok, United Nations, 1973 (Memio), Table 49. p. 42. Based on Kuo 1976.

128

II. *Legal status* — the *de jure*, constitutional, position of a language — ranging from extreme acceptance (the language is declared to be the only one which is appropriate for use in the state) to outright rejection; the language is located on a six point scale:

a) Sole official language e.g. French in France; German in Germany
b) Joint official language e.g. English and French in Cameroun; French, German, Italian and Romansch in Switzerland.
c) *Regional official language* e.g. Ibo as the Regional Official Language of the Eastern Region of Nigeria, Marathi as ROL of the Indian state of Maharastra, etc.
d) *Promoted language* e.g. Pidgin English in West Cameroun where it is used by official agencies but given no official status.
e) *Tolerated language* e.g. immigrant languages in UK which are neither encouraged nor discouraged by the authorities, just ignored.
f) *Discouraged language* e.g. Scots Gaelic actively discouraged by planned suppression after the 1745 Rising.

III. *Language functions* — uses of a particular language by the state rather than those of the individual user.

a) *External wider communication*: a 'window on the world', e.g. English in India or French in much of West Africa.
b) *Internal wider communication*: internal lingua franca, e.g. English in Singapore or Mandarin in China.
c) *Taught but not used as a medium of instruction*: e.g. French in the UK.
d) *Medium at primary level*: e.g. Tribal languages in Tanzania.
e) *Medium at secondary level*: e.g. Swahili in Tanzania.
f) *Medium at tertiary level*: e.g. English in Tanzania.
g) *Medium at post-graduate level*: e.g. English in much of the 'developing' Commonwealth.
h) *Language of public worship*: e.g. classical Arabic in Islamic communities.

6.4.2.2. Language and educational planning — states have certain goals the achievement of which is modified by a number of constraints.

1) *Goals*:
a) purely linguistic — changing the writing system, etc.
b) sociolinguistic — changing the area of use, status etc. of a language.

2) *Constraints*:
a) economic — change costs money and in developing countries that is a scarce resource,
b) political — the extent to which the proposed change(s) further the general political policies of the state,
c) environmental — the structure and efficiency of the educational system.

6.4.2.3. FL or SL situation — A distinction now needs to be made here: the contrast between the learning of the L2 in a situation in which it has no local social function — a 'foreign language' situation e.g. where English is the language: EFL — and one where it has — a 'second language' situation: ESL.

The teaching and learning of English in most of Europe can be defined as EFL, since there are no official functions for English in the individual states of Europe. France, for example, has French as its National Official Language (NOL) and, despite the use of English in some businesses and the occasional educational institution, no foreign language has any official place. The context of learning in such a case makes exposure to the living language more difficult to achieve than it would be where the learner came in contact with the language in his day-to-day life.

The converse situation, ESL, can be found in many Commonwealth countries where English is either the sole official language or one of them. In Singapore, for example, the joint OL status of English, its wide use in business and in face-to-face interaction as a lingua franca between groups with different L1s makes the task of language learning at once more real for the learner and at the same time more relevant, since he knows that in order to function efficiently in Singapore he will need to be fluent in English.

One apparent danger inherent in the ESL situation which was discussed in Chapter 4, is that the day-to-day use of the language by non-natives tends to the creation of non-standard vernacular varieties which, at their most extreme, are not mutually intelligible with the world-wide L1 varieties.

6.5. LANGUAGE TRAINING NEEDS

In Chapter 1, we outlined a simple human-science model of language (see 1.1.2. and Figure 1.2.) which began with the motivation for language — *needs* — and showed the necessity for language to be seen as the result of attempting to satisfy needs through the use of social skills of communication.

What we wish to do here is discuss the kinds of need language learners may have, since our training programme must satisfy those needs if it is to be successful. In doing this, we are taking up again the point we made in chapter 2: the first step in the design of a training programme should be the specification of the needs of the trainees. This may appear self-evident but, until quite recently, the majority of language courses have been created on the assumption that the learner needs the whole of the language for 'general purposes'. It was assumed, that is, that the need was *global* and the course would suit learners of any type.

We have already argued that such a goal is unrealistic and that we would be well advised to try to relate the needs of the learner to the structure of the syllabus in a way which set limits on the items to be taught and the skills to be mastered.

Where the future activities of the learners can be, to some degree, predicted it should be possible, through a thorough job analysis (Step 3 in our procedure for syllabus design; see 2.2.3.) to define the 'training gap' and draw up a syllabus to fill that gap. Unfortunately, most language teaching at school level has to rest on the assumption that the needs are global simply because the future language requirements of the learners cannot be determined in advance. Without assigning children who are still at school to a particular stream which leads to a particular set of occupations which require a specifiable level of competence in the foreign language, there is no way out of this dilemma and we are faced by the situation — all too common in foreign language teaching — where, after as much as 1,800 to 2,000 hours, or even more, of instruction, the learner leaves school unable to string half a dozen sentences together grammatically and incapable of using what little he does know for genuine communication.

Outside the school system and, particularly where the learner is an adult, the possibility of defining needs in terms of skills becomes far greater and, in spite of what we have just said, 'specialized' courses of different types have a relatively long history.

Such courses rest on one of two assumptions about the learner:

1. The mother tongue or the native culture of the learner is taken as primary and the course designed around the 'interference' predicted from his background (see Appendix B on Contrastive Analysis and Error Analysis). Typically, such courses have titles such as *English for Speakers of Polish* or *English for the Arab World*, the first focusing on the L1 as a source of difficulty, the second on the common culture of the 'Arab'.

2. The occupation of the learner is taken as primary — airline staff, bank staff, waiters, etc. — and the language component of the worker's tasks forms the basis of the syllabus (see Appendix A for a discussion of the problems involved in matching the course to the language required for the job).

During the 1960s and 1970s, we have seen a steady growth of courses designed to deal with more and more precisely specified needs: immigrants to Australia and the UK in the early 1960s who needed English to survive in their new homes, *English for Newcomers in Australia* (see Appendix D for an example), English for students — Herbert's *Structure of Technical English* (1965) was an early example — and so forth.

Parallel with, and feeding into, this development has been a growing interest in linguistics in language structures above the level of the sentence — the study of *texts* — at first manifested in work on register (Crystal & Davy 1969, for example) and later on a sociological semantics (Halliday 1973, for example).

6.6. SUMMARY AND CONCLUSION

This chapter has ranged over more than half a century and several disciplines in an attempt to list the influences which have been at work in the creation of a more functional approach to the description and teaching of language.

One result of this growing together of several disciplines has been that the language syllabus designer now has at his disposal far more information than he had 20 years ago.

Now new insights from linguistics and philosophy into the nature of meaning, insights from sociolinguistics into the contexts of language use and from political science and education on the issues involved in language and educational planning are all available to the applied linguist and must be reflected in his course design if it is to satisfy the wide range of interests represented in the activity of language teaching.

If we were asked to pick a single word which epitomized formalist linguistics for the language teacher, the word we would choose would be *sentence*. The sentence is, for formal linguistics, the upper limit of description and hence, for the language teacher whose approach derives from such a linguistics, the largest unit that can be taught. Not that linguists were unaware of larger units of language within which sentences formed constituents; they were aware but unable to discover a suitable structure for language beyond the sentence.

Similarly, if asked, we would choose for functionalists the word *text* or *discourse*, since that demonstrates the attempt of the functionally oriented linguist or language teacher to analyze, synthesize and teach dynamic discourse rather than the decontextualized sentence.

It is for this reason that, at the beginning of the next chapter, before moving on to look at situational language teaching, we wish to discuss the notion of text and illustrate its use — particularly in dialogues — in language teaching.

SUGGESTED FURTHER READING

Bell R. T. (1976), *Sociolinguistics*
Chapters 3 and 7 may be useful as an expansion of what has just been said about the contexts of language use both micro — individual to individual in a small group — and macro — within and among nations.

Mercer N. and Edwards D. (1979), *Communication and Context*
These materials form Part 4 of the Open University course on Language Development and focus on the issue of language and learning in school. Although aimed at L1 usage within the context of formal education, much that is discussed is of relevance to the L2 teacher.

Robinson W. R. (1972), *Language and Social Behaviour*
This book covers much of the area dealt with in Bell (1976) but from a social-psychological rather than a sociological point of view. It is particularly interesting in its treatment of the functions of language.

Searle J. (1969), *Speech Acts*
Based on the theories of Austin, this book by Searle sets out the philosophical rationale behind the idea of the speech act; an idea which has been extremely fruitful in the creation of the notional approach to language teaching.

Stringer D. (1973), *Language Variation and English*
This forms part of an Open University course on Language and Learning and provides an easy access to four key areas of sociolinguistics; the view of language as a system or as a process, the contrast between speech and writing, the social distribution of language and social relationships, social situations and language variation.

7 Beyond the sentence: implications for linguistics and language teaching

We have already suggested that the characteristic which most distinguishes structuralist linguistics and transformational generative linguistics from sociolinguistics is the *formalism* of the first in contrast with the *functionalism* of the second.

This contrast has had important implications for linguistics and for language teaching. With the coming of a more functional view of language the 'sentence barrier' has been broken and attempts have been and are being made to push beyond the sentence and discover how larger units of language are structured. We shall outline the *code, text*, and *discourse* analysis stages by which linguistics has come to its present orientation to its data and also to show how these changing linguistic orientations have affected the teacher, particularly in his choice or creation of written texts and dialogues.

7.1. CODE, TEXT AND DISCOURSE

The description of language above the level of the sentence has progressively focused on the *code*, the *text* and *discourse* (see Widdowson 1971).

Code analysis — 'microlinguistics' as Hill (1958) called it — has been the traditional approach to the description of language during this century, whether in the form of structuralist analysis of texts into their component sentences which were then analyzed by IC Analysis (see 5.1.2.) or the TG generation of sentences from smaller elements. For the language teacher, too, the sentence has been typically presented as the largest unit that can be taught.

Text analysis — 'macrolinguistics' to use Hill's term (*ibid*) — represented by Harris (1952), the work on *register* which we discussed earlier (see 6.2.) and Hasan's work on cohesion (Hasan 1968) approaches the text as a whole and seeks to discover the way it 'holds together'. Analysis is focused on cohesion between sentences — exemplified by pronominalization, anaphoric reference and exophoric reference — by means of which sentences are linked and references are made to parts of the text which have passed and to other parts which are to come. Essentially, text analysis is still formalist since it attempts to correlate linguistic form with linguistic form in order to demonstrate the factors which control textual cohesion. For the language teacher, this is a step forward, since it provides him with some principles for working with larger units of language and for showing the learner that it is not enough to know isolated sentences; sentences must link together otherwise there is no text.

Discourse analysis is a term which has been used for two distinct activities:

the study of the narrative structures of literary texts (Barthes 1966, Todorov 1966, Chatman 1969) and study of the rhetorical *coherence* of records of interaction in which the locus of attention is the way the communicator draws on the resources of the language to participate in the exchange of information (Sinclair & Coulthard 1975 provide a clear example in their analysis of the language of the classroom). It is this second type of discourse analysis which is of such interest to teachers because it directs the attention of teacher and learner to the social functions of language rather than linguistic forms *per se*.

7.2. DIALOGUES AND WRITTEN TEXTS

If we define a *text* as the record of a cohesive and coherent stretch of language, it follows that written passages, written transcripts of speech and audio or video recordings of spoken communication are all texts.

Most ELT textbooks contain, in addition to overtly grammatical material, texts which are intended to give the learner practice in handling longer stretches of language than the isolated sentence. Useful suggestions on how to integrate texts into a course are to be found in a number of books. We have found Byrne (*op. cit.*) helpful at the classroom level and Widdowson (1978) at the more theoretical.

In this section, we wish to concentrate on the *dialogue* not because we find written prose passages uninteresting but because we believe that the changing attitudes which we have been describing in linguistics are best revealed in the type of text the materials-writer selects or produces as an example of a 'dialogue' and also because the 'dialogue' forces us to ask fundamental questions about language and how it is used. In particular, we have to ask how authentic it is and what kind of practice the learner can get from it.

If we take the *formal* items of the *code* as the content of our course, we are likely to present the learner with 'dialogues' which are totally lacking in cohesion and coherence. For example, the following – quoted in the original French in Jespersen 1920; my translation – illustrates the type of text:

'We are in Paris, you are in London'
'Louis and Emelia, where are you?'
'We found the letter.'
'Did you take the book?'
'Have we been to Berlin?'
'Emelia, you are sad'.
'Louis, have you seen Philip?'
'Are we in London?'

As Jespersen points out, the speakers have, to say the least, a very curious sense of location and, in addition, their memories appear to be none too good! There is between the sentences almost 'as little connection . . . as there would be in a newspaper if the same line were read all the way across from column to column' (Jespersen *op. cit.* 11).

Admittedly, such utterly nonsensical material is hardly likely to be produced today but one can still find 'dialogues' which are little more than an excuse to re-present the very same grammatical sequences as the learner has faced in the previous lesson which he has to 'practice' by 'learning by heart', 'dramatizing', 'answering questions' or even reading the dialogue through changing the sex and names of the characters.

The dialogue below is from a Yugoslav secondary school textbook which was first published in 1968.

Looking Around the House

Do you want to see our house?

Yes, please.

I.

There are three rooms downstairs: the sitting-room, the dining-room and the kitchen.

Mrs. Bright: Well, this is our sitting-room.
Mr. Grey: It is very comfortable. It is more comfortable than our sitting-room.
Mrs. Bright: We like this room very much.

Mrs. Bright: This is the dining-room.
Mr. Grey: It is a large room. The furniture is very fine.
Mrs. Bright: It is new.

Mrs. Bright: And this is our kitchen.
Mr. Grey: What a lovely modern kitchen!
Mrs. Bright: It is new too. I like it very much.
Mr. Grey: A new refrigerator, an electric cooker, modern cupboards, a new sink. Fine!

Mrs. Bright: Look, Rex is waiting in the hall.

Mr. Grey: Come here, Rex!

Mrs. Bright: Let's go upstairs now.

Mr. Grey: All right!

EXERCISES

I. Ask questions about the pictures.

II. Describe the pictures.

III. Learn by heart and dramatize.

II.

There are three bedrooms upstairs. The bathroom and the lavatory are also upstairs.

Mrs. Bright: Well, this is our bedroom.

Mr. Grey: The walls are green. The curtains are green. It is a nice colour.

Mrs. Bright: We like green.

Mrs. Bright: This is Nelly's room.

Mr. Grey: It is a lovely little room.

Mrs. Bright: Nelly likes it very much.

137

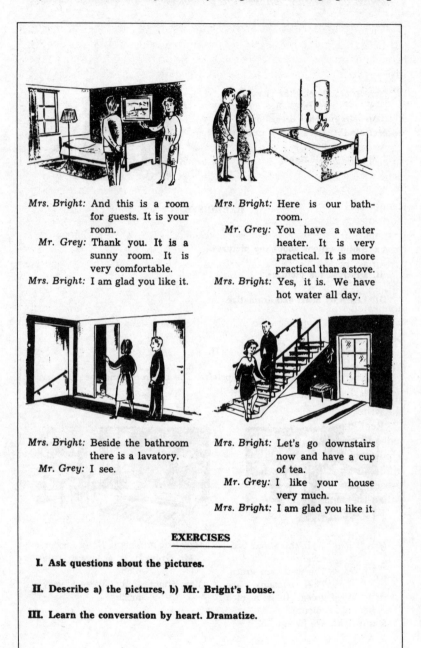

Mrs. Bright: And this is a room for guests. It is your room.

Mr. Grey: Thank you. It is a sunny room. It is very comfortable.

Mrs. Bright: I am glad you like it.

Mrs. Bright: Here is our bathroom.

Mr. Grey: You have a water heater. It is very practical. It is more practical than a stove.

Mrs. Bright: Yes, it is. We have hot water all day.

Mrs. Bright: Beside the bathroom there is a lavatory.

Mr. Grey: I see.

Mrs. Bright: Let's go downstairs now and have a cup of tea.

Mr. Grey: I like your house very much.

Mrs. Bright: I am glad you like it.

EXERCISES

I. Ask questions about the pictures.

II. Describe a) the pictures, b) Mr. Bright's house.

III. Learn the conversation by heart. Dramatize.

There is clearly something odd about this 'dialogue'. We feel that it is artificial; if Mrs Bright and Mr Grey were going around the house they just would not say what is put in their mouths here. The language is very repetitive – *this is . . . , it is . . .* etc. – and the listing of each piece of new furniture and equipment implausible.

However, we are in a dilemma. A full record of an actual dialogue will contain language which is beyond the capabilities of the learners, while a constructed one may well be disconnected and socially inappropriate.

As long ago as 1877, Sweet presented the dilemma in terms which are so clear and appropriate that we must, with some sense of shame at how little we have learned in over a century, repeat them verbatim here:

'The dilemma is this: If the texts are perfectly free and natural, they cannot be brought into any definite relation to the grammar . . . The other horn of the dilemma is that if we try to make our texts embody definite grammatical categories, the texts cease to be natural: they become either trivial, tedious, and long-winded, or else they become more or less monstrosities, or, finally, they are broken up dislocated sentences'. Jespersen too, in 1920, (*ibid.*) makes a crucially relevant point:

'We ought to learn a language through sensible communication . . . Disconnected words are but stones for bread; one cannot do anything sensible with mere lists of words. Indeed, not even disconnected sentences ought to be used . . . '

Are there, then, any criteria for the choice or construction of dialogues? There are, but first we need to attempt to resolve the dilemma of the choice between the 'natural' text – recorded *in situ* as natives interact in a normal and unconstrained way – and the 'artificial' text which is the creation of the writer.

'Real' data will contain, not only grammatical structures which we may judge to be too complex for the learner at the stage he has reached (this is a point related to the whole issue of 'grading' which we have considered in detail in 3.5.), but also incomplete sentences, overlapping speech, pauses, 'ums' and 'ers' and so forth. Consider this extract from an interview with a trawler skipper (Brown 1977.110):

A Is it soon going to be impossible to operate out there if you can't go into Icelandic ports?
B No. I wouldn't say impossible. No.
A Dangerous?
B We can always manage . . . dangerous. Yeah.
A We got a trawler today which is being towed home to Britain precisely because it daren't put into a port.
B mm
A And it has no engine at all.
B mm
A What's going to happen – – –

This is, clearly, acceptable as normal conversation but is it acceptable as a model of English for the learner to copy? In a sense it is. The skipper demonstrates his skill by:

i. Providing feedback to the interviewer; the 'mm' signals both that he has heard and understood and that he does not disagree, or at least, does not disagree so strongly that he wishes to interrupt him.

ii. Changing his own utterance in mid-stream to respond to the question 'Dangerous?'.

Such skilled use of the language corresponds very well with the model we suggested in Chapter 6 (Figure 6.8.) and, as such, is a demonstration of the communicative competence of the skipper not, as the teacher may suspect, his 'inarticulateness'. Clearly, if our aim were merely to teach our learners how to create *grammatical sentences*, we should not wish to present him with a model in which there were occurences of stretches of speech which were not grammatical. However, if our aim is to teach the learner to produce appropriate utterances and to use the language in the way the natives do, such data is valuable. The point is, at what stage do we introduce such skills? Presumably, after the ability to create sentences. If this is the case, we need to 'edit' the data i.e. the skipper's second utterance might become something like this:

A We can always manage somehow. Yes. I agree it would be dangerous though.

Let us now return to Sweet's dilemma and ask ourselves what appears to be wrong with the 'dialogues' we often find in textbooks:

Since 'dialogues' are constructed of language, the errors in them must be classifiable under one of the levels of linguistic description i.e.

a. *Syntax*: the mechanics of producing the form of the message is in some way defective.

b. *Semantics*: something is wrong with the meaning.

c. *Pragmatics*: there is something inappropriate about the social use to which the utterances are being put in the context of the dialogue.

We can usually trust the textbook-writer to get the first two levels correct – not always, but usually – i.e. correct grammar and correct words (in the context of the sentence, that is). What will go wrong, more likely than not, is the pragmatics. There are three key questions to ask here:

1. Is the situation itself *plausible*? Is the situation one which is likely to happen?

2. Is the role played by each of the participants *likely*? Do those involved do what we would expect them to do?

3. Is their language *appropriate*? Do they, that is, choose language which is at the correct level of formality?

The following Monty Python dialogue demonstrates failure on all three counts:

Man:	Hello. I didn't recognize you.
Queen:	But I'm the Queen!
Man:	You don't look at all like you do on the stamps.
Queen:	Don't you speak to me like that, you dirty little nonentity.
Man:	Can you help me change this wheel?
Queen:	Shut your fat gob, you nasty little pile of wombat's do's'.

As Monty Python so perceptively comments, 'A conversation like this could ruin your chances of an OBE'.

Let us return to the Yugoslav dialogue about looking around the house.

If we ask how plausible, likely and appropriate it is we may be able to suggest ways of rewriting it to make it more suitable. Specifically, we need to list what we know of the *participants*, the *setting* of the interaction and the *purpose* of the communication.

a) *Participants*:

Mrs Bright: married woman aged around 35. She is not a widow or divorced person since she refers to 'our' sitting-room, kitchen etc. Her daughter, Nelly, has a 'lovely little room' of her own and so is, presumably, in her pre- or early teens. The Brights appear to be quite well off; the kitchen is well-equipped and the house has three bedrooms.

Mr Grey: no clear indication of age or status but he appears to be staying with the Brights. Perhaps he is an old friend of Mr Bright's or a business associate. The fact that neither Mr Grey nor Mrs Bright uses any form of address – apart from the neutral *you* – suggests that their relationship is neither formal nor informal and strengthens the assumption that Grey is a friend or associate of Mr Bright's rather than his wife's.

b) *Setting*: the Bright's house during the day – there is a mention of the guest room being 'sunny' – the participants are making a tour of inspection.

c) *Purpose*: since Mr Grey is clearly going to stay with the Brights for some time, Mrs Bright is showing him round the house. As they move from room to room Mrs Bright identifies the room, Mr Grey comments on it or on its contents and Mrs Bright follows this up with a comment of her own. We shall look at each of these speech functions in turn and ask whether they are appropriate and whether the language selected for expressing them is also appropriate.

The roles played by the participants appear likely. A guest expects to be shown around the house if he plans to stay for some time. The host or hostess expects to act as guide and both guest and host expect the guest's comments on the house and its contents to be positive, whatever the guest may actually feel!

The situation is plausible except for the anomaly of a clearly Yugoslav – or at least non-British – setting marked by the mention of the stove for heating water with the English names.

The language, however, is less than appropriate. The intriguing thing is that the *functions* are appropriate – the participants produce appropriate *speech acts* — but the selection from the code itself which is intended to carry these appropriate meanings is defective.

We shall tabulate the original words of the first part of the dialogue, the functions they express and, where necessary, an alternative form of words (Figure 7.1.).

Figure 7.1.
Forms and functions in a dialogue

Original Form	Function	Alternative Form
Well.	Making start of speaker's contribution.	Well. Right. OK. Now.
This is our sitting-room.	Giving information.	This is the sitting-room. Here's the sitting-room.
It is very comfortable.	Expressing a valuation.	What a comfortable room!
It is more comfortable than our sitting-room.	Expressing a comparison	(omit)
We like this room very much. etc.	Giving information and accepting Grey's valuation.	Thank you. We like it a lot too.

7.3. SUMMARY

We have spent some time on dialogues in general and on this particular dialogue in order to make a number of points which we feel are important and which we wish to refer back to later in this chapter:

a) Many published dialogues are like this one: the roles are likely and the setting plausible — what the participants are attempting to convey is very much what such role players would wish to mean and the situation in which they find themselves communicating is not an uncommon one. What has gone wrong is partly the selection of functions — the comparison, for example, seems to be inappropriate — but mainly the choice of language items for expressing the functions.

b) The 'dialogue' has the main function in this textbook of practising a small number of recurring grammatical structures which *almost* fit socially but not quite. A more appropriate dialogue would be one which began with the functions and worked back to the forms which could express them.

c) This dialogue shows clearly how, with very little extra effort, we can modify materials which are defective and turn them to our advantage i.e. by building up the dialogue from the question 'what, in this situation, are the participants likely to want to mean?' rather than 'how can we create a dialogue which uses the grammatical structures we have just taught?'

We shall see in section 7.4. the important place dialogues had in the situationalist materials of the 1960s and, in section 7.5., how notional materials also draw on them.

7.4. SITUATIONAL LANGUAGE TEACHING: 'PSEUDO-FUNCTIONALISM'

In the previous chapter, we examined the impact of two formalist theories of language on language teaching. Both theories and the materials we used to illustrate their influence are American (though their origins are in European linguistics) and we may have given the impression that, outside North America, ELT continued with approaches which merely replicated the work of the Early Modern Linguists (whom we discussed in Chapter 4.) and that nothing new was discovered until the situational methodology of the teachers of English to migrants to Australia in the early 1960s.

Nothing could be further from the truth. As we suggested in Chapter 4, the general principles and many of the classroom techniques which are now taken as axiomatic by language teachers can be found in Palmer in the 1920s. During the period discussed in the previous chapter, ELT in Europe and the Commonwealth built on the foundations Palmer laid and developed a methodology which was much more relaxed and opportunist than that in use in America. This technique tended to seek a balance between the grammatical and the situational aspects of language teaching and learning and, especially in the then colonies, a strong 'practical' orientation which stressed the need for learning to be for communicative purposes.

What we intend to do here is to skip over the period from the 1930s to the beginning of the 1960s and take up the story with the appearance of what seemed at the time to be a truly *functional* approach to language teaching which was also a major example of a course in English for Special Purposes (ESP): *English for Newcomers to Australia.*

Although the 'situational' approach can be found in Palmer and the actual techniques on which the Commonwealth Office of Education in Sydney drew in their syllabus design had been worked out in detail in Britain during the 1950s, we can confidently claim that the first fully developed 'situational' course was created in Australia in the early 1960s: *English for Newcomers to Australia* later reissued in Britain as *Situational English* (1965-67).

The materials are a good example of ESP in the sense that they were produced in response to the needs of a clearly defined group of learners: the hundreds of thousands of non-English speaking immigrants who entered Australia in the years after the Second World War. As a group, they demonstrated a degree of linguistic and cultural heterogeneity which made a course focused on the L1 or the home culture and their influence on learning inappropriate; the migrants came from as far afield as Poland and Greece, Spain and Turkey.

Although most of the students were adult beginners, their needs were certainly not 'global'. They did not need the whole of the language. Their need was more limited and, at the same time, very pressing. What the migrants had to learn in a few short weeks was a kind of 'survival level' English so that they could become self-sufficient citizens contributing to and drawing from the society they had entered.

The course designers saw the problem in terms of specifying the situations which the migrant would need to cope with and providing him with the language to allow him to play the appropriate roles in those situations. But, as we saw earlier (6.4), specifying the component parts of a situation and showing how they interrelate is still a task beyond the present capabilities of social sciences, and the predictable co-occurrence of language items with situational ones is a rare rather than common event.

We have dubbed the situational language teaching 'pseudo-functional' because the dependence of the designers on a structuralist description of language locates the materials firmly in the formalist approach despite the fact that the use of the situation suggests functionalism. Indeed, the 'situations' in the materials turn out, on examination, to be little more than props for the routine pattern practice of the formalist approach. However, it would be wrong to damn situational teaching, as exemplified by the Australian materials, with faint praise. They had an important influence on ELT, particularly to immigrants in Britain, which far outweighs their obvious weaknesses.

7.4.1. Situationalist views on the nature of language
Although there is no overt statement of the beliefs of the situationalists — and we use the term here to refer to the text-book writers and teachers who created and used the materials and the method rather than to some group of academics — about the nature of language, it can be assumed, and to some degree deduced from their method, that they accepted the contemporary view of language as a communication code and added to that two small amplifications of that view; that language was used by people to *do* things — to denote, locate, name, label, describe bodily states; etc. — and that language is used by role-players in recurring situations. Both of these ideas had been around in embryo since early in the century and were to be more fully developed in the 1970s.

7.4.2. Situationalist views on the description of language
Without a distinctive view on the nature of language, it is hardly surprising that, on the issue of the description of language, the situationalists followed whatever grammar was readily available; in the early 1960s this clearly meant structuralist grammar.

7.4.3. Situationalist views on language learning
Once again, the prevailing wisdom seems to have been adopted by the situationalists when they came to state their notions of how language is learned.

1. Habit formation is encouraged, implying a behaviourist orientation.

2. Linguistic items have to be learned and manipulated; an echo of the structuralist approach but

3. Sentence patterns (again a structuralist concept) are introduced by ' . . . recreating, in the classroom, situations (in) which it (is) natural to say the sentences he (the teacher) has chosen' (Teacher's Book 1. 4.) and, although the progression through the course is essentially grammatical:

4. Social Formulae are introduced, even when they appear to be too complex for the unit, 'because they are socially useful'. (*ibid*.)

7.4.4. Situationalist language teaching materials

1. The materials adopted an *aural-oral* method i.e. 'new material is heard and spoken by the students *before* they read it and write it'.

2. Actual presentation and practice make extensive use of 'realia'; the contents of the classroom — books, pencils, doors, windows, walls, cupboards, etc. — the bodies and possessions of the teacher and the learners — standing, sitting, walking, giving things to each other, etc. — and a 'kit' of useful objects; pictures, models, bottles, shoes, sticks etc.

3. Role-play is encouraged; students 'meet' each other and say:

> 'Good morning. How are you today?'
> 'Very well thank you. How are you?'

or ask for and are given things:

> 'Give me one please'.
> 'Here you are'.
> 'Thank you'.

or pass between two people who are talking and apologize:

> 'Excuse me please'.
> 'Certainly'.

All these come from very early units — a learner with absolutely no English, who had arrived during the same week from, say, Yugoslavia, would need and would be taught such formulae — and are clearly essential for social survival.

4. The notion of the speech act, never overtly stated, seems to underlie some of the units e.g. the first three units of Book 1 are concerned with *I, you, he, she, it* + BE + something. In syntactic terms, they are concerned with denotative, equative and locative uses of BE. They are presented to the teacher (in the Teacher's Book) in a much more notional or semantic way: 'This pattern stands for all other sentences in which people *identify* themselves or others by making a statement in the simplest terms e.g. 'I am George Scott' . . . A slightly different use . . . is . . . where people wish to *make statements about* their *location* or the location of other people, by saying 'I'm here . . . 'etc. (my emphasis).

In short, the situational method shows an amalgam of American structuralist grammar and behaviourist principles with European pragmatism (in the non-technical sense) and dynamic teaching methods mainly derived from such writers as Palmer (*qv.* Chapter 4).

145

One of its great attractions for the teacher is that each of the three student's books has a companion teacher's book in which the patterns to be taught and suggestions for teaching and practice are clearly laid out, unit by unit.

The weakness of the situational method lies not in the fact that it is eclectic — we have argued already that FL materials ought to be — but that the linguistic description and the learning theory on which it is based are inadequate and the attempt to compensate for those inadequacies by introducing elements from a notional view of grammar and a naive sociolinguistic view of language use was insufficient. Just as the sentence cannot be used as the unit of teaching since it is not the unit of actual speech, so too is the situation inadequate, containing as it does an as yet unspecified set of variables which still await organization into a system.

7.4.5. Summary

At first sight, situationalist teaching gives the impression of being functional in its orientation and, hence, a new *approach*. However, as we have just shown it combines the structuralist view of the nature of language — formalism — and a behaviourist orientation to language learning with a methodology which derives from European language teaching — particularly Palmer — in stressing a greater degree of participation on the part of the learners through the use of dialogues and role-play in particular.

Nevertheless, these differences do not, in themselves, create a new *approach* only a new *method*. It is only with a radically different view of the nature of language that a new approach can emerge. In the next section, we shall argue that notional syllabuses with strongly functional and communicative orientation to the nature of language constitute such a radical shift and therefore represent a new *approach* rather than yet another change in *method*.

7.5. NOTIONAL SYLLABUSES

We now come to a type of syllabus which is truly functional in its approach to language teaching: the notional syllabus. In contrast with situational language teaching which we discussed in the previous section, the notional approach rests on a functional view of the nature of language, a systemic or case-grammar model for the description of language and a cognitive view of language learning.

7.5.1. Notional views on the nature of language

It has already been argued that notional syllabuses constitute a fresh approach to language teaching rather than a change in method by virtue of the view of the nature of language held by those who are responsible for their creation. We must emphasize that the essential difference between the attitude of the designer of a notional syllabus and that of those responsible for earlier syllabuses is the strongly *sociolinguistic* orientation they adopt.

7.5.2. Notional views on the description of language

The attitudes to the description of language on which the makers of notional syllabuses draw have also been discussed earlier in this chapter. All that remains here is to emphasize that any grammatical model with a semantic base – case grammar or systemic grammar for example – can form the linguistic underpinning of the syllabus. The crucial point for the notional syllabus is that the model should concentrate on answering the question 'what meanings are there and how do users express them?'.

Fortunately for the teacher of English or the syllabus designer there are a number of pedagogical grammars available which present, in a form which can be used as the input to a syllabus, semantically oriented models of language.

One of the most attractive is Leech and Svartvik (1975) which, in Part Three – 'Grammar in Use' – breaks down the notions into:

a) *Concepts*: referring to objects, substances and materials, time, place, direction and distance, etc.

b) *Information, reality and belief*: statements, questions and responses, fact, hypothesis and neutrality, attitudes to truth, etc.

c) *Mood, emotion and attitude*: emotive emphasis in speech, volition, permission and obligation, etc.

d) *Meanings in connected discourse*: linking signals, presenting and focusing information, order and emphasis, etc.

Since this is a pedagogical grammar rather than an ELT syllabus, the concepts are grouped in a logical manner but not graded or sequenced for teaching. The next step, if the grammar were being used as the basis of a syllabus would have to be an attempt at grading and sequencing (a problem which we have already discussed in Chapter 3). This might well entail the breaking up of sections a), b) and c) into a larger number of blocs each focused on a single large concept e.g.

i) *Substance*: objects, substances and materials, amount and quantity, abstractions, definite and indefinite meaning.

ii) *Time*: past, present and future, time when, states and events, frequency and duration.

iii) *Space*: position, direction, distance, movement.

iv) *Relationships between ideas*: manner, means, instrument, cause and result, condition and contrast.

v) *Relationships between people*: permission and obligation, degrees of likelihood, attitudes to truth, permission.

Each of these, naturally, subdivides into sub-concepts each of which can be expressed by a range of grammatical forms (see Bell 1980a).

7.5.3. Notional views on language learning

Although there is no absolute necessity for a notional syllabus to adopt a cognitive approach to language learning the prevailing atmosphere in psychology and linguistics has made such a choice almost inevitable and this has been reinforced both by the semantic considerations with which the approach begins and the fact that notional syllabuses first appeared as a result of the attempt to satisfy the needs of adult learners.

7.5.4. The syllabus

The problem faced by Wilkins in designing a syllabus for adult FL learners in Europe (Wilkins 1976) was a fundamental one: how to get from the 'meanings' which the speaker intended to express to the formal structure of the grammar and, ultimately, to the utterances which the speaker can use to actualize those meanings.

In diagrammatic form the problem looks like this:

Figure 7.2.
Notion, grammar and utterance

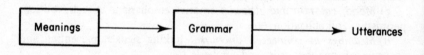

Drawing on the suggestions made by Austin and Searle on the structure of *speech acts* (see 6.1.2. for our earlier discussion of this topic) Wilkins' solution was to set up a pair of intervening categories which were able, as it were, to convert meanings into a form which could be processed by the grammar and converted into sentences — the output of the grammar — which would then be turned into appropriate utterances or, to use Searle's term 'speech acts'.

The first category — *semantico-grammatical categories* (six in all) — has the function of converting meanings into notions which can be dealt with by the grammar. Each category, it will be noted, closely resembles the 'propositional content' of the speech act. Reference is to such notions as time, quantity, space, matter, case, deixis (though the last two are not strictly references to concepts or objects but rather references to relationships between concepts). The focus is, it should be recognized, highly grammatical. Meanings are, of course, also conveyed lexically.

The second category — *categories of communicative function* (8 in all) or to use Munby's term (1978) *micro-functions and attitudinal tones* (7) — has the function of converting grammatical sentences into utterances by relating reference to the orientation of the speaker (i.e. a function very much like the 'illocutionary force' of the speech act) e.g. reference might be made to a point in time by stating the degree of certainty held by the speaker; 'it's 4.30' or 'it might be about 4.30' or 'I don't think it's 4.30 yet', etc.

The model now becomes rather more complex with 'meanings' being converted into utterances by a three-stage process:

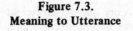

Figure 7.3.
Meaning to Utterance

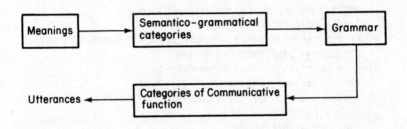

Rather than list Wilkins' or Munby's semantico-grammatical categories in detail (they are easily available in their published work), we shall outline them here and then suggest a grouping of notions which we have found to be useful.

Semantico-grammatical categories
 1. Time
 2. Quantity
 3. Space
 4. Matter
 5. Case
 6. Deixis

Categories of communicative function
(The seven categories are actually Munby's rather than Wilkins').
 1. Certainty
 2. Commitment
 3. Judgement and evaluation
 4. Suasion
 5. Argument
 6. Rational enquiry and exposition
 7. Formulaic communication

Each of these subdivides into between two and ten sub-categories e.g.
Time:
   a) Point of time
   b) Duration
   c) Frequency
   d) Sequence
   e) Time relations

In addition, a sub-category may be further subdivided – *time relations*, for example, into *past, present* and *future* – and, for each meaning, several linguistic forms are likely to be available.

Future time itself can be expressed in English by no less than four separate forms:
   i) *will* + 'bare' infinitive = neutral prediction.
      I will play tennis this evening.
   ii) *be* + *going* + 'to' infinitive = result of present intention or state.
      I'm going to play tennis this evening.
   iii) *be* + verb + *ing*; = result of present plan.
      I'm playing tennis this evening.
   iv) present tense = result of present plan (+ an implication that the activity is habitual).
      I play tennis this evening.

A striking point about this array of notions is the degree to which it reflects the concepts presented in Roget's *Thesaurus* – first published in 1852 but based on ideas initially outlined in 1805 – for example, dimensions, number, order, quantity, etc.

We mention this not with any intention of diminishing the importance of Wilkins' ideas but to show how present-day thinking in linguistics is a reassertion of the rationalism of the eighteenth century and a rejection of the normative formalism of the nineteenth.

7.5.5. Notional language teaching materials

There are now a number of EFL textbooks based on the notional approach. We shall make use of de Freitas (1978.61 f. and 65 f.) on *obligation* and *permission* as our example in Appendix D.

At this point, we wish to make one or two general points about notional materials:

a) Although notional materials can be used for beginners – Wilkins' work for the Council of Europe assumes the need to work towards a 'threshold level' and de Freitas' book has the significant title *Survival English* – the majority appear to be aimed at the needs of the more advanced learner who 'has a good formal knowledge of the language but is not always able to apply this in everyday speech' (de Freitas *op. cit*. iv).

b) Because of the difficulties involved in grading, many avoid the issue altogether by defining themselves as 'handbooks', either as in the case of de Freitas or Bhatnagar & Bell (1979) for reference and classroom or personal practice or, as in the case of Bell (1980a) solely for reference.

c) Similarly, the problem of sequencing is frequently avoided either by presenting notions in what is hoped to be a 'logical' order – an order close to that of the pedagogical grammar on which the materials are based – or even in alphabetical order. Either way, the writer is likely to stress that the static ordering of notions in the book is an inevitable result of the structure of books not the immutable order through which the learner must work.

d) Where the materials contain exercises – not all do, particularly if their purpose is reference and their intended users very advanced – the actual exercises contain verbal interaction between teacher and learners, among the learners themselves – in pairs or groups – and dialogues of essentially the same type as we have been accustomed to since Palmer in the 1930s.

In short, exciting though the notional approach clearly is, its full potential has yet to be realized both at the design level and at the level of use in the classroom.

7.5.6. Summary
In this section we have been outlining a new approach to language teaching – the notional syllabus – which derives from a range of functionalist inputs from linguistics, philosophy and the human sciences. That this is a new *approach* rather than a variation in *method* can, we believe, be demonstrated by pointing to the view of the nature of language accepted by those responsible for notional syllabuses; a social skill which constitutes an open system of elements and relationships which interacts with the context of its use, in contrast with the closed-system context-free view of language accepted by formalist linguists.

The impact of this change of orientation has been, and no doubt in the future will also be, very considerable. Meaning is now in the forefront of the syllabus designer's mind and learning a language is now seen as learning *how to mean* in a wide range of social settings. The emphasis on meaning has had the effect of concentrating attention on the needs of the learner and this, in turn, has given fresh impetus to the design of courses for specific, often job-related, purposes in contrast with the global orientation of earlier courses. In the classroom, the functional orientation has led to activities in which the learner discovers – to quote the title of the influential book by the philosopher Austin (1962) – *how to do things with words*. In essence, a functional approach seeks to provide the learner not only with the linguistic knowledge which permits him to create and understand grammatical sentences – the *linguistic competence* of TG – but also the social knowledge and skill which permit him to produce and comprehend socially appropriate utterances; the *communicative competence* of socio-linguistics.

7.6. CONCLUSION
We began this chapter with an outline of situational teaching methods, since

they appeared to be functionalist in their orientation and, or so we initially believed, for that reason represented a new approach to language teaching.

Situational teaching, we discovered, was actually little more than a new *method* derived from the same *approach* as that based on structuralist and transformational-generative linguistics. However, within situational teaching, as we saw in section 7.4, there were pointers to what was to follow: a new awareness of the relationship between the meaning of an utterance and the context in which it is used and an embryonic appreciation of *notions* underlying the surface structure of utterances.

One crucial shared characteristic in situational and notional teaching has been the attempt to integrate the social-psychological concept of *role* with the semantic notions expressed in language by role-players: an important input from the human sciences to sociolingusitics and sociolinguistically oriented applied linguistics. Indeed, it is the conception of role adopted by situational and notional teaching that marks most clearly their theoretical differences.

Both make use of the notion of *role* but the situational method sees roles as *stereotyped* behaviour patterns and in a situational course the learner is, as it were, 'fitted' to the norm of the role. In such a normative approach, we witness the attempt to *socialize the personality* of the individual learner (the ideas in this section derive, in the main, from Getzels and Thelen 1972).

In contrast, the notional approach is one which seeks to *personalize the roles* i.e. the individual learner is made aware of the expected behaviour of the role-player but — and this comes about of necessity as a result of the emphasis on individual communication needs — is encouraged to modify those expectations to suit his own needs and, ultimately to create behaviours which are *transactional* in nature, containing behaviour which shows a balance between what is expected, what is desired by the individual and what is desired by the other participants in the interaction. In short, a truly functional approach to communication and the teaching of communication skills will imply the increasing of the self-awareness of the individual and his sensitivity to others which will, in the end, result in *appropriate* communication.

SUGGESTED FURTHER READING

Van Ek J. A. (1975), *Systems development in adult language learning; the Threshold Level*
This paper represents van Ek's position on the creation of notional syllabuses for adult learners; a rather more sociolinguistically oriented view than Wilkins'.

Halliday M. A. K. & Hasan R. (1976), *Cohesion in English*
The standard work, to date, on cohesion in English. This is essential reading for anyone who intends to pursue the description or teaching of language beyond the level of the sentence.

Sinclair J. M. & Coulthard M., *Towards an Analysis of Discourse; The English used by Teachers and Pupils*
An important application of discourse analysis to the interactions of the British classroom. The study has powerful implications for ELT both at the level of approach and method.

Widdowson H. G. (1978), *Teaching Language as Communication*
An explication of the 'communicative approach' to language teaching which covers a wide area of classroom applications in addition to the theory which they rest on.

Wilkins D. A. (1976), *Notional Syllabuses*
Wilkins' approach to notional syllabus design derived from his work for the Council of Europe. This should be read in conjunction with van Ek and Trim (1977) in order to gain a balanced view of the efforts which have been made during the past decade by the Council of Europe from which, to a large extent, the notional syllabus has derived.

Epilogue

Running through this book has been the theme that the many methods which have been employed in language teaching during this century can all be subsumed under the heading of a single *approach*. Only with the emergence of notional syllabuses in the last decade, we have argued, has a genuinely new *approach* begun to emerge. Great though the differences are between the attitudes of 'traditional' grammarians, the Early Modern Linguist of the early years of the century, the Structuralists and the Transformationalists in the philosophy and scientific method they employed and, when concerned with language learning — either the acquisition of the L1 or the later learning of an L2 — all, we insist, share a common view of language as *form* rather than *function*. Even the radical shift in goals and methods marked by the development of TG is insufficient, in itself, to constitute a new *approach* in applied linguistics. Renewed attention to the nature of language as a process rather than a form — an acceptance of a functional orientation — seems to us to mark a major watershed and suggest that syllabuses based on notions rather than forms indicate a truly original, though so far only weakly articulated, *approach* and this raises a second issue which must preoccupy applied linguistics in the 1980s; its status as a technology.

Chomsky, in 1969, argued forcefully that neither linguistics nor psychology had reached a level of sophistication which would allow them to support the kind of technology required by language teaching. Applied linguistics, in this view, did not and could not exist. Rather than accept this as a final judgement, applied linguists must surely re-examine the insights available today from the contributing disciplines — not only linguistics and psychology but all the human sciences — in order to set about building itself into a viable technology. Other technologies have achieved a level of autonomy — engineering comes immediately to mind — despite the necessarily incomplete nature of the theories on which they rest and it seems clear to us that applied linguistics can and should make the same effort. Linguistics itself is, in any case, going through a period of self-criticism in the course of which the fundamental assumptions of the discipline are being questioned. In such a context, new insights are bound to emerge and have dramatic implications for applied linguistics in general and for language teaching in particular. New kinds of learners with unexpected needs — particularly very advanced learners whose command of the code is excellent — await us and fresh insights into the nature of language, its social functions and manner of learning will have to be integrated into our response to these new needs; that is the challenge of the 1980s. Eventually, applied linguistics has to gain recognition as an autonomous technology but before that can come about we will have to clarify our thinking about our relationships with our parent disciplines and our clients and tighten up our terminology and procedures; we hope that this book has made a small contribution to this task.

APPENDICES

APPENDICES

Appendix A: Job analysis and ESP—case study on the canteen assistant

In Chapter 2, we were attempting to evolve some general principles of training programme design and to arrange those principles into an ordered series of steps. The outcome was a revision of Boydell's ten steps, modified to take account of the special needs of language training.

In this appendix, we wish to provide an example of the application of the ten steps. The case study is, of course, not intended to be comprehensive, merely illustrative and, we hope, provocative, in the sense of encouraging others to do in detail what we are only able to outline here.

We have taken the canteen assistant working in a self-service establishment which provides hot and cold snacks and drinks. We have selected this particular occupation for two rather different reasons:

a) the job is far from being exotic — everyone knows, or thinks he knows, what such an assistant does — and may therefore suggest more general ideas with a wider range of applications than would a more specialized or rare job and

b) the duties of the canteen assistant in such an establishment are likely to be both physical — setting out displays, replacing them, setting and clearing tables, etc. — and verbal — there will be queries about food or service which the assistant will need to be competent to handle. To be asked to design and run a course for canteen assistants to improve their English seems a not unlikely request these days.

Out of all the duties and responsibilities of the canteen assistant we have chosen for particular attention a single task; dealing with complaints about a meal being cold. We have two reasons for choosing this particular task

a) much of the rest of the communication between assistant and customer in the self-service canteen can be achieved by non-verbal gestures — item selection by pointing, affirmation or rejection by head movements, etc. — but the handling of complaints cannot — we will need to pass on knowledge of and skill in using the code — and

b) we already have a flow-diagram showing the stages and steps involved in the task (thanks, again, to Boydell *op. cit.* 26) so we are only left with the problem of the language content.

STEP 1: IDENTIFY THE NEEDS

Let us assume that we have been approached by the owner, general manager or training manager of a chain of self-service canteens operating in a multilingual society in which English often functions as a lingua franca. He

159

has noticed that the assistants 'have difficulty in speaking English' and that this, he fears, may be making potential customers less inclined to make use of the facilities of his canteens.

An investigation shows that the staff most involved are those who have face-to-face contact with the public but are below the cashier or supervisor level. Company records will show us the total likely target population.

The need for the programme is, according to our client, urgent; he needs some kind of 'crash course' since he claims that the longer the problem remains unresolved the more trade he will lose.

The assistants appear to be the priority group and further investigation suggests that giving them a way of coping adequately with customer complaints in particular should be given priority, since a satisfied customer is far more likely to return than a dissatisfied one.

STEP 2: RELATE STATED NEEDS TO OVERALL AIMS OF THE ORGANISATION

Our client appears to be correct in his assessment of the situation – mishandled complaints are causing a loss of clientele and a reducing clientele, in turn reduces turnover, which, unless facilities are also reduced in step to cut the overheads, will result in a reduction in the profitability of the enterprise; our training seems to be needed and to be in accord with the overall aims of our client's organisation.

STEP 3: ANALYZE THE OCCUPATION OF THE TRAINEES

We have a very rough idea already but now need to go into job analysis seriously:

a) Job description: general statement of the characteristics of the job (taken from Boydell *op. cit*. 6): its purpose, duties and responsibilities.

i. Title:	Counter hand
ii. Department:	Catering – Cafe (Hot Section)
iii. Function:	To serve hot meals as required by customers.
iv. Hours of Work:	9.30 am to 6.15 pm (lunch 10.30 to 11.15; Tea 3.15 to 3.45).
v. Responsible to:	Counter charge hand
vi. Responsible for:	None
vii. Authority over:	None
viii. Duties/Responsibilities:	

1. Comply with instructions received from counter charge hand or supervisor.
2. Comply with food hygiene regulations.
3. Work as a team with other counter hands.

160

4. Clean and polish counter and switch on equipment.
5. Prepare *mise en place*   9.30 to 10.30
6. Place food under counter Sunglow unit.
7. Determine customer's requirements and obtain them from the display unit.   11.15 to 5.30
8. Place pies and pasties on display.
9. Clean and clear the counter, equipment and working area at the close of business   5.30 to 6.15

b) Job Specification: tasks required of the assistant and the knowledge and skills required to carry them out appropriately.

i. *Tasks*: There are a good number and we wish to focus on one which emerges from duty 7 i.e. determine the customer's requirements and obtain them from the display unit. Such a duty, clearly entails a number of tasks, or to be more accurate, one sub-task within that generally formulated task, which we wish to examine here; dealing with a customer's complaint about food which is supposed to be hot, when served, being cold.

ii.*Knowledge*; the assistant must know:

1. The customer's rights.
2. The company's rights.
3. The characteristics of coldness in food.
4. The difference between dishes which are intended to be eaten cold and those which are not.
5. When a complaint is being made.
6. When a customer is satisfied.
7. What to do when a complaint is made.
8. What to do after the complaint has been made, etc.

iii.*Skills*: the assistant must also be able to:

1. Judge whether the food is cold or not.
2. Inform the customer of her judgement.
3. Placate the customer
4. Offer fresh food or a refund as appropriate.
5. Refer or report the incident to the supervisor as appropriate, etc.

c) Further analysis: the more precise description of *tasks* and the analysis of faults. We have decided to focus our attention on one specific task; dealing with customers' complaints about cold food.

Figure A.1.
Dealing with a complaint; algorithm

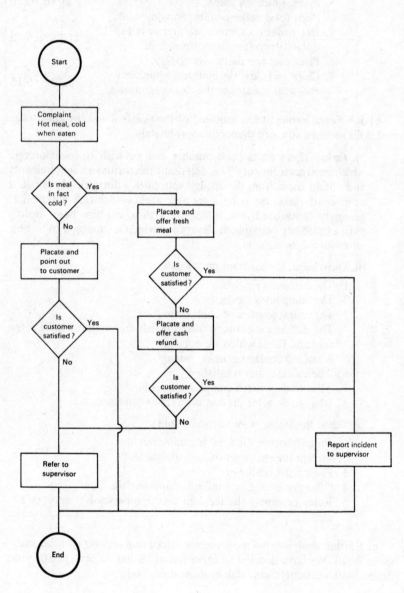

Figure A.2.
Faults Analysis

	Common name of *fault*	What is *appearance* of fault?	What are the possible *causes*?	What *effect* does fault have?	Whose *responsibility* is the fault?	What immediate *action* must be taken	How can the fault be *prevented* from recurring?
A	Cups in vending machine fail to drop.	Tea/Coffee flowing into waste.	1. Fuse. 2. Cups incorrectly loaded. 3. Mechanical.	1. Customer complaint. 2. Loss of profit. 3. Extra work to clean up mess.	1. Service engineer. 2. Canteen assistant.	Check and rectify cup loading.	Train assistant in loading.
B	Hot meal – cold when eaten.	Tastes cold when eaten.	1. Cold plate used. 2. Hot cupboard not switched on early enough. 3. Food not properly heated. 4. Customer talks too long before eating meal. 5. Hold up at cashier desk.	1. Customer complaint. 2. Loss of profit. 3. Loss of a customer.	1.} Canteen 2.} assistant. 3. Cooks. 4. Customer's own. 5. Various combinations of responsibility.	1 Fresh hot meal offered or 2. Cash refund but 3. The customer should be satisfied at all costs.	1. Improved conditions. 2. Further staff training.
C	Lack of variety in meals served.	1. Drop in receipts. 2. Complaints.	1. Inexperienced management. 2. Market and weather conditions. 3. Bad menu planning.	1. Customer complaint. 2. Loss of profit.	Manageress/Area controller.	Reasons investigated and action taken.	Depends on cause as to whether it can be prevented – further guidance and training if manageress is cause.
D	Dirty plate served or about to be served.	Dirt seen on plate by assistant or customer.	1. Water in machine not hot enough. 2. Dirt allowed to dry in. 3. Not properly dried or dirt put on plate by dryer. 4. Staff not trained to withdraw such plates. 5. Lack of hygiene knowledge.	1. Slows down service as plate is withdrawn. 2. Customer complaint.	Canteen assistant.	Plate must not be served if possible. If it is customer should be satisfied.	Further training in use of washing up machine and washing process. Also importance of hygiene.

STEP 4: SPECIFY AND SELECT THE TRAINEES

The likely target population has already been narrowed down to a smaller probable group of trainees — canteen assistants — which may well be reduceable to an even smaller group that requires the training and can benefit from it. We need some kind of test to discover what the assistants actually do and how well that corresponds to what they are expected to do. The shortfall between the actual and the expected constitutes the training gap that our course is to fill.

Whatever test we give, we are likely to find that a small number of potential trainees are not suited to the training we are planning. Some will be too good and others too bad. We are very likely, however, only to lose 10%-20% of our potential students and we can return to those we have decided not to select later when we run a more advanced or a more basic course which suits their particular needs. We might, even, if we have the agreement of our client, be able to make use of the assistants whose proficiency appears to be too great for a course at the level we are planning, as 'tutors' to the others, especially if we intend to use interactive training techniques.

Naturally, the number of trainees we can handle on a particular course will depend on the types of instructional technique we plan to use and whether we are expected to do the teaching alone or with assistance.

To return to testing; if we have a faults analysis available (see Figure A.2.), that will give us both an idea of the areas which need to be covered and a suggestion of questions which we can include in a formal test of knowledge.

Testing skills is more formidable. One way, of many, might be to set up the work situation — ideally, in the actual canteen outside normal working time but we can simulate something like it in the classroom with a little imagination — and have the trainees play out their normal roles while we, our helpers or the other trainees play the roles of customers with complaints. Scoring such a test is difficult. It is hard to see how we can assess the use of a skill objectively at all. Perhaps all we can hope to do is form a subjective judgement of how well the individual has performed and, if at all possible, involve the client in the making of the judgement, since it is he who, in the end, will decide whether our course has been effective or not.

Assuming that we have selected our trainees we can move on to the next step; setting the objectives.

STEP 5: SET THE OBJECTIVES

We have already discussed the range of objectives which need to be considered — key, critical and specific — so all that is required here is a listing of them for this course:

   a) **Key objective**: our key objective is to alter the future behaviour of the trainees i.e. this is the long-term aim of our programme. In this case, the key objective might be expressed as 'being able to deal appropriately with complaints about cold food'.

b) Critical objectives: in contrast with our single, general, long-term key objective, we will have a number of critical objectives — medium term goals which are more specific than the key objective and which make its attainment possible — in this case perhaps four will suffice:

i) Being able to check whether the meal is actually cold or not.

ii) Being able to explain to and/or placate the customer.

iii) Being able to offer a replacement dish or a refund as appropriate.

iv) Being able to involve the supervisor as and when appropriate.

c) Specific objectives: if the key objective represents our overall long-term strategy, our specific objectives are our individual short-term tactics; the activities which constitute the programme. Here we are able to express our specific objectives succinctly: knowing when and how to verbalize the changes in behaviour listed in the critical objectives in a variety of settings. We shall see, in the next step, that this requires of the trainee the knowledge of and ability to select and use appropriately a range of speech acts.

This takes us on to Step 6: the design of the syllabus.

STEP 6: DESIGN THE SYLLABUS

In this step, we need to select the content of the course, grade it from 'easy' to 'difficult' and/or from 'most useful' to 'least useful' and sequence the items in some way which makes learning easier for our trainees.

a) Selection: Since we are committed to a functional approach in the design of our syllabus (though we have yet to state that in this case; see Step 8) we will try to list the speech acts which are needed by the learner and, possibly, select a limited number of formal manifestations of each which we will teach. This selection will in part depend on our feelings about the grading of formal items (an issue which was discussed in detail in Chapter 3) and in part on the level of proficiency in English which our students already have. For example, some may have no way at all of verbalizing a particular speech act. In such a case, we must decide on at least one way which is both easy to learn and useful in a wide range of circumstances. Conversely, the participants may have a passive knowledge of a wide range of possible forms but be unsure of which to use on any particular occasion. In this case, we can be much more opportunist in our methodology and allow forms to emerge which we judge and encourage or discourage depending on their appropriateness at the time.

In the case of dealing with complaints about cold food, the *functions*

165

appear to be *explanation, apology, offering, reporting* and the *speech acts:*

> *Explaining* that the food is hot, if it is i.e. telling the customer that he is wrong.
>
> *Apologizing* to the customer, if he is right.
>
> *Offering* a fresh dish or a refund.
>
> *Referring* the problem to the supervisor.
>
> *Reporting* the incident to the supervisor.

Naturally, for each of these functions there are a considerable number of forms available which can express them or, to use speech act terminology, several things the speaker can do which will 'count as' each of the speech acts.

In addition, since communication is an interactive matter, the assistant will need to recognize that, for example, the customer is, in fact, making a complaint or is, actually, satisfied.

b) Grading: One way of deciding on a grading might be to list the speech acts in the order in which we expect them to occur naturally and match them to the least complex and most widely applicable realizations we can think of.

In the case of the canteen assistant dealing with a complaint about a cold meal, the speech acts – following Boydell's algorithm (Boydell *op. cit.* 26. reproduced as Figure A.1. above) – appear to be, for an interaction with a totally dissatisfied customer:

Customer.	Stating. Complaining.
Assistant.	Checking. Placating, Offering.
C	Rejecting.
A	Placating. Offering.
C	Rejecting.
A	Referring.

The actual realizations might take the form of:

C	This soup is cold.
A	Please let me check. I'm sorry. It is. Can I get you another bowl?
C	No. I don't want another one.
A	I'm sorry. Would you like your money back?
C	No. I want to see the Manager.
A	I'll call the supervisor. This gentleman's soup was cold when he got it and he wants to complain to you about it.

This is, of course, a rather crude dialogue. We really need to add in some additional words and phrases which have the function of holding the interaction together, e.g. the customer is likely to begin with a signal which attracts the assistant's attention; 'Miss', 'Waitress', etc. Similarly, the point at which the assistant hands the problem over to the supervisor is likely to be marked by a sequence:

A   Informing customer of next action.
         Attracting the attention of the supervisor.
         Introducing the supervisor to the customer.
         Explaining the nature of the problem to the supervisor.
         Taking leave of the customer.

The realizations of these functions as speech acts could take the form of utterances such as:

A   I'll call the supervisor, sir.
         Miss Jones.
         This is Miss Jones, the supervisor, sir.
         This gentleman's soup was cold when he got it and he wants to complain to you about it.
         I'm sure Miss Jones will be able to help you sir.
         Please excuse me.

One problem with attempting a grading here is that a dependence on grammatical grading may do more than fail to help us, it may in fact lead us into attempting to teach quite unnatural forms. We will probably be forced into teaching the forms which occur naturally no matter how grammatically complex they appear to be. After all, if we are trying to help people to do what is done by more skillful communicators we are obliged to teach what really happens rather than what we would like to happen.

c) **Sequencing**: Fortunately, in this case, the sequence of speech acts can be determined with considerable accuracy. The structure of the interaction itself carries within it the sequence of verbal actions and, as the algorithm clearly shows, the points at which alternative paths become available are marked by 'yes-no' decisions.

We come next to the creation of the materials – in the broad sense of whatever activities we decide to make use of to assist learning – and their implementation.

STEP 7: CREATE THE MATERIALS

In our discussion of Step 6, we suggested that the speech acts might be realized in a particular way and began to write a dialogue.

We can capitalize on this by manipulating the interaction so as to create interactions of greater and greater complexity which will, of necessity, contain speech acts which are qualitatively and quantitatively more complex.

The simplest interaction would be one in which the customer is wrong i.e. the soup is not actually cold. This would require the speech acts:

C	Stating. Complaining.
A	Checking. Placating. Explaining.
C	Expressing satisfaction.
A	Reporting the incident to the supervisor.

Perhaps the dialogue could have the form:

C	This soup is cold.
A	Let me check for you. Oh dear, it seems hot to me. I hope that's all right sir.
C	Oh yes. It is quite warm isn't it? Thank you.
A	Miss Jones. We've just had a customer complaining that the soup was cold and it wasn't . . . . .

At the other extreme would be an interaction in which the customer refused to be placated and insisted on complaining to the supervisor i.e. the interaction follows the 'no' decisions in the algorithm; the dialogue would look like the one we gave in Step 6.

There are, in fact, no less than six routes through the algorithm i.e. six highly plausible interactions each with strongly associated speech acts. We can use the degree of complexity in the route as a measure of grading and present the interactions from simplest to most complex. Of course, we will never be absolutely sure that the customer will react in exactly the way we have predicted. People can, in principle, do and say anything they like at any time but the fact remains that they tend to keep fairly closely to the behaviours we predict, at least in a relatively stylized interaction such as this.

Not only can we make the interaction more complex but, by reducing the amount of control we have over the language content in the role-play make the verbalization more challenging for the learner. For example, we could start off with dialogues fully written out and ask the trainees to memorize them and act them out. We could then introduce variations in intonation, gesture, etc. which would signal differences in *manner*: polite–rude. The next step might be to give the role-players cue cards with the functions on them – *placate, point out* – rather than their realizations: 'I'm sorry', 'Oh dear this is unfortunate', etc. Finally, we can arrange a completely free role-play in which we would provide the trainees with a vague specification of the situation and the roles they were to play, e.g. 'You are an angry customer with a bowl of cold soup', 'you are the assistant', 'start'. The final step would be as close to the real work situation as we can make it in the classroom and, for that reason, the end of our task; we, by this stage, would have made ourselves redundant.

STEP 8: DECIDE ON EDUCATIONAL STRATEGY

We have been implying throughout this discussion an attitude to education which regards learner and teacher as equal adults working together to complete a task (see our earlier comments in 2.2.8.). It is for this reason that we have been concentrating on setting up learning situations in which the trainees can learn from each other as they simulate the interactions which commonly take place in their day-to-day contacts with their customers and each other.

Such an orientation seems to follow too from our commitment to the teaching of function rather than form – not that the forms no longer need to be learned; they must be since it is through them that functions are manifested – and to provide us with the means of making both learning and practice meaningful for the learner.

STEP 9: TEST THE EFFECTIVENESS OF THE PROGRAMME

We suggest in Appendix C (13) that there are four types of question we could ask about the 'success' of a training programme:

a. Are the trainees happy? If not, why not?
b. Did the training work? If not, why not?
c. Is the knowledge being used? If not, why not?
d. Is the knowledge helping the organization? If not, why not?

The first of these forms the basis of a popularity rating for the course. We can ask the participants whether they enjoyed the course, whether it covered the right topics, whether it was pitched at the right level for them, whether it was long enough or too long, etc. In the case of this particular study, we might also ask if the trainees would have preferred the course to have been held in normal work time (assuming we held it outside work time).

The value of this kind of rating is that it gives us an indication of what 'went well'. Its weaknesses is that, as we will point out in Appendix C, entertainment may well be rated high and learning relatively low by the trainees.

The second question concerns attainment and could be reformulated as 'have they learned what we taught?'. Like the first question, this is aimed at validating the course i.e. checking on its efficiency. But the two questions do differ in focus. The first asks the trainee to assess his teacher and the course he taught. The second, in contrast, asks the teacher to judge the learner and the course. Together they provide some degree of internal assessment.

The third question relates to the applicability of the course to the receiving system. Together with question four, it provides an external measure of the usefulness of the course to the client and his organisation. This question focuses on the changed behaviour of the trainees after the course i.e. it seeks to show the degree of improvement in work efficiency which has resulted from the course.

The fourth question also looks at the changed behaviour of the trainees but from the point of view of the organisation as a whole i.e. it attempts to measure the degree to which the changed behaviour influences the organization.

Attainment can be measured by working the trainees through the kinds of exercise we were suggesting in Step 7, but we will be more satisfied — and so will the client — if the newly acquired knowledge and skill can be demonstrated to carry over into the 'real world' of work. To investigate this we would need to carry out follow-up studies; observe the trainees at work and attempt to assess the improvement in their behaviour.

The final type of assessment is best carried out by the client or at least by our being given access to the facts and figures the client has at his disposal. We might find that the more competent assistants appeared to be attracting more customers, that the number and gravity of complaints had decreased and that the profitability of the company had increased. This suggests — though it cannot be shown to be a definite causal relationship — that our course has had a beneficial influence on the client's organization; this was what we planned for in Step 2 when we attempted to relate our programme to the overall aims of the organization.

STEP 10: PROVIDE FEEDBACK TO ALL AREAS

The answers we receive from the four questions posed in the previous step will provide a good deal of feedback. The participants can be told how, as a group, they rated the course, how much they learned, to what extent they are applying the contents of the course in their work and how important this is to the organization.

Our clients can be given much the same information plus our suggestions for further courses; more advanced courses for the personnel or courses for other grades.

Finally, we can give ourselves feedback which will enable us to revise the course. Some parts will have been well received well learned and widely applied on the job. Others will have been less satisfactory. We will need, on the basis of such feedback, to work right through the ten steps again as we redesign the programme.

In this case, we might find for example, that our trainees were a little shy of role-playing in the early stages of the course. Perhaps we should try showing them some films first rather than pushing them immediately into acting out the roles themselves. And so on.

Appendix B: Contrastive analysis and error analysis

In Chapter 2 — as part of Step 3: the analysis of the occupation(s) of the learner(s) — we suggested that the recognition of the need for training frequently arises as a result of the perception of a 'gap' between the expected knowledge and skills of the potential trainees and the current extent of their knowledge and skills. What is most likely to throw this deficit into relief is the extent to which the job-holder makes mistakes in his work and one of the ways of working towards a syllabus which will satisfy both the learner and the client is to base what we intend to teach on what we discover needs to be taught i.e. on a faults analysis.

Figure B.1.
Faults Analysis

RECOGNITION Common *name* of fault	DESCRIPTION *Appearance* of fault	EXPLANATION Possible *cause* of fault	CORRECTION *Prevention* recurrence of fault
Saleable apples thrown out	Saleable apples in garbage	Faulty grading caused by: a) Carelessness	a) Give practice in handling and piling.
		b) Misclassification	b) Explain grading system. Give practice in grading.

This appendix is concerned with the analysis of 'faults' produced by L2 learners and seeks to provide, in so far as it is possible, a step-by-step procedure which the teacher can follow in order to recognize when an error has occurred, describe what it is and explain why it exists.

1. ERROR ANALYSIS

All language teachers and language learners are aware that learners make mistakes; as Dulay & Burt (1974) charmingly put it 'You can't learn without goofing'. For the teacher several issues arise in relation to mistakes:
   a) Are mistakes systematic or random?
   b) Are there levels of seriousness, some mistakes being trivial and others being crucially important?

c) Are there any ways of explaining why particular mistakes occur with particular learners?

d) How can we set about answering these questions?

Rather than attempt to give answers here to these questions, let us look a little more closely at the problem, sort out the terminology and contrast the attitude of structuralist linguists and post-structuralist linguists to the whole issue of error.

1.1. Errors, mistakes and lapses

Corder (1967 and 1971) put forward a useful distinction between three types of 'fault': the grammatically incorrect form — termed *error* — the socially inappropriate form — the *mistake* — and the 'slip of the tongue/pen': the *lapse*. We might consider these in order, since most of us would agree that errors, as we have just defined them, are more serious and more in need of correction than mistakes and that lapses may well require no corrective action at all.

1.1.1. Errors

An error is a sure sign that the learner has not mastered the code of the target language. Why he has not mastered it and why the form of the error is as we observe it rather than a different form are questions which we will raise in a moment. If an error indicates faulty knowledge of the grammar of the L2, we must define the error as something which arises as a result of L2 learning and is not, therefore, to be found in the L1 user of the language. The pre-school child certainly produces utterances which, if judged by the standards of adult grammar, are errors but the native adult, by definition does not.

1.1.2. Mistakes

In contrast, both L1 and L2 users of a language make mistakes — social gaffs of varying degrees of seriousness — but the native is far more likely to realize that his behaviour has been judged to be socially unacceptable and is also far more likely to take steps to remedy the mistake than is the L2 user. The learner may fail to read the non-verbal feedback from his hearer correctly and so miss the cue that he has just produced an utterance which, perfectly grammatical though it may be, breaks some social rule of which he is unaware. Even if he is aware that something has gone wrong he may not know the 'repair strategies' for putting it right or, if he does know them may be unable to get the forms across quickly enough to be effective.

The fact that the L2 user is operating not only with a foreign code but also in an alien environment further strengthens the view that part, perhaps a large part, of our teaching of foreign languages should be concerned with the social context in which the language is used.

1.1.3. Lapses

Since face-to-face communication is a 'real-time' activity, all speakers whether native or not make slips — or lapses as we are calling them here —

and the teacher can for all practical purposes ignore them, unless they recur so frequently that the hearer becomes disturbed by them or they are not the kind of lapse commonly made by natives.

1.2. Procedure.

Figure B.2. provides us with an algorithm (based on Corder 1971) for recognizing and describing *errors* and *mistakes*. It does not supply any means of

Figure B.2.
Error Analysis; Procedure

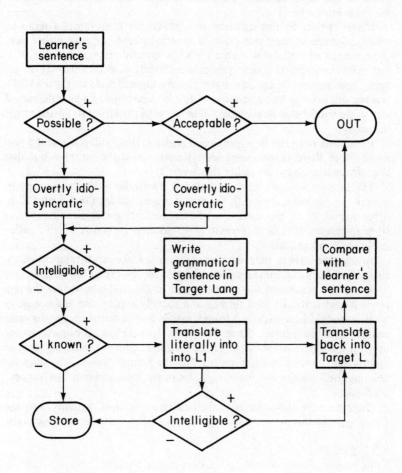

dealing with *lapses* — we have, in any case, decided to ignore them — and, except by implication, gives us no way of explaining why particular errors occur.

1.2.1. Recognition

Taking the learner's sentence as our input data, we ask first 'Is this sentence *possible* in the target language?' This is a question about the formal structure of the learner's sentence not about its likelihood or appropriateness. We are asking whether, irrespective of the context, a native could create the sentence i.e. is the learner's sentence well-formed in terms of the rules of the grammar of the target language? Do the elements which appear in it occur in the target language code and, if so, do they occur in this order, with this intonation, etc?

If our answer to this question is negative, we have found a sentence which contains at least one error. If we try to be descriptive rather than prescriptive, we will label such a sentence 'overtly idiosyncratic' i.e. it is not native-like and its strangeness is immediately obvious to us. If we are being prescriptive — and we have already argued that, in the end, the teacher will need to be prescriptive but, it is to be hoped, in an enlightened way — we will label it ungrammatical in terms of the structure of the target language.

If our answer to the first question is positive, there still remains the possibility that there is something idiosyncratic about the sentence but that the idiosyncrasy is *covert* rather than *overt*.

To discover whether we are looking at a *mistake* rather than an *error*, we ask the second question 'Is the sentence *acceptable* in *this* context?' In other words, given the intention of communicating *this* meaning on *this* topic to *this* participant in *this* setting would *these* be words which a native could use appropriately?

A negative answer here defines for us a *mistake*; an utterance which, though grammatical, breaks some social rule for the use of the language.

A positive answer to this question and to the first tells us that the sentence is grammatically well-formed and socially appropriate and is exactly what we would have expected from a native. Such a sentence, for the error analyst, is of no interest. Since the learner 'got it right', it cannot provide us with information about the errors he makes. But we must not assume lightly that 'getting it right' means that the learner 'knows' the rules for creating the sentence and for using it. He might have achieved this 'success' by chance.

Once we have the answers to the first two questions, we leave the stage of recognition and move on through the algorithm to the description stage.

1.2.2. Description

Returning to a sentence which we have judged to be either not possible in the target language or inappropriate in a particular context — overt or a covert idiosyncrasy — the first step in describing the nature of the *error* or *mistake* is to ask 'Is the learner's sentence intelligible?' i.e. can we work out what he intended to mean?

If we can understand what he was trying to say, we can compare his sentence with that which would be produced by a native and, with such a comparison, list the *errors* or *mistakes*.

If, on the other hand, we cannot understand, we may need to refer to the learner's L1, since this may give us a clue to his intentions. Hence we ask 'Do we know his L1?'. If we do, we can carry out a contrastive analysis (see section 4 below for more detail) of a literal translation of the learner's L1 equivalent, the target language equivalent and the learner's actual sentence, assuming, of course, that the literal translation is itself intelligible.

Where we do not know the learner's L1 or where the literal translation still does not make sense to us, we are left with nothing more we can do. If we cannot deduce the meaning from the forms we have available, we cannot work out the nature of the error.

We might add that the question 'Do we know his L1?'' taken at face value can only reveal information about errors not mistakes. Perhaps we should interpret the question far more liberally to include in the term 'L1' the social conventions of language use in his community. Such an interpretation would allow us to describe mistakes as well as errors.

1.2.3. Explanation

Recognition and description of errors and mistakes is far from simple but, at least, the data is tangible and the techniques we can draw upon well established in descriptive linguistics. Explanation is a far more difficult task. To realize that an error or mistake has occurred and to specify the forms which express it is a simpler enterprise than hypothesising about the processes in the learner's mind which have caused the fault to occur. While we can be relatively sure that the first two stages reflect the facts, we will never be able to give more than plausible suggestions as explanations of the facts. Indeed, there may well be more than one plausible 'explanation' and between them different degrees of importance.

When we attempt to 'explain' the appearance of a particular error or, more generally, type of error in the speech or writing of a learner, group of learners or category of learner, we are asking 'Why did he say (or write) this?'. To attempt to answer such a question is to bring us back to the second of the fundamental questions with which we began this book 'How do people learn languages?', since our 'explanation' will be a reflection of our answer, stated or merely assumed, to that question. Small wonder, then, that the way in which the structuralist linguist sought to explain learners' errors should differ so markedly from the explanations favoured by more recent applied linguists influenced by TG and by cognitive psychology. Not only does this difference manifest itself in the explanatory methodology of the two schools of linguistics but, even more fundamentally, it can be clearly seen in the attitudes adopted towards error *per se*.

We shall deal first with the question of attitude to error and then move on to a discussion of contrastive linguistics and the claims made for it by applied linguists since the mid 1950s.

2. ATTITUDES TO ERROR

Learners make mistakes and errors and teachers have to respond appropriately to them. But how should we respond? We surely all believe that we should correct errors somehow but which ones and how much? We also know that too much correction can be counterproductive – the learner can become discouraged if we are too critical of his efforts – but too little can be equally counterproductive – the learner has no yardstick for judging his output and may be discouraged by a teacher who appears to be uninterested in him.

We are, once again, faced by a dilemma. We want the learner to be *accurate* – not to make errors – but also to be *fluent* – which certainly entails lapses and, unless he is paying a great deal of attention to what he is saying, mistakes and errors too. An accurate non-fluent speaker may well bore his hearer who has to wait patiently while the learner slowly and painfully brings out his grammatically correct sentence. The fluent inaccurate speaker, conversely, may well fail to get his message across at all. We need a sensible compromise between accuracy and fluency; a compromise which can only be arrived at pragmatically in the classroom and must derive from the teacher's knowledge of his own students and from his personal professional expertise.

How should we view errors? Bluntly, do we feel that they are 'good' or 'bad'. We are about to look at two views on this: the structuralist which assumed that errors were 'bad' and the more recent TG-influenced view that, far from being 'bad' errors are a necessary part of learning and therefore 'good'.

We apologize for putting the distinction in such a simplistic way but we feel that, in the end and for all manner of reasons, this is what it comes down to.

2.1. Structuralist views

Structuralist linguists – in particular Fries and Lado – based their approach to language teaching (as we saw in Chapter 5) on the behaviourist belief that to learn is to change habits. Errors in their view:

a) Occur when new habits have to be acquired or old ones modified or replaced.
b) When the features of the L2 differ from those of the L1 the learner. Conversely, where the structures are the same there will be no problems.
c) Consist of failing to respond with the correct response to a particular stimulus.

In addition, as we saw earlier (see 5.1.3.) one of the assumptions made by structuralist linguistics was that bilingual speakers – and therefore L2 learners — tend to 'carry over' features of the L1 into the L2. These features can and will be from all levels of the language structure — syntax, semantics and pragmatics — but in this section, solely for convenience of illustration, we shall limit our discussion to the phonological level.

This belief in the transfer of features was, of course, in keeping with the tenets of behaviourism which most structuralist linguists had adopted as an explanation of the phenomenon of language learning: stimulus — response — habit. For the structuralist an error was, of necessity, a failure to respond automatically to the stimulus and, worse, to allow errors to appear at all was dangerous, since an error could itself become a stimulus which could then reinforce itself and make the 'bad habit' more deeply ingrained. In such a view the learner might 'practise mistakes' and make them harder to eradicate.

Lado in his very influential book *Linguistics across Cultures* (1957) states the structuralist position very plainly: 'Many linguistic distortions heard among bilinguals correspond to describable differences in the languages involved'. Such a statement is a programme for large-scale work in describing the differences and working out how they correspond, i.e. contrastive linguistics. We shall return to this in Section 3, since what concerns us here is the question 'How do features of the L1 transfer into the L2?' i.e. the phenomenon, termed 'interference' at the time, is, presumably, some kind of process; how does it work?

The key mechanism at work in interference was thought to be *interlingual identification*; the perception of a feature in the L2 in terms of an already understood feature in the L1. We realize that we are using the term 'feature' in a highly ambiguous manner but this is intentional since we wish to reassert, despite the fact that we intend to keep to phonological examples, that interlingual identification was thought of as operating at all linguistic levels in the language of the bilingual.

A simple phonological example of a probable error caused by and L1 user of English misinterpreting the Hindi /k/ phoneme in word initial position and reproducing it as [g] (see Figure B.3.).

For example, the Hindi word /kam/ 'work' begins with a non-aspirated /k/. In English /k/ in word initial position is aspirated. Therefore, the learner argues, the Hindi /k/ by virtue of its lack of aspiration must be the nearest equivalent sound which has no aspiration in English i.e. a voiced rather than a voiceless velar plosive — /g/. This will not only lead him to 'hear' the Hindi /k/ as /g/ but to use /g/ as the first sound in the word /kam/ i.e. */gam/ a nonsense word in Hindi. If, however, he is told by his teacher that the first sound is a 'k' not a 'g' he is likely, still following the phonological rules of English, to produce /kam/ as [k^{h}ɑ:m] i.e. just as he would realize the English word *calm*. This too would be wrong since he would be signalling a phonemic contrast between /k/ and /k^h/ which though part of Hindi system would, in this case, be the selection of the wrong phoneme.

The Hindi learner of English is just as likely to be misled but in the opposite direction. Rather than fail to retain the distinction between /k/ and

Figure B.3.
Interlingual Identification: English–Hindi

English learner of Hindi

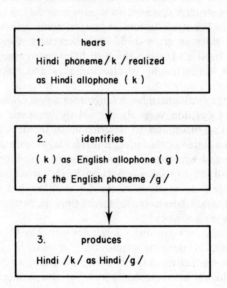

1. hears
Hindi phoneme / k / realized
as Hindi allophone (k)

2. identifies
(k) as English allophone (g)
of the English phoneme /g /

3. produces
Hindi / k / as Hindi /g /

/kʰ/ he will, when learning English, overemphasize the distinction. In those environments in which the English /k/ – and /t/ and /p/ – are aspirated, he will make the aspiration excessively noticeable to his hearers.

This brings us to a subdivision of 'interference' in phonology into four sub-types. Each of which we shall illustrate with English–Italian examples.

2.1.1. Sound Substitution

The most straightforward form of interference is the substitutuion of a sound from the L1 for one in the L2. Both Italian and English possess an /r/ phoneme but realize them differently. The Italian /r/ is realized either as a flap [ɾ] or a trill [r] in contrast with the English post-alveolar friction-less continuant [ɹ].

A speaker of English wishing to mimic an Italian speaking English might go no further than substituting an 'Italian /r/' for the 'English /r/'. Conversely, to mimic an Englishman speaking Italian, the mimic may do little more than reverse the process.

2.1.2. Underdifferentiation

The example of /kam/ produced as */gam/ or */kʰɑ:m/ by the English learner of Hindi which we discussed above can be classified as a case of underdifferentiation. The learner has failed to recognize in the L2 a phonemic distinction which exists only at the allophonic level in the L1. A further example, this time from Italian, might be the way in which the lack of an /i:/ − /ɪ/ distinction in the L1 often leads the Italian learner of English into blurring the contrast between such minimal pairs as *beat* and *bit*. Conversely, the English learner of Italian may, because of the lack of contrast in his L1 between 'single' and 'double' consonants, fail to signal the difference between, for example, *casa* 'house' and *cassa* 'cash desk'.

2.1.3. Overdifferentiation

The reverse of underdifferentiation, overdifferentiation, can occur when the L1 contains phonemic contrasts which are lacking in the L2 but are imposed on it by the learner in his attempts at producing it. The single-double consonant phenomenon we have just mentioned may provide an example here. The possession of such a contrast in Italian can lead the learner of English to attempt to impose the distinction on English and this is particularly likely where the learner sees double consonants in the written form of the language. He might well produce *bigger* as *['bigger] or *little* as *['littel] or even *['litteli].

2.1.4. Reinterpretation of distinctions

So far we have been considering rather straightforward problems of identification but not all 'interference' is so simple to explain. Since the phoneme has always been thought of as consisting of a complex of sounds, or better 'features', the learner may well seize on one which is crucial in his L1 and use that to make a phonemic distinction which he has perceived when, in fact, the feature he has selected plays only a secondary role in the L2. Another Italian example may help to make this point clear. English possesses a /ɑ:/ − /æ/ contrast which distinguishes such minimal pairs as *bard* and *bad* (in RP). In Italian no such phonemic distinction exists but, and here is the problem, there are [ɑ:] sounds and 'short' [a] sounds which can be mistaken for the RP /ɑ:/ and /æ/. However, the occurrence of the [a] is conditioned by its phonetic environment: before 'double' consonants. Hence, the L1 speaker of English, hearing the words *fato* and *fatto* − 'done' and 'fact' − and lacking the single-double consonant distinction in his mother tongue may well perceive the contrast between the two words as being carried by the vowels rather than, as it is, by the consonants. In this way, he may well realize *fato* correctly as [fɑ:to] but incorrectly realize *fato* as *[fæto] instead of [fatto] with a 'double: /t/.

2.1.5. Summary

The structuralist attempt to explain language learning in stimulus-response terms and to see in the structure of the L1 the major source of interference and error formed the basis of most thinking in Applied Linguistics until the end of the 1960s by which time many contrastive studies had been published and linguistics itself was moving rapidly to a reorientation (which we have discussed in Chapter 5) which was to have a profound effect in language teaching.

We shall turn now to post-structuralist views on error.

2.2. Post-Structuralist Views

With the emergence of TG in the late 1950s and its denial of both structuralist linguistics and its associated behaviourist psychology came a reorientation of the discipline which was to have profound effects not only on linguistics itself but also on applied linguistics.

The changes which had most impact on applied linguistics were:

1) The acceptance of a cognitive psychology as a more plausible explanation of human language acquisition and learning.

2) The recognition of the autonomy of pidgin and creole languages as languages in their own right rather than mixed or degenerate versions of other languages.

The first change has immediate implications for our attitude to errors. We assume:

a) Learning a language implies making assumptions about the structure of the language.

b) On the basis of these assumptions the learner formulates hypotheses about the structure of the target language which he tests out on native speakers.

c) His incorrect hypotheses — his errors — give us direct access to the assumptions he is making about the new language.

If we accept this, it follows that errors are of enormous value to the teacher, since they show us what the learner is thinking and guide us to the teaching he needs to correct his false assumptions and move closer to the actual system of the target language.

The second change also has implications for our view of errors not, as we have just described, singly, but as a system.

a) Pidgin languages and creole languages arise when a group of learners attempt to learn a new language either without overt teaching or with the help of teachers who are willing to settle for a means of communication which falls short of the norms of the L1 version of the target language.

b) Pidgin and creole languages represent a system which is neither the L1 of the learners nor the L2 at which they were aiming i.e. a compromise system which contains elements of both but which is neither.

c) Pidgin and creole languages are fossilized systems which ceased to change at a particular point in their development i.e. they are, fixed in time, the assumptions about the target system held at that time by the learners.

How then, we might ask, do pidgin and creole languages differ from the 'language' of the L2 learner? In terms of the code and the way it came into being, we would argue that there is no significant difference. What difference there is relates to the degree and extent of fossilization. In the pidgin and creole languages, contact with the target language was, for various reasons, curtailed with the result that the movement of the learners' systems towards the target ceased. In the case of the foreign language learner, where contact is still maintained change, often rapid change, continues.

By the late 1960s papers were beginning to appear which claimed the same kind of autonomy for the learner's system as had been claimed for the pidgins and creoles. Most important were those by Corder (1967) on *idiosyncratic dialects*, by Nemser (1971) on *approximative systems* and Selinker (1972) on *interlanguages*.

What then of the notion of interference and of the mechanism of interlingual interference which brings it about?

The post-structuralist linguist will not deny that interlingual identification takes place. He will accept it as one of the 'central processes' of language learning (see Selinker *op. cit.*). Where he parts company with the structuralists is on their assertion that interlingual identification is the only or even the major process involved. For him the structure of the L1 is important in influencing the way the learner copes with the target language data since it predisposes him to perceive that data as though it were mother tongue data but contrastive analysis, helpful though it might turn out to be in some instances, cannot supply the whole explanation and certainly will have little predictive value for the course designer.

We need now to look at the claims made for contrastive analysis; a strong claim by the structuralists and a weak claim by those who followed them.

3. CONTRASTIVE LINGUISTICS

As we have seen, applied linguistics has been concerned to explain the nature of language use by learners and, in particular, to assign to the learner's L1 some degree of responsibility for that behaviour. In essence, the point at issue is the extent to which the structure of the L1 is a *cause* of the errors which the learner produces in his attempts to use the target language.

There are two polar views on this and a range of compromise positions between them:

a) The strong claim that the 'deviant' behaviour of the learner is the direct result of the transfer of the 'habits' of the L1 into the L2.

b) The weak claim that the structure of the L1 provides only a partial explanation of the phenomena involved in L2 learning.

3.1. Strong claim
Those who make the Strong Claim are clearly committed to contrastive analysis not only as a means of explaining error but also as a technique for

predicting error. Once the areas of contrast have been isolated, the teacher can devise drills which will practise errors away before they ever have a chance to emerge and become established as habits.

The strong claim is, then, highly predictive in that it assumes that, armed with a contrastive analysis of the languages involved, the teacher will have a clear picture of the problem areas even before the learner has started to learn.

As Fries (in his introduction to Lado *op. cit.*) declares 'the most efficient teaching materials will be those that are based upon a scientific description of the language to be learned, carefully compared with a parallel description of the language of the learner'.

3.2. Weak claim

Since those who make the weak claim insist that the structure of the L1 is only one of many influences at work in the learning process, it follows that contrastive analysis may be of some value in explanation of errors but cannot have a strong predictive value. For those who make the weak claim, *post facto* analysis of the errors currently being made by learners is likely to be of far greater value in designing the syllabus than any *a priori* comparison of the languages involved.

4. CONCLUSION

In this appendix we have been considering the nature and treatment of learners' errors. We have seen how, at one extreme the language used by the learner is thought of as a series of deviations from the norm of the target language and his errors no more than unfortunate failures to behave appropriately: failures which can be explained almost entirely by reference back to the 'language habits' he has carried over with him from his mother tongue.

At the other extreme, we find a belief in the language of the learner as a system in its own right – created by his intellectual effort to make sense of the new system – in which his errors stand out as the signposts he is setting up as he maps his way across the alien terrain. Some of his signposts are, to be sure, in the wrong place or facing the wrong way but they are the only clear indicators we have of what he is attempting to do and, as such, the greatest help we, as teachers, can get in our attempt to devise materials to help his learning.

Finally, present-day thinking still accepts that the L1 will have an influence on the way the learner comes to terms with the L2 but today few would argue that it is the only or even the chief influence and would place contrastive analysis and error analysis together as techniques which can provide the teacher with insights into the learning process.

SUGGESTED FURTHER READING

Bell R. T. (1973), *The English of an Indian Immigrant; an Essay in Error Analysis'*

Probably the first published attempt at actually carrying out an error analysis on a text; a 20-minute conversation between the author and an Indian immigrant in the UK.

Richards J. (ed.) (1974), *Error Analysis: Perspectives on Second Language Acquisition*
A collection of 11 influential papers on error analysis. Particularly important are papers 2, 3, 4, 6 and 9.

                              (1980), 'Error Analysis' *Annual Review of Applied Linguistics*
A survey of the growth of the notion of error analysis from the late 1960s to the present together with a comprehensive bibliography of over 100 items half of which are annotated.

Svartvik J. (ed.) (1973), *Errata; Papers in Error Analysis*
A collection of 17 papers on error analysis among them Johansson's on including the factor of 'irritation' in the hearer of an error.

Appendix C: Language testing

The purpose of this appendix is to pick up the problems of testing which we were only able to touch upon in Chapter 2 — in Step 9 — i.e. to expand on the general principles of test construction and use in the evaluation of courses (Section 1) and individuals (Section 2) and to give examples of language tests.

1. TRAINING AND TESTING

We suggested in Chapter 2 that there were three models of training — the ballistic, the guided and the adaptive system respectively — which could be distinguished from each other by the extent to which they provide feedback. We wish to consider the three systems in some detail here since we shall argue later (see 1.2.) that language teaching tends to be stuck at the level of sophistication of the second system — the guided — and that we must recognize and satisfy the need for external evaluation in our course design and testing procedures (see Brethower & Rummler 1979).

1.1 Model 1: the ballistic system
The ballistic system (illustrated in Figure C.1. below) is clearly far too unsophisticated for our needs — it lacks any element of feedback. The learners are, as it were, loaded into the process and fired out of the other end, presumably in some changed form! There is no provision for checking the output and hence no feedback which would permit planned change in the selection of the input — the students and, indeed, teachers — or the design of the process itself, i.e. the course. Of the three systems we are describing here, it is the weakest since it is unresponsive to the need for change and, because of its inability to justify its existence, very vulnerable to attack by dissatisfied clients who may seek to cut it back or even dismantle it.

1.2 Model 2: the guided system
The guided system, unlike the ballistic, attempts to validate the programme by testing the behaviour of the participants at the end of the course. This is typically done in two ways:

a) *Qualitative evaluation*: this is essentially 'subjective' and while quantitive evaluation (b) normally consists of the teachers testing the learners, qualitative evaluation is normally the reverse — the learners are asked to pass judgements on the course and on the trainers. At its silliest, such 'evaluation' takes the form of getting the participant to fill in a questionnaire only on

Figure C.1.
Model 1: the ballistic system

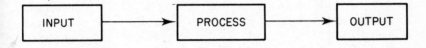

how much he 'enjoyed' the course or how much he 'liked' a particular trainer. Our experience with such questionnaires – and they are very common in management training courses – is that they throw up no consensus at all and even if they did the trainer-designer may well have good reasons for disregarding the feedback provided when he came around to redesigning the programme. At its best, such evaluation can highlight the degree of customer resistence to a new technique or topic and can be used as a kind of market research device. Unfortunately participants' evaluations can be used illegitimately as a method of assessing and evaluating the individual trainer. We feel very strongly that this *is* illegitimate: the ability to help others to learn and the ability to amuse others can hardly be equated, otherwise teachers and comedians would be interchangeable and, our experience tells us, they are not!

b) *Quantitative evaluation*: this is the use of immediate, individual, 'objective' post-course attainment tests which seek to demonstrate the degree to which the individual learner attained the stated aim of the course. In language courses, such tests have been commonplace for decades and despite the fact that they are examinations or tests (see 1.4. for some discussion on the differences between the two) of knowledge or linguistic form rather than, as many would prefer to-day, of communicative ability, they do provide the teacher with 'facts' which are presented in the form of percentage 'passes' or 'failures' or particular grades in public examinations and so forth. Some proficiency tests in English – the Michigan Test of Oral Comprehension in English for example (see 4.3. below) – were specifically designed to provide before, during and after measures of this kind. On the basis of such figures and on the assumption that the change in the test scores is a direct result of the course through which the learners have gone – and there are rather serious philosophical objections to such an assumption – we can set about revising the syllabus and making it, in our terms, more *valid* and more *efficient*.

Figure C.2.
Model 2: the guided system

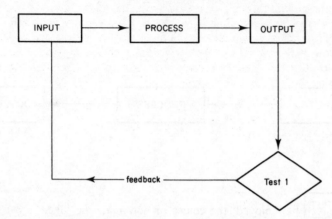

The guided system, then, attempts to gather feedback by applying quali-tative and quantitative measures to the output. This makes it rather more responsive to change and more able to cope with it. Faced by a client who wishes to curtail their activities those who operate within a guided system have some defences they can put up when challenged to justify their exis-tence and expenditure. They have data at hand which will show, for indi-vidual programmes or for the training set-up as a whole, the cost per student hour or per trainer hour, the ratio of planning and preparation time to classroom contact hours to time spent in evaluation and, dubious though we might be about the absolute validity of the 'test results' we have, we can argue and demonstrate that, for example, a reduction of the amount of time made available for the design of a course shows up as 'poorer' results at the end.

This unfortunately, is about as far as most language trainers go in evalu-ating their courses. We say 'unfortunately' because those in the outside world, our clients, on whom we are financially dependent, apply a different set of criteria when they judge effectiveness and until we learn to go out into the outside world and check there in our clients' terms how well our programmes are being accepted we are still very vulnerable indeed. The questions we would like to ask however are complex and the cost of asking them will be high.

1.3. Model 3: The adaptive system
This is the most sophisticated of the three systems. It is responsive to feed-back from its participants − and teaching staff − through what we have labelled 'Test 1' and through 'Test 2' to feedback from the clients and the other occupants of the receiving system to which the learners return (as *output* from the training process and as new *input* to the office, company, society at large).

Test 2, like Test 1, will ask quantitative and qualitative questions but, unlike Test 1, which was inward-looking and seeking to validate, in its own terms, the process through which the learners have just come, the questions will now concern the usefulness — in terms of the stated goals and objectives of the client organizations — of the output; how much better can they now do their jobs? Can they now take on greater responsibilities? Are they (to put it very bluntly) now *worth* more to the company as a result of passing through the training programme?

Figure C.3.
Model 3: the adaptive system

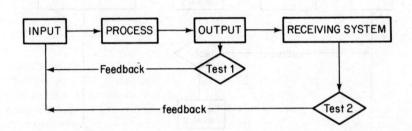

Given these two very distinct types of feedback, we are now in a far stronger position to defend our arrangements and to support, internally and externally, changes which we may wish to make. If asked to justify ourselves to our clients, those working with an adaptive system can refer to the clients' *own* evaluation and use that not only as a defence but as a vehicle for gaining further support for our specific type of training and, indeed, for training in general.

The problem, however, is to work out what levels of evaluation there are, what questions we can usefully ask at each level and how we can set about the evaluation.

There appear to be four levels of evaluation:

(a) *Popularity ratings*: we ask 'were the participants happy with the course?' and related questions.

(b) *Attainment ratings*: we ask 'did the course teach the knowledge and skills we intended it to teach?'

(c) *Applicability ratings*: we ask 'is the new knowledge being used back on the job?'

(d) *Influence ratings*: we ask 'is the application of the new knowledge and skills having a positive effect on the organization?'

We can fit these four levels into Model 3 — the adaptive system — and show at which testing point we can ask the questions.

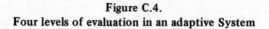

Figure C.4.
Four levels of evaluation in an adaptive System

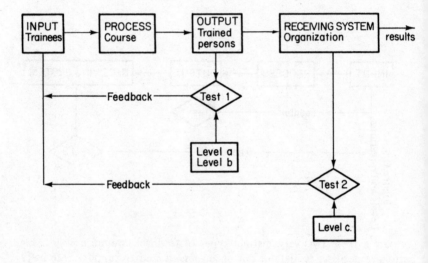

At each of the four levels, we have about half a dozen kinds of question we need to ask, not *to* any particular group or *about* any particular data but questions about questions:
1. What questions would we like answered?
2. What can be measured that will answer these questions?
3. What learning or performance dimensions are we trying to measure?
4. What data sources can be tapped to help us measure?
5. What alternative data-gathering methods are there?
6. What evaluation criteria should we apply to each question?

We are now in a position to put our comments on levels of evaluation and this list of question-types together to form a coherent matrix which should help us decide who to ask what about what:

Figure C.5.
Levels and questions

Trainees → TRAINING COURSE → Trained persons → JOB/ORGANIZATION → Results

LEVEL	a	b	c	d
QUESTIONS WE MIGHT ASK	Are the trainees happy? If not, why not?	Did the training work? If not, why not?	Is the knowledge being used? If not, why not?	Is the knowledge helping the organization? If not, why not?
MEASURE WHAT?				
MEASUREMENT DIMENSIONS				
DATA SOURCES				
METHODOLOGY				
CRITERIA				

This provides us with 6 × 4 matrix i.e. a minimum of 24 questions. Naturally, in each cell a potentially large number of answers could be found e.g. if we ask if the trainees are happy and discover that they are not we have several possible explanations: the trainees were not properly selected, the knowledge or skills we tried to teach were not relevant to them or ill-presented or insufficiently or inappropriately practised. Any one of these answers would lead us on again to ask 'why'? Should we check our selection procedure? Should we check on the real needs of the trainees? Were our trainers sufficiently well prepared for the course?

Rather than attempt to fill in all the cells and follow up all the potential answers — a virtually infinite task — we would prefer to refer the interested reader to Brethower & Rummler (*op. cit.*), who make an attempt at partially filling the cells and on whom this section on evaluation heavily rests.

We wish to move on now to a consideration of the practical problems involved in testing and to illustrate and comment on some typical tests. First we shall turn to the issue of the inherent unreliability of measuring instruments as a prelude to discussing language tests as a special case of 'measuring'.

1.4. Problems with measuring instruments

The process of evaluation — using examinations or tests — involves the use of measuring instruments. We attempt to show how well individuals score on our tests both against some preconceived standard ('criterion-referenced testing') and against each other ('norm-referenced testing': see comments on Test 8. 4.8. of this appendix). But all measuring instruments contain within them inherent flaws which make them prone to error. This is true no matter what kind of measuring device we are using and is particularly the case where we are concerned with the 'measurement' of some aspect of human behaviour as we so frequently are in the human sciences; anthropology, sociology, psychology, education, etc.

Error can be traced to any or all of three sources:

a) The *sampling procedures* employed in the choice of the questions and/or the choice of those to be questioned; *qualitatively* — right people? right language? — or *quantitatively* — right number of people? right amount of language?. Typically, this type of error shows up when the candidates find the questions too difficult or too easy and the test fails to *discriminate* between those whom we believe to be good at whatever it is we are attempting to measure and those whom we believe to be bad. Sometimes, though, we may deliberately choose a test which does not discriminate (see Test 4. 4.4. of this appendix).

b) The *behaviour of the informants* (or, in the case of testing, the examinees). One example of this type of error is the case of the student who, in contradiction of our expectations, scores spectacularly well or badly on the day. Such an error can be compensated for by giving more than one test and averaging out the results, e.g. three short tests on different occasions will be more satisfactory than a single longer test.

c) The *behaviour of the investigators* (here, the examiners or markers). The worry in the mind of the tester, in this case, is that the scores would have been different, either absolutely or in relation to the ranking of the individual examinees, had a different marker graded the tests. Examinations are particularly prone to this weakness and it is for this reason that public examinations — for example finals examinations universities — make use of several markers for each candidate. In this way, the 'hard' and 'kind' markers can be made to cancel each other's errors out.

There are, in short, two key questions on which the tester must be satisfied: is the test *valid* — does it measure what it purports to measure? i.e. how relevant is it? — and is it *reliable* — if it is re-used with the same candidates will it continue to give results which are not significantly different, assuming that the candidates have received no instruction between the test and retest? (We take up the question of the characteristics of a 'good' test in section 3).

Fortunately, there are many accepted and easily available statistical techniques on which the tester can draw to satisfy himself on the reliability and some aspects of the validity (empirical validity; see 3.1.c of this appendix) of his tests (we do not wish to go into them now but refer the reader to Harris 1969, Chapter 12). However, the appropriateness of these statistical methods hinges on the extent to which the procedure we have adopted is *objective* rather than *subjective* and it is to this issue which we now turn.

Testing involves us in three steps:
a) The setting of the questions.
b) The answering of the questions.
c) The marking of the answers.

If we contrast examinations and tests, it is clear that the test can be objective in its setting, answering and marking but that the examination is likely to be subjective either at all three stages or, with effort, can be made objective only in its marking. There are several reasons for this. The typical examination contains essay-type questions which require the candidate to carry out rather vague instructions — 'describe', 'compare', 'contrast' — and, in addition, it is virtually impossible to decide whether the individual questions are of equal difficulty. Marking is more often than not subjective 'impression marking' despite the fact that the 'impressions' are frequently clothed in a spurious objectivity by being presented numerically as a percentage mark or a degree classification.

Tests, conversely, can be objective all through and it is for this reason that we shall continue our discussion by looking at tests rather than examinations.

2. TYPES OF TEST

In section 1, we have been concerned primarily with the evaluation of *courses*. In this section we move on to a consideration of the problems involved in the evaluation of *individuals*; typically our concern is with adult FL learners rather than school children, since the aims of school language teaching are often at variance with those of the adult education sector. When we are faced by the decision to select or design a test, we need to take into account the same variables as we considered when designing a course: *why* do we wish to test? — what purpose have we in mind? *What* do we wish the test to show us? — what do we wish to test? what knowledge and skills are to be included in the content of the test? — *how* shall we set about selecting or creating a device which will answer the first two questions? — how shall we design it? — and finally, *who* is to be tested and by whom? Who is to participate in the testing process?

2.1. Purpose

There are four reasons for having a test: to indicate future ability, to discover what is already known, to discover what has been learned and to discover what is still to be learned.

There are four test types which seek the answer these questions:

a) *Prognostic* (or *aptitude*) *tests*: these attempt to discover an individual's potential for acquiring a particular skill, e.g. a specific foreign language or foreign languages in general. Such tests typically make use of artificial language data which the individual is expected to manipulate and 'make sense of'. The rationale for this is that the test is a simulation of the code-learning in which the learner is to be involved and hence provides us with evidence of his overall ability to cope with the alien structures of a new language. An easily accessible example is 'Novish' (see 4.1. below). Alternatively, the individual might, if we assume that the ability to analyze language is a pre-requisite for learning, be given 'scrambled sentences' in his L1 and we might record the time it takes him to reorder the elements to form a coherent sentence (see 4.2 below).

b) *Proficiency tests*: these attempt to discover what the testee already knows. Language tests of this type are not based on the content of any particular course or skill but aim to assess *global* ability. Typically, proficiency tests are much used in the placing of individuals in learning groups appropriate to their level of knowledge — beginner, intermediate, advanced, etc. — or for deciding how many salary increments are to be given to an employee for his skill in a required language. There are several internationally recognized proficiency tests in English. Among the best known are the TEOFL test (available from Educational Testing Service, Princeton New Jersey), and the Davies Test (not commercially available; enquiries to the British Council). We reproduce part of one proficiency test — the Michigan Test of Aural Comprehension in English — later in this appendix (see 4.3. below).

c) *Attainment* (or *achievement*) tests: these, in contrast with the aptitude and proficiency tests, seek to determine the extent to which a learner has mastered the contents of a particular course. For this reason, they contain — or should contain — only test items based on what has been taught.

Many textbooks contain tests of this kind either at the end of the course as a final check or else as a test at the end of a number of units of instruction (we give an example of a simple attainment test in 5.4. below).

d) *Diagnostic Tests*: these may be thought of as the converse of the proficiency test since their aim is to discover not what is known by the candidate but what he does *not* know. Indeed, a proficiency test might be used as a diagnostic test if the intention of the tester was to discover what needed to be learned and should therefore be included in future teaching. Some textbooks (for example Alexander's *New Concept English*) include pre-unit tests, others (for example Bhatnagar & Bell's *Communication in English*: see 4.6. below) suggest that the first part of each unit can be used as a diagnostic test to discover if the learners need to continue with the unit or can move on to the next.

As we have just suggested, it is not uncommon for a test originally intended for one purpose to be used for another. At times this can be acceptable — Heaton's use (in *Create and Communicate 4*) of two past GCE 'O' level papers as proficiency tests is legitimate in the context of the aim of the textbook: to prepare candidates for that examination — but at others one may be rather sceptical. Consider the typical GCE 'A' level examination in this light. The history examination, for example, is actually an *attainment* test. It tells us the extent to which the candidate has mastered a particular course content. However, many employers are likely to mistake the test for one of *proficiency* in history arguing 'He's got a grade B in 'A' level History'. In fact, he has not. He gained a 'B' grade in the examination set by a particular Examining Board in a particular year on, let us say, nineteenth century European History and the Tudors and Stuarts. Worse, institutions of tertiary education often, for want of a better measure, use the examination as a *prognosticator* of the student's potential for future study. An Admissions Officer is likely to argue 'He did pretty well in History, so he ought to be able to minor in Philosophy'. Small wonder that there is no significant correlation between 'A' level grades — except for the General Paper — and final degree classification!

2.2. Content
What is to be put in a language test is, clearly, language but, and this brings us full circle to the question with which we began this book, what do we consider language to be?

The *formalist* answer that language consists of a code made up of elements which combine to make grammatically correct sentences will lead us to construct tests which stress such formal characteristics and the interrelations between forms and the cognitive aspects of meaning. Testees will be expected to create or select what is judged, by external and normative criteria, to be possible in terms of the rules of the code. The overwhelming majority of language tests today are of this type.

The *functionalist* answer is that language is more than the code and meaning more than context-free referential meaning i.e. that language is also the skilled use of the code in the creation and comprehension of socially acceptable utterances and texts. Acceptance of this view will lead us to create tests which are *pragmatic* rather than purely *syntactic* and *semantic*; tests in which the syntax and all four levels of semantics — conceptual, logical, attitudinal and organizational (see Leech and Svartvik 1975. 12f) — are involved. Although such tests are still far from common, the new orientation to language teaching which we have been discussing in this book necessarily demands that all language tests become pragmatic, in the sense in which we have been using the term, and a number have, indeed, already appeared (see Oller's discussion 1979).

2.2.1. Tests of linguistic form

Traditionally, language skills have been thought of, taught and tested, as fourfold:

a) *Productive Skills*: speaking and writing.

b) *Receptive Skills*: listening and reading.

Some tests have been frankly labelled 'Test of Reading' or 'Test of Aural Comprehension' but many have been vaguely entitled 'X Test of English'. The four-way division has, of course, been recognized as a convenient fiction not only because actual language use necessarily involves the ability to integrate several skills at once but also because within each gross skill there are several subskills which are called upon simultaneously.

The breakdown of skills into their formal linguistic components has, over the years, closely followed the then current levels of descriptive linguistics, so there is no need to reiterate them here.

2.2.2. *Tests of linguistic function*

Recent advances in linguistics and, in particular, sociolinguistics have led language teacher and hence language testers to the realization that language tests need to be pragmatic i.e. that they should require the test to be, as far as possible, a simulation of the realities of actual language in use.

As we shall see (in Section 4) many classroom activities can be turned around to act as tests — 'cloze' procedure, dictation, translation and, in keeping with the increasing use of role-play as a means of activation notional syllabuses, the kind of exercise we suggested for the canteen assistant (see Appendix A. Step 7.).

Pragmatic tests satisfy two 'naturalness criteria':

a) They require the examinee to produce language in a genuine context and in the face of the normal 'situational constraints' experienced by actual communicators (see 6.4.1.).

b) They require the examinee to utilize the language to make appropriate links between the code and extralinguistic features, e.g. he is expected not only to comprehend but also to infer, to speak and also to predict the hearer's response.

2.3. Design

Once we have decided *why* we are testing and *what*, we can consider *how* we are to design the test. The essential distinction here is between *discrete point* testing and *integrative* testing, (the distinction comes from Carroll 1961).

a) *Discrete point tests* seek to discover the knowledge of the testee on individual distinct points of the phonology, syntax and lexis of the language being tested. Minimal pairs in phonology provide one example (see 4.4. nos. 19.20 which attempt to test the distinctions *sinking – singing – thinking* and *ice – eyes* respectively), the past-future-present distinction (see 4.3. no. 17 which tests *used – is going to use – is using*) an example for the syntax and the *chocolate milk – milk chocolate* distinction (see 4.3. no. 18) for the lexicon. The actual procedure for discrete point testing has frequently (though not always and not obligatorily) been multiple-choice in which the candidate is provided with a cue question plus a number of possible answers. His task is to select the answer which most closely fits the cue (as in 4.3. which is a test wholly constructed in this way).

b) *Integrative tests* are the exact converse of discrete point tests, since they attempt to test several elements and perhaps skills at the same time. The distinction between the discrete point and integrative test is most clearly seen in the complex area of testing comprehension, where discrete item tests would direct the examinee to choose an appropriate word or definition in place of selected vocabulary item (see 4.5. for example) an integrative test would require more of the candidate. He might, for example, be expected to make an inference for the information provided in the text, e.g.

'He turned the heating on'. 'He was:
  i) Tired
  ii) Cold
  iii) Hot
  iv) Hungry

We can see from this example the extent to which the integrative test attempts to extend the notion of context from that of the isolated sentence as in the discrete item test to the larger context of connected discourse i.e. from the purely conceptual level of meaning to the logical and, in part, organizational. Recent revisions of the TEOFL Test have begun to move its design in the direction of integrative tests and away from their earlier discrete point orientation (see Oller & Spolsky 1979 for further discussion).

The next step, historically, in test design was, inevitably, towards a special case of the integrative test which would involve all four levels of meaning and expand the context beyond that of the language *per se* to the extra-linguistic context of the interrelation of language as a system to the human use of that system for communication, i.e. pragmatic tests which we discussed earlier (see this Appendix 2.2.2.). We shall limit ourselves here to outlining some of the design features of pragmatic tests.

Even during the heyday of discrete point testing which co-occurred with that of structuralist linguistics there were tests which attempted to be pragmatic. Most obvious is the test of proficiency in spoken English in which the candidate would be expected to talk about a particular topic or engage in a discussion with the examiner. The Foreign Service Institute Oral Interview with its well-known rating scale provides a good example (see 4.8.). But early 'pragmatic' tests were not limited to 'orals'. A test which required some ostensive behaviour as an answer – the handling of realia, the carrying out of an action, role-play – can be thought of as 'pragmatic' in the sense of requiring the candidate to do something natural with the language (see 4.6. below). More surprisingly perhaps, dictation, 'cloze' tests (see 4.7. below) and even translation have pragmatic characteristics (see Oller 1979 esp. chs 2 & 3), since they cannot be answered adequately merely by manipulating the code, i.e. they require knowledge of the code and its relationship with its context of use.

2.4. Participants
At first glance, this variable appears to resolve itself into the straightforward question 'who is to be tested?' and to require of the test designer or administrator that he takes into account the psychological and sociological characteristics of the examinees. On reflection however, it becomes clear that the question is actually more complex and contains at least two sub-questions: who is to test whom? and who is to select or design the test?

2.4.1. Testers
We noticed earlier in this appendix (1.2.) that evaluation can be carried out not only in the traditional way – teacher assesses learner – but in the reverse manner. We might add that self-assessment provides an additional source of information which as teachers we should welcome.

Self-assessment (based essentially on the work of Oskarsson 1977) has considerable value as a means of continuous feedback both for the learner and the teacher. Furthermore, the evaluation of the learner of his own level of achievement may confirm or contradict that of the teacher and so lead to fruitful discussion between them of what to tackle next. Indeed, self-assessments on the part of the participants can provide an extra input for the course designer, since they focus the planner on areas in which the learner feels insecure; areas which the designer on his own may not have anticipated and therefore failed to include in the course (see Bell 1980c for an outline of the use of self-evaluation in the design of an ESP course). In short, how well a learner is coping or expects to cope consists, in part, of how well he believes he *is* coping; self-assessment gives us access to these beliefs in a way which teacher-assessment does not (we give an example of a self-assessment test in 4.9. below).

2.4.2. Designers
We need to distinguish between commercially available, ready-made tests

and those designed, administered and scored by the teacher. Both types have particular strengths and weaknesses:

a) The public test is ready-made and can be obtained together with its question booklets, answer sheets, scoring devices and instructions for administration. This makes it convenient for the teacher who has only to select a test and administer it. The private teacher-made test involves the teacher in a good deal of effort which is avoided by using a public test.

b) The public test is the result of substantial research and development which the individual teacher cannot hope to match.

c) The public test is statistically *reliable* (see section 3.2. below) i.e. scores, when the test is repeated, are not subject to significant fluctuation and so those who have taken the test maintain their rankings relative to each other. The private test is likely to be far less reliable.

d) The public test also discriminates, i.e. it distinguishes the best from the worst in a statistically acceptable manner: a 'normal distribution' is one in which the majority obtain 'middling' scores while on either side of them there is a small 'tail' of high scores and low scores. The private test may fail to satisfy this criterion.

e) The public test is also *valid* (see 3.1. below on types of validity) i.e. it tests what it sets out to test and does so within stated degrees of tolerance: an essential characteristic of any appropriate test.

f) The public test, however, has an inherent weakness. Its very globality — seeking to test *any* individual or group on a particular skill — makes it a poor fit with the characteristics of any specific group. This is, as we pointed out earlier (in section 1.4. of this appendix) a problem with all measuring instruments, the more general the scope of the instrument, the less it will apply to the unique individual. It is on this point that the teacher-made test comes into its own. The teacher knows his learners and can tailor his test to suit them. If he does so he can be sure that the reliability at least of his test is greater than that of any public test.

We would strongly urge the teacher to make up and administer regular and frequent tests of this kind. They will provide him with the diagnostic information he needs to revise his syllabus and ensure that what he is teaching is what the learners need. (We give an example of a very simple diagnostic test made up by the author to test the past and past-participle forms of irregular verbs — see 4.4. of this appendix — and would also refer the teacher to Green (1963) whose excellent little book, *Teacher-made Tests*, is full of practical advice for the would-be test-maker).

3. THREE ESSENTIAL CHARACTERISTICS OF A TEST

We have already touched upon the general problem of the inherent inaccuracy of measuring instruments (in Appendix C, Section 1.4.) and one or two features which appear to be obligatory if a test is to be successful. What we intend to do now is to list the three key characteristics of the 'good' test in order to help the teacher create or select tests which suit his own purposes.

e evaluate a test we are forced to ask two fundamental questions: this test actually test? and how well does it do it?

st which measures what we want measured and measures it in a hich we find acceptable is a *valid* test. If it does this without significant variation when the examiners and other test conditions are not altered it is a *reliable* test. And, if it can do this with ease and economy, it is a *practical* test.

We shall examine the qualities of validity, reliability and practicality in turn before moving on, in Section 4, to providing examples of a number of types of language test.

3.1. Validity

Validity is concerned with relevance; does the test actually measure what we want it to measure and does it do it well enough for us to have faith in the results?

There are, in fact, four kinds of validity, the first — content validity — being concerned with what is being tested and the remaining three — construct, empirical and face validity — with the extent to which the measurement is satisfactory.

a) *Content validity*: if the tasks which the candidates are required to perform in the test are a true reflection of the skills which are actually required in real life, the test can be said to have content validity. Much of the dissatisfaction felt about discrete item tests has stemmed from the feeling that they lack content validity i.e. filling in the appropriate blank in a multiple-choice test, for example, bears little relationship to the skills required for genuine communication in a language.

b) *Construct validity*: if the test is able to satisfy some previously stated theoretical requirement, it can be said to possess construct validity. The term 'construct' is used here in the sense of 'theoretical construct' or 'assumption' either about the nature of language or about the nature of language learning and the test designer who held a particular belief about these issues would assign greater or lesser degrees of construct validity to a test to the extent that its results appeared to confirm or deny what he believed. For example, the linguist who holds to a view of language as communication in context will assign low construct validity to a test which is based on the assumption that language can be described as a contextless code. A more conservative linguist will, naturally, given his formalist view of language, assign a high construct validity to the very same test. We shall see in a moment (in (d) below) that this is not the only kind of subjective assessment of validity which we shall meet.

c) *Empirical validity*: if the test results correlate positively and strongly with some trustworthy external criterion, the test can be said to possess empirical (or 'pragmatic' or 'statistical', to use two alternative terms) validity.

Time is normally taken as a key variable here — whether the correlation is carried out simultaneously or with some subsequent criterion — and this provides a subdivision of empirical validity into two varieties:

    i. *Concurrent* (or status) validity: a typical example might be where a group of students is given the test and is immediately rated by an experienced teacher.

    ii. *Predictive* validity: in contrast, we might give the students the test and, after a period of time has passed, have them rated again in some way.

d) *Face validity*: if the test is accepted as appearing to be appropriate by those who administer it and those who take it, it can be said to have face validity. It may seem a trifle odd to include such a clearly subjective matter in a list of essential characteristics but, subjective or not, the assessment of those involved will affect the choice or the rejection of a test. Even if a test possesses all the other characteristics but lacks face validity, it will not be selected and its manifest good points will never be known.

3.2. Reliability

Reliability is concerned with the precision of the measurement made possible by the test; does the test measure what it measures sufficiently accurately for us to have confidence in its results?

It may appear from this specification that reliability and empirical validity are the same thing. They are not. Empirical validity is demonstrated by correlating test results with some external criterion in which we have faith; a strong positive correlation implying a high degree of empirical validity. Reliability, on the contrary, is a measure of the efficiency of the test as a measuring device *per se*. Demonstrating reliability involves the correlation of the test not with other criteria but with itself by, for example, the 'split-half' procedure or the use of an equivalent 'parallel form' in order to show how consistent it is (see Allen & Davies 1977.17).

The reliability of a test can be reduced by sources of error extrinsic to itself — the examiners and the test situation — or intrinsic: a lack of stability or equivalence.

a) *Extrinsic sources of error*; since those who administer the test and those who take it are human beings with different backgrounds and, on any given occasion, different personal reactions to the situation they are in, and since the situation may itself contain elements which are not conducive to the taking of the test, many factors can combine to make the test less 'fair' for one individual than for another. We have already discussed such problems (in 1.4.) and tests these days are normally constructed in such a way as to minimize error deriving from such sources.

b) *Intrinsic sources of error*; more serious are sources of error within the test itself:

i. *Stability*: a stable measuring device would give the same reading when used to measure the same object twice, assuming that there had, between the two measurements, been no actual change in the object measured. For example, a thermometer placed in water at boiling-point at sea-level should always measure 100°C. A thermometer which gave readings which fluctuated between 95°C and 105°C would obviously be most unstable and unreliable. A stable test, then, ought to give the same results when administered to the same candidates twice in succession, assuming no teaching between the two trials. Naturally, human beings being what they are, a perfect repetition of the scores is highly unlikely. The tester, of necessity, seeks an acceptable correlation between the two sets of scores and, if satisfied, by using, for example, the 'test-retest' procedure (Heaton 1975.155) declares the test to be reliable, at least in respect of its stability.

ii. *Equivalence*: one measuring device is equivalent to another if, when used to measure the same object, they give the same reading. Two thermometers, for example, are equivalent if, plunged into the same boiling water, they both read 100°C (or any other temperature for that matter so long as it was the same). In testing, it is not unusual for several equivalent versions of the same test to be produced — not only to increase security but also to provide a mechanism for demonstrating improvement during a course — and for the correlation between them to be given by the authors.

3.3. Practicality

Practicality is concerned with the useability of the test: can I, in my situation, with my students and my resources use this test?

It may appear mundane to include such considerations in our discussion of the characteristics of a 'good' test but we must accept that a test which is perfect in its validity and reliability but difficult to administer or score or which is expensive may well fail to gain acceptance just as it might if its face validity is low.

Two parameters appear to be involved

a) *Economy*: the cost in time, money and personnel of administering a particular test.

b) *Ease*: the degree of difficulty experienced in the administration and scoring of the test and the interpretation of the results.

3.4. Summary

The ideal test would be one which was reliable in that it provided dependable measurements, was valid in that it not only measured what it was supposed to measure, supported what we already believed about the nature of language and of learning and agreed with trustworthy outside criteria but also looked as though it did all these things. In addition, it would be cheap and easy to use. Such a test is, of course, at the end of the rainbow and we are still looking!

4. SOME EXAMPLES OF LANGUAGE TESTS

In this section we shall give nine examples of language tests and comment on them. One or two, it should be noted – the first, 'Novish', for example – were not originally designed as tests but we have included them to support the point we made earlier (see 2.2.2.) that many classroom teaching methods can be used as tests.

4.1. Novish

Although originally designed to demonstrate programmed learning techniques (see Howatt A in Allen & Corder 1974) we are suggesting here that the artificial language 'Novish' might be used as an aptitude test for FL students.

The only change required to turn the materials into a test is to mask the answers – in the right-hand column – and, perhaps, add a final question along the lines of 'why does Novish use *gru* and *stil* in short answers?'.

Language Aptitude Test
This test concerns part of the grammar of an artificial language called 'Novish'. All you need to know about the language is that *sademane* = 'this is' and *min* = 'man' so that a sentence such as *Sademane min* = 'this is a man'. The meanings of other nouns will become clear as you do the test, since each is introduced by a picture.

Short form answers in Novish (1)   ANSWERS

1	Ki poi sademane?	Ye, gru
2	Ki min sademane?	Ye, gru.
3	Ki weimin sademane?	Ye, gru.
4	Ki pooni sademane?	Ye, gru.
5	Ki min sademane?	Ye, gru.
	Ki weimin sademane?	Ye, gru.
	Ki pooni sademane?	Ye, gru.

201

6		Ki tre sademane?	Ye, gru.
7		Ki tavl sademane?	Ye, stil.
8		Ki bukh sademane?	Ye, stil.
9		Ki pokit sademane?	Ye, stil.
10		Ki tavl sademane?	Ye, stil.
		Ki bukh sademane?	Ye, stil.
		Ki pokit sademane?	Ye, stil.
11		Ki min sademane?	Ye, gru.
		Ki tavl sademane?	Ye, stil.
		Ki tre sademane?	Ye, gru.
		Ki pooni sademane?	Ye, gru.
12		Ki tavl sademane?	Nu, gru.
13		Ki bukh sademane?	Nu, gru.
14		Ki pokit sademane?	Nu, gru.
15		Ki poi sademane?	Nu, stil.
16		Ki weimin sademane?	Nu, stil.

17		Ki pooni sademane?	Nu, stil.
18		Ki pokit sademane?	Nu, gru.
		Ki poi sademane?	Nu, stil.
		Ki tavl sademane?	Nu, gru.
		Ki tre sademane?	Nu, stil.

4.2. Scrambled sentences

The five sentences below were suggested to me by Eugene Winter (of Hatfield Polytechnic) as a possible way of testing comprehension. Like the Cloze Test (see 4.7 for an example) these sentences do discriminate rather well between native and non-native users of English. One reason for this can be found in the need for the candidate to put the words into an acceptable syntactic order. This requires of the candidate a knowledge of lexical collocation and an expectation of what can reasonably be expected to go with what.

Speed is also a good indicator: the natives completing the task far more rapidly than the non-natives. The 'norms' should be taken as no more than suggestions of the time one might expect an educated adult L1 user of English to take.

The test might also be used as an aptitude test if one assumes that syntactic analysis is a skill required by the L2 learner of a language.

Scrambled sentences
The five sentences below contain in each case the words which make up a complete and grammatically correct English sentence but in each case the words have been rearranged in a random order.

Your task is to put the words back into an appropriate order as quickly as possible.

There is often more than one possible answer. Write out the first one you think of.

After each sentence has been completed make sure you note how long the task took you.
1. Can a defined ignorance of safely sheer authority the and young wishful-thinking be as towards the mixture attitude of.
2. On which conscious from reading an only a superior grammar can and command intelligent of come mastery a language depends of vocabulary.

3. Repression of always likely totalitarian into a government activity nearly measures suspects against extreme subversive alarms.
4. Since shy publisher has ever poverty-stricken finding many of writers a willing manuscript are notoriously for a despaired writer of his publishers.
5. Who stanzas most takes a life of the man a view compresses personal and few it is into a poet introspective.

Answers and Norms
These 'answers' consist of one of the several possible solutions which are available in almost all cases.

1. The attitude of the young towards authority can be safely defined as a mixture of wishful-thinking and sheer ignorance.
   (19 words − 3 minutes)

2. A superior command of language depends on a conscious mastery of vocabulary and grammar which can only come from an intelligent reading.
   (22 words − 7 minutes)

3. Subversive activity nearly always alarms a totalitarian government into measures of extreme repression against likely suspects.
   (16 words − 7 minutes)

4. Many a writer has despaired of ever finding a willing publisher for his manuscript since publishers are notoriously shy of poverty-stricken writers.
   (22 words − 10 minutes)

5. A poet is a man who takes the most introspective personal view of life and compresses it into a few stanzas.
   (21 words − 20 minutes)

4.3. The Michigan Test of Aural Comprehension of English
This test, originally designed in the late 1940s, was used in placing non-native students in classes in American Universities. It should be noted that only the first third of the test is reproduced here i.e. the first 20 questions in which the 'clues' are in picture form. The last 40 questions are in the more normal written form.

Questions

Example 1. There is a square, a circle and a triangle on your paper. Which is the triangle?
Example 2. The man played the violin.
Example 3. He is sitting on a chair.
Example 4. He closed his suitcase by sitting on it.

1. Mother said 'John. Please close the window'.
2. John said 'Have you found the ball?' Charles said 'I'm still looking for it'.

204

3. It's a lovely day and he's going fishing.

4. The man played a concert on the new piano at half past seven. When did he play?

5. It's his hat that fell in the water, not he.

6. He's going to eat with his sister.

7. The nice young man took off his hat in the elevator at nine o'clock. Who took off his hat?

8. The dog is further from the ball than the cat.

9. You're a lucky boy; she saw your picture and was very happy.

10. The boys had the bird tied with a string.

11. The boy is as tall as the girl.

12. Somebody turned the radio on too loud. Will you turn it down a little?

13. He wasn't able to maintain his balance.

14. The dog was bitten by the man.

15. He is giving her his hat and coat.

16. The fat man with the cigar is having his house painted.

17. The girl used the telephone.

18. The little boy likes milk chocolate.

19. She is sinking.

20. The horse's eyes were cold and piercing.

4.4. Crossword Puzzle

This is a teacher-made attainment test designed to test knowledge of irregular past and past participle forms. It would be given to a class at the end of a block of teaching on irregular verb forms and it is assumed that the vast majority of the class would be able to complete the crossword correctly. The test intentionally does not discriminate. Its function is to provide some measure of what has been learned but, and perhaps more importantly, it gives even the poorer student the chance to, for once, 'get it right'. It surely does no harm to encourage the weaker student, does it?

Puzzle

This puzzle can be completed if you know the past tense and past participle forms of the irregular verbs we have been studying. In each case, there is a clue to help you make the right change to the words in italics so as to turn it into the correct past form. Be careful though; sometimes what you have to do is leave the word as it is.

4.5. Vocabulary Test

This is another teacher-made test which makes use of the multiple-choice format we saw in the Michigan test (4.3.) to force the candidate – who is assumed to be an L1 speaker of a Romance language: French, Italian, Portuguese, Spanish or Roumanian – to grapple with 'false friends': lexical items which share a similar form but differ in meaning between the L1 and English. The test was made up by Mrs Carole Robinson of Oxford College of Further Education.

CLUES

Across

2. He said he *will* have read the book if he had had the time. (5)
4. You are too late he has already *go*. (4)
5. Where did you *put* your coat? (3)
6. I was so hungry that I *eat* all the food. (3)
8. The ten of them *drink* 100 bottles of beer last night! (5)
9. You have *mistake* me for someone else. (8)

Down

1. I didn't know what to *do*. (2)
2. Last year they *go* by sea to England. (4)
3. They *leave* three months ago. (4)
4. I'd like to *go* to England too. (2)
7. Have you *eat* your dinner yet? (5)
8. Your lights are too bright: please *dim* them. (3)

SOLUTION
Across: 2. would 4. gone 5. put 6. ate 8. drank 9. mistaken
Down: 1. do 2. went 3. left 4. go 7. eaten 8. dim

Vocabulary Test
Read the following passage and then answer the questions at the end of it.

The managing director reported that the actual cost of producing the new de luxe model washing machine would be adequately covered by the expected returns for the product and the concurrence of its appearance with the new Parnall model was vital if his company was to retain its reputation in the field of high quality consumer goods.

The words and phrases below have been taken from the passage. Choose the word or phrase on the right which is closest in meaning in each case, i.e. a, b or c.

1. the actual cost
   a. the cost at the present time
   b. the cost itself
   c. the existing cost
2. producing
   a. manufacturing
   b. supplying
   c. advertizing
3. adequately covered
   a. well hidden
   b. permitted
   c. more than balanced
4. expected returns
   a. machines sent back
   b. refunded money
   c. profit margin
5. concurrence
   a. competition
   b. simultaneity
   c. rivalry
6. vital
   a. necessary
   b. essential
   c. lively

Answers
1. b 2. a 3. c 4. c 5. b 6. b

4.6. Pragmatic diagnostic test
The test below was originally designed as a classroom activity (in Bhatnagar and Bell 1979.231f) to teach the expression of personal emotions.

Since the text consists of a 'half-dialogue' the exercise or test requires the learner to fill in the blanks with appropriate utterances, by recording or in writing.

TEST

Imagine that you are B in the dialogue below. Listen to what A says and provide appropriate responses. Make sure what you say fits with what A says next as well.

207

1. A.   How's your son doing at University?
   B.
   A.   Oh. I'm sorry. I only asked.
   B.
   A.   Well. It has in a way. My own son is at University too you know.
   B.
   A.   All right then. I won't ask in future. Goodbye.

2. A.   How's your son doing at university?
   B.
   A.   That's good. You must feel very proud of him.
   B.
   A.   Very well it seems. He passed his Part 1 exams and has been accepted to major in physics.
   B.
   A.   Yes. We're pretty lucky with our children aren't we?
   B.
   A.   And to yours. See you soon.
   B.

4.7. Cloze test for comprehension

A cloze test consists of a cohesive text in which words have been blanked out. For ELT the frequency is often every fifth word, though it is possible to make the removals more or less frequent or even to remove certain formal items – prepositions, logical and temporal connectors, etc. – and require the examinee to fill in the blanks as appropriate.

This test was originally part of the teaching materials in a course of first year Indian university students (Bhatnagar and Bell *op. cit.* 145) aimed at teaching reference to the notion of 'frequency'.

Test

In this passage you will see that every fifth word has been blanked out. Your task is to fill the blanks with a single appropriate word in each case. There is often more than one acceptable answer and we shall be timing you so do not spend time trying to choose between equally correct alternatives.

When snow becomes compressed — a long period of — freezing it congeals into — and forms ice-streams — as glaciers . . . As we —, the summits of many — are covered with snow — the year round. The —, however, varies in different — of the world — according to the weather — of a particular year. — snow-line is normally as — as about 8,000 feet — the Alps, but on — equator it is as — as about 16,000 feet. — rain and snow mix — fall together they produce —. Sometimes, however, it will — again as it reaches — ground, and create a — dangerous thin layer of —.

Time taken: mins   secs

4.8. Foreign Service Institute oral interview

So far all the tests we have been looking at have shared the same characteristic; each has consisted of a predetermined series of tasks set by the examiner to be carried out by one or more candidates at once and assessed by the examiner against the performance of the group as a whole, i.e. they have all been norm-referenced tests.

This test and the next are, in contrast, forms of assessment which depend on judgements of individual knowledge and skill by an examiner or examiners against a set of predetermined objectives i.e. they are criterion-referenced tests.

The Foreign Service Institute Oral Interview consists of an interview between the candidate and, normally, two interviewers. The candidate is assessed during the interview on his overall ability to communicate in the language against a five-point scale ranging from one — lowest — to five — highest — and, simultaneously, on his command of accent, grammar, vocabulary, fluency and comprehension. The scores on each of these — this time on a six-point scale — are weighted, totalled and, finally, converted into a point score to give an FSI Level of between 0+ to 4+ (lowest to highest) on a nine-point scale.

1. Proficiency Levels

Level 1: *Able to satisfy routine travel needs and minimum courtesy requirements.* Can ask and answer questions on topics very familiar to him or her; within the scope of his or her very limited language experience can understand simple questions and statements, allowing for slowed speech, repetition or paraphrase; speaking vocabulary inadequate to express anything but the most elementary needs; errors in pronunciation and grammar are frequent, but can be understood by a native speaker used to dealing with foreigners attempting to speak his or her language. While elementary needs vary considerably from individual to individual, any person at level 1 should be able to order a simple meal, ask for shelter or lodging, ask and give simple directions, make purchases, and tell time.

Level 2: *Able to satisfy routine social demands and limited work requirements.* Can handle with confidence but not facility most social situations including introductions and casual conversations about current events, as well as work, family, and autobiographical information; can handle limited work requirements, needing help in handling any complications or difficulties; can get the gist of most conversations on nontechnical subjects (i.e. topics that require no specialized knowledge) and has a speaking vocabulary sufficient to express himself or herself simply with some circumlocutions; accent, though often quite faulty, is intelligible; can usually handle elementary constructions quite accurately but does not have thorough or confident control of the grammar.

Level 3: *Able to speak the language with sufficient structural accuracy and vocabulary to participate effectively in most formal and informal con-*

versations on practical, social, and professional topics. Can discuss particular interests and special fields of competence with reasonable ease, comprehension is quite complete for a normal rate of speech; vocabulary is broad enough that he or she rarely has to grope for a word; accent may be obviously foreign; control of grammar good; errors never interfere with understanding and rarely disturb the native speaker.

Level 4: *Able to use the language fluently and accurately on all levels normally pertinent to professional needs.* Can understand and participate in any conversation within the range of his or her experience with a high degree of fluency and precision of vocabulary; would rarely be taken for a native speaker, but can respond appropriately even in unfamiliar situations; errors of pronunciation and grammar quite rare; can handle informal interpreting from and into the language.

Level 5: *Speaking proficiency equivalent to that of an educated native speaker.* Has complete fluency in the language such that his or her speech on all levels is fully accepted by educated native speakers in all of its features, including breadth of vocabulary and idiom, colloquialisms, and pertinent cultural references.

2. Supplementary Scales
Comprehension
1. Understands too little for the simplest type of conversation.
2. Understands only slow, very simple speech on common social and touristic topics; requires constant repetition and rephrasing.
3. Understands careful, somewhat simplified speech directed to him or her, with considerable repetition and rephrasing.
4. Understands quite well normal educated speech directed to him or her, but requires occasional repetition or rephrasing.
5. Understands everything in normal educated conversation except for very colloquial or low-frequency items or exceptionally rapid or slurred speech.
6. Understands everything in both formal and colloquial speech to be expected of an educated native speaker.

Accent
1. Pronunciation frequently unintelligible.
2. Frequent gross errors and a very heavy accent make understanding difficult, requires frequent repetition.
3. 'Foreign accent' requires concentrated listening and mispronunciations lead to occasional misunderstanding and apparent errors in grammar or vocabulary.
4. Marked 'foreign accent' and occasional mispronunciations that do not interfere with understanding.
5. No conspicuous mispronunciations, but would not be taken for a native speaker.
6. Native pronunciation, with no trace of 'foreign accent.'

Grammar
1. Grammar almost entirely inaccurate except in stock phrases.
2. Constant errors showing control of very few major patterns and frequently preventing communication.
3. Frequent errors showing some major patterns uncontrolled and causing occasional irritation and misunderstanding.
4. Occasional errors showing imperfect control of some patterns but no weakness that causes misunderstanding.
5. Few errors, with no patterns of failure.
6. No more than two errors during the interview.

Vocabulary
1. Vocabulary inadequate for even the simplest conversation.
2. Vocabulary limited to basic personal and survival areas (time, food, transportation, family, etc.).
3. Choice of words sometimes inaccurate, limitations of vocabulary prevent discussion of some common professional and social topics.
4. Professional vocabulary adequate to discuss special interests; general vocabulary permits discussion of any nontechnical subject with some circumlocutions.
5. Professional vocabulary broad and precise; general vocabulary adequate to cope with complex practical problems and varied social situations.
6. Vocabulary apparently as accurate and extensive as that of an educated native speaker.

Fluency
1. Speech is so halting and fragmentary that conversation is virtually impossible.
2. Speech is very slow and uneven except for short or routine sentences.
3. Speech is frequently hesitant and jerky; sentences may be left uncompleted.
4. Speech is occasionally hesitant, with some unevenness caused by rephrasing and groping for words.
5. Speech is effortless and smooth, but perceptibly non-native in speed and evenness.
6. Speech on all professional and general topics as effortless and smooth as a native speaker's.

Although the five separate scales are intended to supplement the overall general assessment, each of the five factors is given a different weighting — grammar the heaviest and accent the lightest — as in the table below:

FSI Weighting Table

Proficiency Description ⟶	①	②	③	④	⑤	⑥	
Accent	0	1	2	2	3	4	_____
Grammar	6	12	18	24	30	36	_____
Vocabulary	4	8	12	16	20	24	_____
Fluency	2	4	6	8	10	12	_____
Comprehension	4	8	12	15	19	23	_____
						Total:	[ ]

The next step is to take the total score and convert it by reference to the Conversion Table into an FSI Level.

FSI Conversion Table

Total Score	Level	Total Score	Level	Total Score	Level
16–25	0+	43–52	2	73–82	3+
26–32	1	53–62	2+	83–92	4
33–42	1+	63–72	3	93–99	4+

4.9. Self-assessment

Once the notion of criterion-referenced tests was accepted, the next logical step was to relate criterion-reference to the general movement in language teaching towards a more learner-centred view of learning and arrive at a form of test which the learner applied to himself: self-assessment.

The test below derives from those designed by Oskarsson (1977) for the Council of Europe – the 'general assessment' sections for speaking, writing and reading are taken directly from Oskarsson – but with the difference that the specific activities on which the candidates are asked to rate themselves were arrived at after a needs analysis related to the particular pre-defined group of learners: Factory Inspectors in Singapore (see Bell 1980c for more information).

After the completion of the questionnaires, a 'language profile' can be easily built up for each individual – his personal view of his own proficiency – and that matched with the results of other tests and the evaluation of the officer's superiors, to give a broad and, it is hoped, balanced picture.

HOW TO COMPLETE THE QUESTIONNAIRE

This questionnarie is divided into three sections:
1. *Speaking*:
   a General assessment.
   b Specific activities.

2. *Writing*:
   a General assessment.
   b Specific activities.

3. *Reading*
   a General assessment.
   b Specific activities.

General assessment
In each case there are five statements — ranked from 5 (highest) to 1 (lowest) level of proficiency — from which you should choose the one which best fits your assessment of your own proficiency.

Circle the number to the right of the statement which seems to you to fit best.

You may also find the statements useful as descriptions of the values of the numbers in the specific activities section.

Specific Activities
In each case, there are descriptions of situations or activities — 8 for speaking, 6 for writing and 6 for reading — with a five-point scale to the right. For each activity, circle the number which best fits your feeling about your proficiency in that activity. Remember that 5 is the highest and 1 the lowest and that the General Assessment sheet spells out the general meaning of each number.

SPEAKING: GENERAL ASSESSMENT	
I speak the language as well as a well-educated native.	5
I speak the language fluently and for the most part correctly. I have a large vocabulary so I seldom have to hesitate or search for words. On the other hand, I am not completely fluent in situations in which I have had no practice with the language.	4
I can make myself understood in most everyday situations, but my language is not without mistakes and, sometimes, I cannot find the words for what I want to say. It is difficult for me to express myself in situations in which I have had no opportunity to practice the language. I can give a short summary of general information that I have received in my native language.	3
I can make myself understood in simple everyday situations, for example asking and giving simple directions, asking and telling the time, asking and talking about simpler aspects of work and interest. My vocabularly is rather limited, so it is only by a great deal of effort that I can use the language in new and unexpected situations.	2
I can just about express very simple things concerning my own situation and my nearest surroundings, for example asking and answering very simple questions about the time, food, housing and directions. I only have a command of very simple words and phrases.	1
I do not speak the language at all.	0

SPEAKING: SPECIFIC ACTIVITIES					
1 Face-to-face questioning as part of an investigation at a factory	5	4	3	2	1
2 Discussion with colleagues on matters related to your work.	5	4	3	2	1
3 Receiving and dealing with telephone enquiries from the public	5	4	3	2	1
4 Making telephone calls to occupiers to give or check information	5	4	3	2	1
5 Dealing with face-to-face enquiries at the office from members of the public	5	4	3	2	1
6 Interviewing witnesses, etc. in the office	5	4	3	2	1
7 Presenting evidence and being cross-examined in court	5	4	3	2	1
8 Any other activity involving the use of spoken English (please specify)	5	4	3	2	1

WRITING: GENERAL ASSESSMENT	
I write the language as well as a well-educated native.	5
I write the language rather easily and for the most part correctly. I only make occasional grammatical mistakes and spelling mistakes. When writing about subjects in which I have had no opportunity to practise the language I need to use a dictionary.	4
I can formulate written messages or give a coherent account of things connected with my own life, my interests, needs and wishes, but I make mistakes in both grammar and spelling. I often cannot find the words for what I want to express. I can write down from dictation a normal prose text about a familiar subject. I may make spelling mistakes and mistakes due to a lack of words.	3
I can formulate simple written messages connected with my own life and my needs, but there are often grammatical and spelling mistakes and a wrong choice of words. I can write down from dictation a simple text about everyday subjects. There are often spelling mistakes and mistakes due to a lack of words.	2
I can formulate very simple messages connected with my own life. I only have a command of very simple words and phrases.	1
I cannot write the language at all.	0

WRITING: SPECIFIC ACTIVITIES					
1 Writing reports on inspections of factories	5	4	3	2	1
2 Writing reports on investigations of accidents	5	4	3	2	1
3 Writing letters and notices to the occupiers of factories	5	4	3	2	1
4 Updating records	5	4	3	2	1
5 Writing minutes of meetings	5	4	3	2	1
6 Any other activity involving the use of written English (please specify)	5	4	3	2	1

READING: GENERAL ASSESSMENT	
I read and understand the language as well as a well-educated native	5
I understand everything or nearly everything written in the language within non-specialized fields. There may be words I do not understand in difficult texts	4
I understand most of what I read in simple texts dealing with familiar subjects such as leisure interests, current affairs and living conditions. I understand most of a normal private letter dealing with everyday things such as the family and their doings, etc. I understand the main contents of a normal newspaper article about a plane crash or the opening of a new underground line, for example, but not all the details.	3
I understand the meaning of simple written instructions about the way, time, place and similar things, and also understand the essential things in simple texts dealing with familiar subjects such as common leisure interests, current affairs and living conditions.	2
I understand the main points of a simple text and simple written directions for familiar things.	1
I cannot read the language at all.	0

215

READING. SPECIFIC ACTIVITIES						
1	Reading general files.	5	4	3	2	1
2	Reading factory records.	5	4	3	2	1
3	Reading workmen's records.	5	4	3	2	1
4	Reading files concerned with legal matters, e.g. statements, solicitors' letters, etc.	5	4	3	2	1
5	Reading the Factories Act and related legislation.	5	4	3	2	1
6	Any other activity requiring the reading of English (please specify)	5	4	3	2	1

SUGGESTED FURTHER READING

Allen J. and Davies A. eds. (1977), *Testing and Experimental Methods; Edinburgh Course in Applied Linguistics* vol. 4. Oxford, London.
This volume of the Edinburgh Course in Applied Linguistics provides the reader with two views of tests – as measuring instruments in their own right and as constituents of experiments – and a selection of useful statistical procedures.

Harris D. (1969), *Testing English as a Second Language* McGraw-Hill, New York.
A valuable book since it not only provides an introduction to the field but also attempts to give the practising teacher the ability to produce and administer his own tests.

Heaton J. B. (1975), *Writing English Language Tests* Longman, London
One of the Longman Handbooks for Language Teachers, this gives the classroom teacher an introduction to testing, advice on test construction and, most usefully, a substantial section dedicated to practical work through which the teacher can practice writing tests.

Jackson S. (1968), *A Teacher's Guide to Tests and Testing* Longman. London.
This book is one of the simplest and most clearly written books on the general subject of educational testing and as such gives the teacher a straightforward introduction to testing problems and to the associated statistical techniques.

Lado R. (1961), *Language Testing: the Construction and Use of Foreign Language Tests* Longman, London
Now rather dated this book sets out the fundamental principles of struc-

turalist linguistics in relation to language testing. It is still essential background reading for the student who is seriously interested in testing.

Oller J. W. Jr. (1979), *Language Tests at School* Longman, London
An excellent and up-to-date survey of the field full of cogent argument and thought-provoking discussion. Represents current thinking in testing and is particularly valuable for its treatment of pragmatic testing problems.

Valette R. M. (1967), *Modern Language Testing; a Handbook* Harcourt Brace & World, New York
Provides, like Harris, the principles of language testing but unlike most books in the field gives many examples in languages other than English, French, German and Spanish.

Appendix D

The purpose of this appendix is to take a little further the points we raised in our earlier discussion of types of language syllabus — grammatical, situational and notional — by providing examples of structuralist, transformational, situational and notional teaching materials. In this way we hope to flesh out the arguments put forward in the body of the book (particularly in Chapters 3, 5, 6 and 7) with selected sections of what we hope are fairly typical texts.

In order to make it easy to compare the four examples, we have limited them to a single unit dealing with the same topic: the modal verbs *can, should,* etc. expressing such notions as ability, permission, obligation, etc. Although, of course, we realize that the lack of a one-to-one correspondence between form and function makes strict comparability impossible, we feel that there is enough in common to make the exercise worthwhile.

1. POINTS OF COMPARISON

It is possible to look at language teaching materials from any point on a continuum between comparing whole courses with other whole courses to comparing the way a series of courses tackle the teaching of a particular point. We have chosen the latter, micro perspective, for a number of reasons. First, the broader issues concerned with syllabus design have already been discussed in the text, so it would be somewhat redundant to raise them all again in this appendix. Secondly, the choice of a single and common teaching point — particularly one so notoriously problematic as the modals — seems to us to provide an opportunity to see the extent to which supposedly new ideas derived from linguistics and psychology actually manage to cope with what we all know to be a very tricky topic indeed. Finally, we feel that a close study of a small sample from the four methods will crystalize for the reader the essential differences (and many similarities) between them in a way which we may have failed to do in the body of the book.

Even so, unless we are to comment on each text in an *ad hoc* way, picking out points in a purely random manner and hence failing to provide a framework for comparison, we need some kind of procedure or, at the very least, a taxonomy of points to look out for; a check list. Very useful in this respect is the paper by Candlin and Breen (1979) in which they propose just such a check-list; four major issues which need to be investigated and evaluated when teaching materials are being examined or prepared. Each contains, in addition, a number of sub-points:

a) The relationship of the materials to the situation – sociological and psychological – in which they are to be used and to the curriculum within which they constitute a resource.

b) The nature of the content of the materials: their focus, sequence, subdivisions and continuity and the theory of language implicit in them.

c) The nature of the activities involved in the use of the materials: the procedures, types of participation, roles played by learner and teacher and the theory of learning implicit in them.

d) The extent to which the materials are amenable to modification in the new directions suggested by recent work in applied linguistics, the stressing of activities as against the mere presentation of models, the acceptance of the fact of variability and unpredictability in language as against the imposition of a convenient but fictitious normative and predictive form of the language, etc.

Rather than take up each of these issues in our discussion of the following materials and risk being repetitive, we shall make use of four of their 20 points:

i) *Content*: what language data and information about language is contained in the selected sequence of materials?

ii) *Activities*: what are teachers and learners expected to do when they work through these materials?

iii) *Theory of Language*: what theory of language is implied by the materials – particularly their content – and is the theory overtly referred to by the writer?

iv) *Theory of Learning*: what theory of learning is implied by the materials – particularly the activities – and is it ever overtly referred to by the author?

2. STRUCTURALIST MATERIALS

We have already discussed the general features of structuralist teaching materials and the methodology underlying them (see 5.1.4.). We now wish to take an example from the extremely well-known 'Ann Arbor' materials issued between the early 1940s and the mid-1960s by the English Language Institute of the University of Michigan (see Fries & Lado 1943, 1954, 1958, 1964 and Krohn 1971).

Probably the best-known of the Ann Arbor series is Fries and Lado's *English Sentence Patterns* (1958) from which we have chosen half of Lesson XI (pages 95–98) which deals with modal verbs.

LESSON XI

1. CAN, SHOULD, MUST, WILL, MIGHT, MAY.
   1a. I CAN READ ENGLISH. CAN YOU READ IT?
   (Statements and questions)

1b. CAN YOU PRACTISE NOW? YES, I CAN.
     (Short answers)
2. A pattern of connected statements.
   2a. JOHN CAN'T GO AND I CAN'T EITHER.
        MARY CAN GO AND BETTY CAN TOO.
   2b. (AND . . . TOO contrasted with . . . AND . . . EITHER)
   2b. MARY CAN GO BUT JOHN CAN'T.
        (. . . BUT . . .)

1a. Key examples: I CAN READ English. Can you READ it?

Observe the position of CAN, SHOULD, etc.
Observe the form of the Class 2 words.
Previous pattern (lesson IV):

		John	is	speaking English
	Is	John		speaking English?

New pattern:

		John	CAN	SPEAK	English.
		He	SHOULD	STUDY	everyday.
		You	MUST	SPEAK	English in class.
		The class	'LL	FINISH	the book next month.
		I	MIGHT	GO	to Chicago next week.
		You	MAY	SMOKE	in the dormitory.
		John	MUSTN'T	SPEAK	Chinese.
		He	SHOULDN'T	GO	to the movies every night.
		You	MUSTN'T	SPEAK	your native language here.
		The class	WON'T	FINISH	The book this month.
		I	MIGHT NOT	GO	to Chicago next week.
		You	MAY NOT	SMOKE	in the classroom.
	CAN	John		SPEAK	English?
	SHOULD	he		STUDY	everyday?
	MUST	we		SPEAK	English in class?
	WILL	we		FINISH	the book next month?
When	WILL	we		FINISH	the book?
Where	MAY	the students		SMOKE?	

SENTENCE PATTERNS

COMMENTS

(1) Use CAN, SHOULD, MUST, WILL ('LL), MIGHT, MAY in the positions of HE: after the subject (JOHN, HE, etc.) in statements; before the subject in questions. Don't use DO in questions with CAN, etc.

(2) Use the simple form of the Class 2 word (SPEAK, PRACTISE, etc.) with CAN, SHOULD, etc.

(3) Use CAN, SHOULD, etc., with I, YOU, WE, THEY and HE, SHE, IT. Do not add -S to words like CAN.

(4) CAN'T, SHOULDN'T, MUSTN'T, WON'T, MIGHT NOT, MAY NOT are the negative forms.

Illustrative examples

Paul studied French for five years. He CAN speak it well.
Betty never practises her piano lessons. She CAN'T play well.
Paul is young and strong. He CAN work hard all day.
Peter is old and weak. He CAN'T work hard.
Mary is going to have an examination next week. She SHOULD study for it this week. She SHOULDN'T go to the movies.
Automobiles are dangerous. We SHOULD drive carefully. We SHOULDN'T drive fast.
Mrs Smith is sick. She MUST stay in bed. She MUSTN'T get up.
A red light means 'stop.' Drivers MUST stop. They MUSTN'T go.
We're going to have a programme next week. We'LL have it on Friday night. All of the students WILL be there. They WON'T go to the movies that night.

NOTE: WILL is equivalent to BE + GOING TO in most situations.

John invited me to his house tonight. I MIGHT go, but I MIGHT stay home. I don't know.
I sometimes see Mary in the library. I MIGHT see her tomorrow. I MIGHT NOT see her. I don't know.
Betty asked 'MAY I open a window?' Her mother answered, 'No. You MAY NOT open a window. I'M cold.'

Exercise XI
Betty asked her father, 'MAY I go to the concert tonight?'
He gave her permission. He said, 'Yes, you MAY go.'

Practice

Exercise 1a.1. (To practise MAY, CAN, etc. in proper position.)
Substitute the words. For example:
I can play the piano.

speak Spanish	I CAN SPEAK SPANISH.
they	THEY CAN SPEAK SPANISH.
may	THEY MAY SPEAK SPANISH.
ask for a visa	THEY MAY ASK FOR A VISA.

1. should	9. we
2. she	10. study tonight
3. write home	11. must
4. I	12. he
5. might	13. speak English
6. go to the dance	14. can
7. John	15. finish the lesson
8. will	16. you

17. should	25. go to Detroit
18. must	26. might
19. practise every day	27. they
20. John and Mary	28. visit the museum
21. they	29. can
22. should	30. return tomorrow
23. we	31. should
24. will	32. must

Exercise 1a. 2. (To practise questions with CAN, MUST, MIGHT, etc.)
Convert the statements into questions. For example:

I can hear the band.	CAN YOU HEAR THE BAND?
They may miss class tomorrow.	MAY THEY MISS CLASS TO-MORROW?
Professor Brown will give a speech today.	WILL PROFESSOR BROWN GIVE A SPEECH TODAY?

1. Mary should answer the letter.
2. She may use my pen.
3. The students must practise every day.
4. They should study in the evening.
5. John can play the organ.
6. He will play tonight.
7. We must report to the office now.
8. We can go to lunch later.
9. Mr Brown will explain the lesson to you.
10. You should wait for him.
11. Paul must see a doctor immediately.
12. He might have pneumonia
13. Mary may keep the book for seven days.
14. She should return it next Monday.

Exercise 1a. 3. (To produce the negative forms of CAN, MAY, etc.)
Listen to the affirmative statements about John. Produce corresponding
negative statements about Mary. For example:

John can go.	MARY CAN'T GO.
John may go.	MARY MAY NOT GO.
John should go.	MARY SHOULDN'T GO.

1. John must study hard.
2. John will go tomorrow.
3. John may smoke.
4. John can play the piano.
5. John might visit us.
6. John must practise every day.
7. John will go to Chicago on Saturday.
8. John must wait for his brother.
9. John can pronounce the words.

10. John should come to the programme.
11. John might attend the concert.
12. John may live in an apartment.

Exercise 1a. 4. (To practise comprehension of SHOULD, CAN, etc., and to produce statements with SHOULD, CAN, etc.) Answer the questions. For example:

John's a pianist. What can he do?
HE CAN PLAY THE PIANO.
A South American is going to study in the United States. What should he do?
HE SHOULD LEARN ENGLISH.
Paul and Jim permit John to play their piano. What may John do?
HE MAY PLAY THEIR PIANO.

1. Peter goes to the movies. His mother permits it. What may he do?
2. John doesn't speak English. He needs it. What must he do?
3. John needs a lot of practice in English. What should he do?
4. Paul is going to take a train to Washington, D.C. What might he see there?
5. Paul is going to take a train to Washington, D.C. Who might he see there?
6. We had presidential elections in 1944, 1948, 1952, and 1956. What will we have in 1960?
7. Women may vote in the United States. The Constitution gives them permission. What should they do?
8. Mary is a bad student. What should she do?
9. Mary is a singer. What can she do?
10. The students drive cars on the campus. They have permission. What may they do?
11. Fred is sick. Who must he see?
12. Mr Smith is a Professor of English. What can he do?

2.1. Content

The content of the sample is exclusively the modal verbs, *can, should, must, will, might* and *may* and the focus of the lesson is the forms of the modals and the syntactic relationships into which they enter in declarative and interrogative sentences.

It is significant that meaning is totally ignored. The learner, it would seem, is left to his own devices to deduce the meanings of each form from the examples and exercises to which he is exposed.

The meanings which appear to emerge from the data are:

can	=	ability
should	=	obligation
must	=	obligation

223

will	=	future reference
might	=	conjecture
may	=	permission

None of the other meanings of the modals are implied by the examples — assuming that the teacher is consistent in his stressing and intonation — and that the student is not referred forward — to lesson XXII more than 100 pages later — to the point where more (by no means all) of the meanings are introduced.

The only 'note' which, at first reading, looks as if it might have something to do with meaning — 'WILL is equivalent to BE + GOING TO in most situations' — turns out either, if actually a semantic comment, to be plain wrong or, if not, to be purely syntactic: 'situation' here certainly refers to the syntactic context rather than to the sociolinguistic setting of the use of the sentence.

The layout of the lesson follows that outlined in the introduction to the book:

1. *Outline*: the key examples followed by brief descriptions of the patterns to be learned.

2. *Frame*: preceded by a Key Example, the Frame introduces the pattern to be learned in three stages:

    a) *Attention pointer*: a sentence focusing the attention of the learner on the essential point of the pattern, e.g. 'Observe the position of CAN, SHOULD, etc'.

    b) *Structural pattern*: the pattern to be taught presented in the form of a substitution table, e.g.

John	CAN	SPEAK	English
He	SHOULD	STUDY	every day

More often than not, as in this case, the pattern is preceded by a previously taught pattern for contrast and comparison, e.g.

John	is	speaking English
Is	John	speaking English?

    c) *Comments*: a number of comments — here four — which summarize and verbalize the formal characteristics of what is to be learned, e.g.

    'Use the simple form of the Class 2 word (SPEAK, PRACTISE, etc.) with CAN, SHOULD, etc.'

3. *Illustrative examples*: demonstrating the use of the pattern in a range of syntactic environments, e.g.

    'Paul studied French for five years.

    He CAN speak it very well.'

4. *Practise*: a number of exercises by means of which the learner manipulates the elements of the pattern. We shall be looking in some detail at the exercises in this sample in the next section (i.e. 2.2.).

5. *Notes*: usually in the form of footnotes these are directed at the teacher − pointing out particular teaching problems, or at the learner − drawing attention to a form which needs to be recognized rather than learned for active use, e.g. '*You will also hear this pattern without THAT: THE PROFESSOR IS SO BUSY HE CAN'T LEAVE HIS OFFICE' (from Lesson XXV.239).

6. *Review of the key examples*: this can consist of as little as a list of the patterns or as much as a revision exercise. Lesson XI has only a list.

2.2. Activities

Fries gives precise instructions to the teacher on the activities which he is to encourage and, in addition, justifies his recommendations by reference to the behaviourist tenets of structuralist applied linguistics (see 5.1.4. on this). In the revised version of *English Sentence Patterns* (*English Sentence Structure* 1971) Krohn spells out in even greater detail what is expected. Since he claims that his own book contains much material from the 1957 book and covers ' . . . the same topics . . . and in approximately the same order . . . ' (Krohn, *op. cit.* Preface), we feel no compunction in drawing on his directions and applying them to the sample we have chosen.

1. *Outline*: the teacher presents the key examples and the students repeat them in chorus.

2. *Frame*: the teacher introduces the pattern orally but 'briefly'. Alternatively, the frame may be written up and comments drawn from the students.

3. *Illustrative examples*: these too are presented orally and repeated by the class. Teachers are advised to keep ' . . . any remarks about structure preceding the exercises . . . as short as possible (since) it is not necessary to explain everything in detail . . . keep discussions about structure brief . . . ' (Krohn *ibid.*). In any case, as Fries insisted in his 'Teacher's Introduction' − 'The entire process so far should not take much more than 15% of the time devoted to that pattern. The remaining 85% of the time should be devoted to PRACTICE' (Fries *op. cit.* xiv).

4. *Practice*: both Fries and Krohn recommend chorus responses in the exercises leading to individual responses if class size and time permit − 'With a class of approximately ten students it is possible and desirable for each student to recite individually at least once for each exercise' (Fries *op. cit.* xv) but, Fries continues, even with large classes ' . . . when students are trained to keep the same rhythm in group recitation, it is often possible for the teacher to detect individual errors and correct them' (*ibid*). Lesson XI section 1a contains four exercises:

1. Substitution to practise the placing of the modals in sentences e.g.
I can play the piano
speak Spanish   I CAN SPEAK SPANISH

they	THEY CAN SPEAK SPANISH
may	THEY MAY SPEAK SPANISH
ask for a visa	THEY MAY ASK FOR A VISA

2. Substitution to practise questions with the modals e.g.

I can hear the band	CAN YOU HEAR THE BAND?
They may miss class to-morrow	MAY THEY MISS CLASS TO-MORROW?

3. Substitution to practise the negative forms of the modals e.g.

John can go	MARY CAN'T GO
John may go	MARY MAY NOT GO
John should go	MARY SHOULDN'T GO

4. Substitution to practise comprehension of the modals e.g.

John's a pianist. What can he do?

HE CAN PLAY THE PIANO

A South American is going to study in the United States. What should he do?

HE SHOULD LEARN ENGLISH

Paul and Jim permit John to play their piano. What may John do?

HE MAY PLAY THE PIANO

2.3. Theory of language

In Chapter 5 (5.1.1. and 5.1.2.) we discussed structuralist views on the nature of language and on the description of language. This example of teaching materials amply demonstrates the adherence of the writers to structuralist linguistic theory. Particularly significant is the instruction 'observe the *position* of CAN, SHOULD, etc. and 'the *form* of the Class 2 words' (our emphasis). The reference back to an earlier *pattern* and the use of the term 'Class 2 words' rather than 'verbs' also relate directly to the 'slot-and-filler' and IC Analysis grammars of structuralist linguistics.

The avoidance of semantic considerations and of any attempt to contextualize the examples or the exercises mark the materials off as thoroughly structuralist and would do so even if we were to halt our examination here and not continue to look at the activities which, as we shall see, typify the psychological correlate of structuralist applied linguistics: behaviourist psychology.

2.4. Theory of learning

We discussed the theory of learning most commonly associated with structuralist linguistics earlier (see 'Structuralist views of language learning' 5.1.3.) — behaviourist psychology — and intend now to examine the materials drawn from *English Sentence Patterns* in order to demonstrate the extent to which they reflect behaviourism in their content and, most particularly, in their activities.

The commitment to *practice* (some 85% of the allocated time is expected to be given over to this) and the drastic reduction of time made available for explanation by the teacher or attempted explanations of structure by the students typify materials with a behaviourist psychology as their base.

Notice too that the role of the teacher and that of the learner is strictly delimited: the teacher retains total control — terms such as 'trained' in relation to chorus work and 'recitation' in relation to student output demonstrate this very clearly — and the learner merely has to do as directed. The teacher, that is, provides the stimulus, the learner the response.

When we examine the exercises themselves, we realize just how mechanical they are. In virtually every instance, the teacher's cue sentence contains the actual item required for the learner's answer, e.g.

They may ask for a visa

should

They should ask for a visa

Even where some manipulation of the structure is called for, the item is, once again, provided, e.g.

Mary should answer the letter

Should Mary answer the letter?

The negation exercise works in just as mechanical and predictable a way, e.g.

John must study hard.

Mary mustn't study hard.

Presumably the change from John to Mary is some sort of concession to discourse!

The fourth exercise — to practise comprehension and to produce statements using the modals — looks more promising but turns out to be in part mechanical and in part requiring of the learner a high degree of knowledge of the lexis of English and assuming a set of common presuppositions, e.g.

John's a pianist. What can he do?

He can play the piano.

The *can* is supplied by the second sentence of the teacher's cue but the production of *play the piano* as a response to the stimulus *a pianist* surely demands more of the learner than mere automatic response?

What is the 'proper' response to these?

Paul is going to take a train to Washington DC.

What might he see there?

Paul is going to take a train to Washington DC.

Who might he see there?

Mary is a bad student.

What should she do?

2.5. Summary

The short extract of materials drawn from the Ann Arbor series typifies structuralist language teaching materials of the 1960s. The content is limited to a small set of structually similar items, focused on the correct rendering of the forms of the items and their correct placement in sentences. The sentence as a syntactic unit is taken as the model unit to which the student is exposed. Neither semantics within the structure of the sentence nor cohesion between sentences is taken into account. The student is expected to deduce meaning from the examples and exercises and in this enterprise it is impossible to see how he cannot but be confused by the apparent synonymy of *must* and *should*, both of which clearly mean 'obligation'.

The activities are totally teacher controlled, the learner being required only to respond mechanically to the teacher's stimulus. On the only occasion that creativity is called for (the fourth exercise), it is far from clear how the learner can judge whether his intended answer is appropriate or not.

The theory of language underlying the materials is pure structuralism with its IC analysis, 'slot-and-filler' grammar and total commitment to the description of language as form.

The theory of learning underlying the materials — indeed actually expanded upon in the Teacher's Intdoduction — is that of behaviourist psychology, amply exemplified by the 'min-mem' and stimulus-response nature of the exercises.

3. TRANSFORMATIONAL MATERIALS

We discussed the general features of materials influenced by TG in Chapter 5 (5.2.4.) and now wish to provide a more extensive example of such materials by reproducing part of Rutherford's *Modern English* (1965) specifically the first, revision section on modals (Rutherford *op. cit.* 23–25).

Modals

Presentation

UTTERANCE DISCRIMINATION

A

| I You He She We They | can should 'll | come. wait. sing. leave. work. etc. | I You He She We They | can't shouldn't won't | come. wait. sing. leave. work. etc. |

Explication

You can	sing,	can't	you?	Yes, I	can.
They should	try,	shouldn't	they?	Yes, they	should.
She 'll	come,	won't	she?	Yes, she	will.

(What)	can	you sing?
(Where)	should	they try?
(When)	will	she come?

Can, should, and *will* are modals. They form part of the auxiliary and precede all other parts of the verb phrase (VP).

Each modal has only one form for all persons and numbers.

The modals, like *be*, are unstressed except when negative or in final position. Stressed and unstressed modals assume the following shapes:

	Stressed	Unstressed
can	/kæn/	/kən/
should	/ʃud/	/ʃəd/
will	/wil/	(/l/ (after vowel)
		(/əl/ (after consonant)

The range of meaning of these modals is somewhat as follows:

Can indicates ability and feasibility (present and future).

He can swim.

The doctor can see him now.

The doctor can see him tomorrow.

Be able to may be substituted for *can*.

He's able to swim.

Can (and *could*/kud/) also indicates permission.

(Can)
(Could) I see that newspaper please?

Should indicates constraint or weak obligation.

They should speak English in class.

Ought to is synonymous with *should* (They ought to speak English in class.) but does not usually occur in the negative or interrogative.

Will indicates futurity.

We'll see him this afternoon.

Its negative is *won't*/wownt/).

Verification

RESTATEMENT

1. He isn't able to swim.
   He can't swim.
2. You're able to speak English.
   (I)
   (We) can speak English.
3. I'm able to drive a car.
4. They aren't able to see very well.

5. She's able to translate Chinese.
6. We weren't able to understand it.
7. He's able to fly a plane.
8. You're able to read two languages.
9. They're able to borrow from the bank.
10. She isn't able to communicate.
11. We're able to solve the problem.

ASSOCIATION

1. newspaper
   $\binom{Can}{Could}$ I (see that) newspaper, please?
2. phone call
   $\binom{Can}{Could}$ I (make a) phone call, please?
3. cigarette
4. drink of water
5. pencil
6. question
7. a few words
8. address and phone number
9. radio
10. information
11. match
12. sandwich
13. reservation
14. an aspirin

FIXED COMMENT

1. If he studies, he'll pass.
   He should study.
2. If we wait, it'll be too late.
   $\binom{You}{We}$ shouldn't wait
3. If I don't try, I won't succeed.
   You should try.
4. If they listen, they'll learn.
5. If she loses it, she'll be in trouble.
6. If you don't ask, you won't find out.
7. If he leaves now, he'll have plenty of time.
8. If we leave now, we'll miss the last act.
9. If I don't practise, I won't be able to play.
10. If they work hard, they'll finish tonight.
11. If she eats candy, she'll have weight problems.
12. If you don't keep records, you won't have the information.

REPLY/REJOINDER

1. I'll see you again, won't I?
   (Yes, you will.)
2. Where can I make a phone call?
   (You'll find a phone in the hall.)
3. We should all work hard.
   (We know that.)
4. Will this class meet next week?
5. You can read Greek, can't you?
6. When should you register for the course?
7. It'll probably rain tomorrow.
8. Can you read technical journals in English?
9. You should be able to make speeches in English, shouldn't you?
10. Who'll be at the party tonight?
11. I'm not able to find a new apartment.
12. Should I open one or two windows?
13. You'll be in the lab this afternoon at five o'clock, won't you?
14. What can I wear to the reception?
15. We should always accept helpful advice.

3.1. Content

Like the structuralist materials we examined in the previous section, these too are exclusively concerned with modals but, in contrast with the earlier materials, only three are presented to the learner: *can, should* and *will.* In the sample we have selected, the three modals are presented, explained and practised in their positive and negative declarative forms and in their positive interrogative forms.

In contrast with the previous example, the meanings of the forms are referred to overtly in the text with the caveat that there is a 'range of meanings' which is to be further explained in a later section (Section 91 f).

The layout of the lesson follows that laid down in Rutherford's introduction:

1. *Presentation*: two sets of utterances – one positive, the other negative – presenting the forms of the three modals with all persons, singular and plural and a range of verbs both transitive and intransitive.

2. *Explication*: a frame showing a range of forms for the modals set in the syntactic context of short sentences together with the appropriate intonation contour. This is followed by a description of the form and meanings of the three modals and a comment on the phonological contrast between their stressed and unstressed forms, e.g. /ˈkæn/ – /kən/.

3. *Verification*: four exercises – restatement, association, fixed comment and reply~rejoinder – which are designed to teach the learner skill in manipulating the modals.

We shall comment on the exercises in the next section under the heading 'activities'.

3.2. Activities

According to Bowen & Stockwell in their Foreword to the book, the materials 'should challenge the attention and interest of the intermediate student who wants to bridge the gap between the manipulative activities of a beginning class and the skills necessary for meaningful and nonpredictable communication in a social situation' (Rutherford *op. cit.* viii) and they do this by 'offering interesting and insightful innovations in drill types . . . ' (*ibid.*). Rutherford too claims that his course 'develops through drill work' the ability of the student to distinguish between structures which share a common deep structure and those whose deep structures are in contrast (Rutherford *op. cit.* ix). The function of the 'verification' section is, he tells us, that it provides a means whereby the grammatical point of the unit can be ' . . . manipulated through a wide variety of oral drills . . . ' (*ibid.*).

This, however, is all the indication the teacher is given on methodology and one can only assume that it is the author's intention that the techniques so clearly described by Fries (see his instructions in section 2.2. of this appendix) should be taken over by the teacher who is using these materials.

The activities contained in the 'verification' are:

1. *Restatement*: an exercise in which the student is provided with the clue (or stimulus?) 'BE + (n't)able' which he is expected to restate (transform?) using the appropriate form of *can*, e.g.

He isn't able to swim → He can't swim.

2. *Association*: an exercise in which the learner is provided with a cue − a noun phrase − which he is expected to include in his response which takes the form of a request, e.g.

newspaper → $\begin{Bmatrix} \text{Can} \\ \text{Could} \end{Bmatrix}$ I see that newspaper please?

3. *Fixed Comment*: an exercise in which the student is given the cue 'If . . . . . . ' and responds using 'should', e.g.

If he studies, he'll pass → He should study.

4. *Reply ~ Rejoinder*; an exercise in which the learner is required to answer questions and rejoin to statements', e.g.

I'll see you again, won't I? → Yes, you will.

Where can I make a phone call? → You'll find a phone in the hall.

3.3. Theory of language

In the Foreword to the materials, Bowen and Stockwell indicate the allegiance of the author to TG 'It is based on generative-transformational theory, an exciting and significant advance in the history of linguistics' (Rutherford *op. cit.* viii) and Rutherford himself claims the 'linguistic orientation of the work is that of *generative*, or *transformational-generative* grammar . . . ' (Rutherford *op. cit.* ix original emphasis).

The influence of TG on the materials can be seen, according to the Foreword (*op. cit.* viii) in ' . . . explaining patterns and meanings on the basis of the deep structure of English . . . presenting the structural and semantic correspondence between related sentences . . . ' (*ibid*.). In short, we should expect to find indications in the content of the fundamental assumptions of TG (see Section 5.2. for an extended discussion): the notions of linguistic universals — demonstrated in the contrast between deep and surface structure — the infinite productivity of finite means and the enormous creativity of the individual language user, to list but three.

It should be recognized, in fairness, that the example we have chosen comes from the preliminary unit which is intended as a quick resumé for the student and is therefore perhaps less typical than it might be but, this said, it is difficult to see how TG is reflected in the materials any more than it is in the structuralist materials of the Michigan School. The focus of the unit is on the forms of three modals and the syntactic relationships into which they enter. There is a great deal more semantic information provided than in the earlier example but still no consistent attempt to provide the learner with a cohesive text (other later units do contain dialogues which are 'the source of all the material to be treated in the unit' (*ibid*.) or any of the 'natural social contexts' referred to in the Foreword.

In short, the content looks worryingly like that of the Ann Arbor materials and the influence of TG minimal.

3.4. Theory of learning
We are told in the Foreword (*op. cit*. viii) that the author ' . . . assumes intelligence and high motivation' and that these will be applied rather than 'mimicry' in the grasping of the rules of English (*ibid*.). The author himself outlines the major tenets of cognitive psychology as they impinge on language learning and use ' . . . a person's verbal behaviour is the result not of reinforced habit but of the "internalization" of an intricate set of abstract rules, which enable him to fashion an infinite number of novel sentences' (*ibid*.). So the commitment to cognitive psychology is plain but the processes required of teacher and learner look suspiciously behaviourist: 'This book . . . develops through *drill* work the student's ability to distinguish forms having similar surface but different underlying deep structure' (*ibid*. emphasis added) and again the point is ' . . . *manipulated* through a wide variety of oral *drills* . . . ' (*ibid*. emphasis added).

To be sure Exercises 2 and 4 seem to require of the learner some degree of 'creativity' but to what extent is this any more than what is expected in the fourth of the exercises we presented in the previous — structuralist — example? In any case, our concern at the uncertainty of the criteria for a 'correct' response in those exercises must be equally expressed here.

3.5. Summary
This example from Rutherford's *Modern English* seems fairly typical of materials which express an allegiance to TG. The allegiance is stated but there is little in the content to show that the writer really accepts the theory or can present his syllabus in a way which truly reflects it. The associated psychology — cognitive psychology — is likewise espoused but hardly

reflected in the activities which, except for minor innovations, look very much like those of the structuralist era.

It is an irresistible temptation to quote Bowen and Stockwell's Foreword here, 'Much of the work, however, that has gone under the name of applied linguistics either has only the most tenuous links with linguistic theory of any variety or has grown, in the cases where linkage does exist, from inadequate comprehension of the nature of the linkage' (*op. cit.* viii).

4. SITUATIONAL MATERIALS

In chapter 7 (section 7.4.4.), we outlined the situational method and gave one or two examples of situational materials. Here we wish to provide a more extensive sample drawn from *Situational English*: the Commonwealth 1965 revision and reissue of the 1956 *English for Newcomers to Australia*.

In order to make comparison easy between this and the two previous samples of ELT materials — structuralist and transformational — we shall present and comment on units 41 and 42 (Commonwealth office of Education 1965. Student's Book 2. 1-9).

4.1. Content

Like the structuralist and transformational materials we have just been examining, these materials are also solely concerned with the presentation and learning of modals but whereas the structuralist lesson content consisted of the forms of no less than six modals — *can, should, must, will, might, may* — the transformational materials dealt with only three — *can, should, will* — as do the two units presented here, i.e. *can, must* and *may*.

The forms of the modals are presented and taught in positive and negative declarative structures, positive questions and long and short answers, while the meanings — overtly referred to in the Teacher's Book — taught are:

can = 'to be physically capable of', e.g. *I can touch the table = I am physically capable of touching the table.*

= 'to have the skill', e.g. *I can speak English = I know how to speak English*

must = 'it is compulsory to', e.g. *You must walk on the path = It is compulsory for you to walk on the path.*

may = 'it is permitted to', e.g. *may I come in? = is it permitted for me to come in?*

Each unit is laid out in the Teacher's Book in the same way:

1. *Introductory comments:*

a) *Syllable stress*: a list of lexical items required for the unit marked with their primary stresses.

b) *Teaching kit*: suggestions for realia and audio-visual aids which may be useful in the teaching of the unit.

c) *Notes*: comments which provide the teacher with linguistic information about the content of the unit or pedagogical suggestions for the activities which will promote the learning of the content.

UNIT 41

CAN – CAN'T

He's touching his head.
He's touching the table.
He <u>CAN'T</u> touch the ceiling.

Question	Long Answer	Short Answer
Can you touch the ceiling?	– No, I can't touch the ceiling.	– No, I can't.
Can he touch the ceiling?	– No, he can't touch the ceiling.	– No, he can't.
Can you touch the moon?	– No, we can't touch the moon.	– No, we can't.
Can she put the table in her pocket?	– No, she can't put the table in her pocket.	– No, she can't.
Can a dog open the window?	– No, it can't open the window.	– No, it can't.

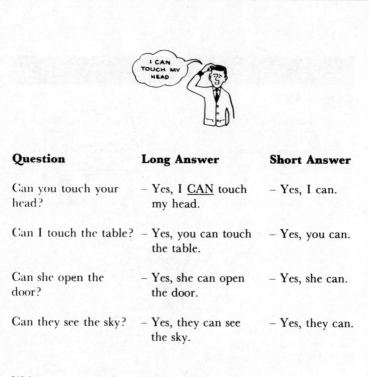

Question	**Long Answer**	**Short Answer**
Can you touch your head?	– Yes, I <u>CAN</u> touch my head.	– Yes, I can.
Can I touch the table?	– Yes, you can touch the table.	– Yes, you can.
Can she open the door?	– Yes, she can open the door.	– Yes, she can.
Can they see the sky?	– Yes, they can see the sky.	– Yes, they can.

Write.   I can't write <u>without</u> a pen.
Wash your hands. I can't wash my hands <u>without</u> water.

I You He She We They	can't	buy bread open the door paint the ceiling cut cake	without money. without a key. without a brush. without a knife.

can + not = cannot = CAN'T

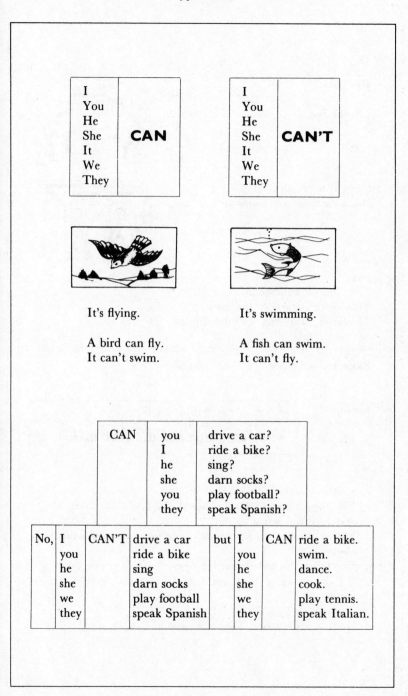

	I You He She It We They	CAN

	I You He She It We They	CAN'T

It's flying.

A bird can fly.
It can't swim.

It's swimming.

A fish can swim.
It can't fly.

CAN	you I he she you they	drive a car? ride a bike? sing? darn socks? play football? speak Spanish?

No,	I you he she we they	CAN'T	drive a car ride a bike sing darn socks play football speak Spanish	but	I you he she we they	CAN	ride a bike. swim. dance. cook. play tennis. speak Italian.

Do This:

Lift the box.

Carry it to the door.
Don't carry it to the window.

Say:
They're lifting the box.
They're carrying it to the door.
They aren't carrying it to the window.

Exercise A: Write "can" or "can't":

Example

> A dog — run but it — talk.

Answer

> *A dog can run but it can't talk.*

1. A fish — swim but it — fly.
2. I — speak Chinese but I — speak English.
3. A dog — run but it — fly.
4. You — cut meat without a knife, and you — buy bread without money.
5. I — touch the top of that big tree.
6. I — make tea without water, and I — make a cake without flour.
7. A parrot — fly but it — play tennis.
8. He — cut the string. He hasn't a knife.

Exercise B: Give short answers:

	Can you swim? (Yes)	Can they play tennis (No)
Example		
Answer	*Yes, I can.*	*No, they can't.*

1. Can she open the door without a key?   (No)
2. Can he drive a car?   (Yes)
3. Can I speak English?   (Yes, you)
4. Can you see the moon?   (Yes, we)
5. Can he ride a bike?   (No)
6. Can a fish swim?   (Yes)
7. Can a dog fly?   (No)
8. Can she play football?   (No)

Exercise C: Make questions:

Example	You can swim.
Answer	*Can you swim ?*

1. He can speak French.
2. They can lift the box.
3. She can cook.
4. He can play football.
5. You can play cards.
6. Peter can ride a horse.
7. Mary can darn socks.
8. A bird can fly.

MUST – MUSTN'T

You <u>must not</u> go out here.
= You <u>mustn't</u> go out here.

You <u>must</u> go out here.

must not = must nøt = MUSTN'T

The traffic light is red.
You <u>mustn't</u> go across the street.

The traffic light is red.
You <u>must</u> stop.

You <u>mustn't</u> drive a car on
the footpath.
You <u>mustn't</u> ride a motor-bike
on the footpath.

You <u>must</u> drive a car on the
road.
You <u>must</u> ride a motor-bike
on the road.

Left – Right

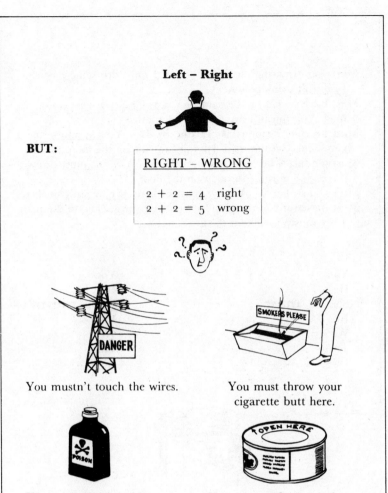

BUT:

> <u>RIGHT – WRONG</u>
>
> $2 + 2 = 4$ right
> $2 + 2 = 5$ wrong

You mustn't touch the wires.

You must throw your cigarette butt here.

You mustn't drink this.

You must open the tin here.

You mustn't walk on the grass.

You must walk on the path.

Must you drink the medicine? – Yes, <u>I must</u> drink the medicine. <u>I mustn't</u> drink poison.

Must I drive a car on the road? – Yes, <u>you must</u> drive a car on the road. <u>You mustn't</u> drive on the footpath.

Must he ride a motor-bike on the road? – Yes, <u>he must</u> ride a motor-bike on the road. <u>He mustn't</u> ride on the footpath.

Must she throw her cigarette butt there? – Yes, <u>she must</u> throw it there. <u>She mustn't</u> throw it on the floor.

Must you sit here? – Yes, <u>we must</u> sit here. <u>We mustn't</u> sit there.

Must they walk on the path? – Yes, <u>they must</u> walk on the path. <u>They mustn't</u> walk on the grass.

I You He She It We They	**must**

I You He She It We They	**mustn't**

<u>MAY I?</u>

May I May we	come in? sit down? smoke? use your telephone? close this window? go now?

Yes, certainly.

At the Doctor's

PETER: I'm ill. I have a sore throat and a temperature.

DOCTOR: You must go to bed. You mustn't go to work. I'm giving you a prescription. Here's the prescription. You must take it to the chemist's, and you must get the medicine.

PETER: May I smoke?

DOCTOR: No, you mustn't smoke, and you mustn't talk.

PETER: May I sit in the garden?

DOCTOR: No, you mustn't sit in the garden. You must go to bed.

Do This:

Here's a book.
Turn to page eight.

I'M TURNING TO PAGE EIGHT

Now look at page nine.   I'm looking at page nine.

Say:

He's turning to page eight.
He's looking at page nine.

Exercise: put in "not":

Example	You must take this hammer.
Answer	*You mustn't take this hammer.*

1. He must read the letter now.
2. They must smoke cigarettes.
3. We must open the door.
4. She must buy a car.
5. She must break the cups.
6. He must drop this parcel.
7. I must go to bed.
8. You must cut the paper.

d) *Imperative drill*: a drill which teaches – often revises – an imperative form which the teacher will need to present the new content of the unit.

2. *Patterns*: a number of sentence 'patterns' which demonstrate the syntactic characteristics of the items being taught (cf the 'structural pattern' of the 'Frame' in the typical structuralist lesson; 2.1.). Each is presented and drilled and practised in a written exercise, all of which is available in the student's materials.

The content of units 41 and 42 is laid out in exactly this way:

Unit 41: five patterns:
    a. I can't touch the ceiling.
    b. I can touch the table.
    c. He can write.
    d. Can you see the watch?   – Yes, I can.
                             – No, I can't.
    e. I can't write without a pen.

Unit 42: three patterns:
    a. You mustn't smoke in here.
    b. You must walk on the footpath.
    c. May I come in?

The teacher is not only given clear directions on how to present and practise the content (see the next section for discussion of the activities) but also information on the semantics of the modals – as we have just seen – and alerted to the need for the students to distinguish between /æ/ and /ɑ:/ i.e. between the stressed forms of *can* and *can't* as pronounced by those varieties based on southern rather than northern English.

4.2. Activities

An examination of the students' materials will show how difficult it is to deduce from them alone what activities the authors might consider appropriate for any particular item of content. This, according to the 'note for teachers' at the beginning of each students' book, is intentional, since the students' books 'are *not* intended for self-study without a teacher. Each of the three Students' Books is matched by a corresponding Teacher's Book (which) provides a general statement of the principles of the Australian Situational Method (on which the course is based) and provides ... guidance on ... the ... teaching ... of the materials ... ' (*Situational English* 1965. v. original emphasis).

In the Teacher's Book – we are referring to that which relates to Students' Book 2 but each Teacher's Book contains the same introductory remarks – the teacher is provided with an outline of a lesson plan for a one-hour lesson:

Part I (approximately 20 minutes)
    1.   Pronunciation exercise – recognition and production
       .. about 10 minutes.
    2.   Rhythm and intonation exercise . . . . . . about 5 minutes.

3. Imperative drill . . . . . . about 5 minutes.

Part II (approximately 25 minutes)

1. Revision of earlier sentence-patterns and vocabulary required for the teaching of the new sentence-pattern . . . . . . about 5 minutes.
2. Presentation and first drilling of the new sentence-pattern . . . . 5–10 minutes
3. Further drilling and consolidation of the new sentence-pattern . . . . . . 10–15 minutes

Part III (approximately 15 minutes)

Further developement of the new sentence-pattern through one or more of the following activities:

1. Reading specially prepared material in controlled English either from the blackboard or from the Students' Book.
2. Recall exercises from reading material on the blackboard.
3. 'Seen' dictation, from material previously treated on the blackboard for reading or recall . . . .
4. Oral or written answers to comprehension questions.
5. Written exercises . . . .
6. Oral or written self-expression exercises . . . .
7. Language games (based on) the new . . . pattern.
8. Songs . . . .
9. Work on the cultural background of the English-speaking peoples, and their environment.
10. Stories told by the teacher, using the range of language the students have learnt.

In this particular case, the authors divide the unit into presentation and drilling.

a) *Presentation*: use students to demonstrate ability by commanding one to carry out certain actions, e.g. *Touch your head*, and, as he does so, to provide a commentary on what he is doing, e.g. *I'm touching my head* — and getting the class also to comment, e.g. *He's touching his head.*

Next the student is ordered to do the impossible, e.g. *Touch the ceiling* — and when he fails he is told *You can't touch the ceiling* and he responds *I can't touch the ceiling* and the class comments (like a Greek chorus) *He can't touch the ceiling.*

Finally, the teacher makes utterly impossible demands *Touch the sky, Put the table in your pocket*, etc. to elicit appropriate responses — and stages situations in the classroom which further make the point of ability versus inability, e.g. *I can't see my hand / the class*, etc.

b) *Drilling*: using the patterns:

He can't touch the box
They can't see the pen

The teacher uses 'pronoun gestures' and 'call words' (cf. the substitution practice in 2.2.4.).

The work on the rest of the patterns proceeds in essentially the same way.

4.3. Theory of language
In Chapter 7 (7.4.1. and 7.4.2.), we discussed the view of language and the description of language held by those who evolved the situational method for ELT. We made the point then, that these teachers and curriculum designers were, in so far as they had any clearly formulated theory of language, committed to a structuralist view of language as form and structure; essentially the theory espoused by structuralist linguists whose ELT materials we have already examined.

The Teachers' Books of the *Situational English* series claim to provide 'a general statement of the principles of the . . . Method . . . ' and to provide the teacher with such guidance as 'a treatment of teaching techniques; guidance on lesson planning; a graded section on the teaching of English pronunciation; and detailed suggestions for aural/oral teaching and practice of the material . . . ' (*Situational English* Part 2; students' book *ibid.*). This being so, it should prove possible to quote overt acceptance or covert allegiance to a particular theory of language.

Unfortunately, there is actually no overt statement but it is a far from difficult task to recognize the structuralist theory of language which underlies the materials. The Teachers' Book tells us that an ELT course must concentrate on 'three fundamental features of the English language' (*op. cit.* 1f); pronunciation features, grammatical features and vocabulary. The teacher's attention is drawn to the *sentence-pattern* and to the ability of the descriptive linguist or learner to *substitute* 'appropriate . . . words or phrases at certain points in the pattern' (*op. cit.* 2.). Very much a structuralist view of language. The acceptance of this position comes out even more clearly in the authors' statement of principles: 'the syllabus followed by *Situational English* is a syllabus of *grammatical points*, i.e. of items which function in *sentence* structure' (*op. cit.* 3). The selection of content, then, is based on the sentence as a unit and the ability of the syllabus designer to discern items which can − 'slot-and-filler' style − substitute within sentence 'patterns'. Discussions of grading also reveal a structuralist orientation, 'simple functional items are introduced early in the course in simple sentence-patterns and more complex . . . items and more complex sentence-patterns in which they appear are left until later in the course' (*ibid.*).

So far, it would appear that these materials are in no way an advance on the structuralist materials of the mid-1950s and, in many ways, such a judgement is far from harsh. But one innovation in content stands out: the introduction of 'social formulas' into the syllabus long before their 'proper' place in terms of formal grading because they 'are needed early . . . because they are socially useful' (*ibid.*).

However, to be just, the theory of language accepted by the writers of these materials is structuralist but a curiously tempered structuralism which through the pervading influence of European linguistics − in particular Palmer whose contribution to applied linguistics we outlined in Chapter 4 − retained the feeling that language was more than mere structure, i.e. that 'usefulness' was an essential criterion for content selection even if it clashed with formal criteria of simplicity of structure.

We shall see in the next section that very much the same feelings about behaviourism — diluted by a sense of individual and social influence — pervades the theory of learning accepted by the creators of those materials.

4.4. Theory of learning

We argued in Chapter 7 (particularly in sections 7.4.1.-7.4.5.), that the situational method by accepting the prevailing wisdom of the day in both linguistics and psychology — structuralism and behaviourism — defined itself not as a new approach but merely as a methodological variant of structuralist applied linguistics.

Just as the content of the sample we have been discussing reflects very clearly the structuralist preoccupation with the sentence and with its formal characteristics so the activities reflect behaviourist psychology; presentation of new material orally rather than in writing, 'new material is heard and spoken by students *before* they read it and write it' (*Situational English op. cit.* 7), drills which aim at giving the learner the ability 'to say each sentence, as the situation demands, without hesitation and with acceptable speed, sentence rhythm and intonation' (*Situational English op. cit.* 10) etc.

However, it would be unjust to leave this discussion here having given the impression that the situational method is nothing more than a trivial variant of the older structuralist methodology. There is more to it than that. Even though the syllabus is formal — the object of the course is to teach *sentences* — there is a serious attempt not only to present and practise the formal items by simulating 'real language in use' but also to tie the formal items to tangible realia so that their meanings can be deduced by the learner. The authors argued that an unfamiliar 'situation would prevent students from learning the meaning of the sentence-pattern' (*op. cit.* 7) and that the teacher was obliged to 'create situations which will be meaningful for the students' oral practice of the new sentence-pattern' (*op. cit.* 24).

Finally, the rather obvious point might be made that the situational method contains within it a substantial range of exercise types. A comparison of the list in Section 4.2. of this appendix with the tiny number of activities proposed by the creators of the structuralist and transformational materials makes this clear.

4.5. Summary

Although the authors of *Situational English* make no overt claim to follow any particular school of linguistics or psychology, it is clear that their *essential* allegiance was to structuralism and behaviourism.

Nevertheless, there are features in these materials which mark them off from those of the Ann Arbor English Language Institute (which we examined in Section 2 of this appendix) and show the influence of European — particularly British — language teaching, e.g. the attempt at contextualization, the aural-oral technique, the concern that the student should be involved in deducing relationships between sentences and between sentences and their 'context of situation' (the term, which is used several times in the teachers' books, clearly ties the writers to the linguistics of Firth and the applied linguistics of Palmer in particular: see 6.2.1. and 4.3. respectively) and, finally, the enormous range of classroom activities which are suggested.

5. NOTIONAL MATERIALS

We discussed notional materials in Chapter 7 (in section 7.5.) and provide a very brief example of them there. In this section, we shall provide a more extended illustration of notional teaching materials by taking de Freitas' sections on obligation and permission – expressed by *must, have (got) to, should, ought to, had better* in the case of the first notion and *may, can, could*, etc. in the second – in his *Survival English* (de Freitas 1978. 61f and 65 f.).

5.1. Content

Part of the content of this sample is identical to that of the three examples we have just been discussing, i.e. modal verbs. But, since the whole orientation of the notional syllabus is towards the presentation of linguistic forms as exponents of meanings rather than as forms in their own right, not all modals are represented here and some forms which are not modals but, and here is the crucial point, share the same or closely related meanings, are included. The focus is meaning. The forms are, in a sense, secondary.

The two sections cover between them the two notions of obligation and permission:

Obligation subdivided into:

    a) *Obligation*: expressed by *must* and *have (got) to.*

    b) *Moral duty*: expressed by *should, ought to* and *had better.*

Permission subdivided in terms of formality into:

    a) *Formal*: expressed by *could I (possibly)?*

    b) *Informal*: expressed by *can I? may I?* subdivided by degree of tentativeness into:

    c) *Tentative*: expressed by *is it all right if I . . . ?* and *is it all right (for me) to . . . ?*

    and either formal or informal:

    d) *Unmarked*: expressed by *do you mind if I . . . ? I wonder if I could . . . ?* and *do you think I could . . .?*

In contrast with the structuralist materials (see Section 2 of this appendix) and the situational materials we have just looked at (see Section 4) where the learner was expected to deduce the meanings of the formal items himself but in common with the transformational materials we examined (in Section 3), these materials give the learner the meanings of each form; indeed, the meanings are so central to the sequencing of items in each section

Obligation *

* See also page 59 on *Necessity*.

What do you say when you feel you have an obligation or a duty to do or not to do something? You may also wish to remind or ask others about their obligations or duties, or to release them from these. Here are some of the things you might say.

MUST I FILL IN THE WHOLE FORM?

NO, YOU NEEDN'T.

A

Must I	fill in the whole form? fill it in now? provide a photograph? write in ink/type it? sign my name? put it in an envelope? post it?	*obligation*
Do I have to		
Have I got to		

B

Yes, you must./No, you needn't.
Yes, you do./No, you don't.
Yes, you have (to)./No, you haven't.
Yes./No.

A (I think) . . .

I should **I ought to**	call the doctor. I don't feel well. call the Police. There's been an accident. write to my parents. I haven't written for ages. return this book to the library. It's overdue. go to bed. It's late.	*moral duty*

B

Yes, (I think) you should/you ought to/(you'd better).

No, I don't think you should/you ought to/(you'd better).
No, you shouldn't/you oughtn't/(you'd better not).

you can't get out of it *

1 **What would you say, using the expressions in Sections A and B, if you hadn't:**
1 paid your rent
2 been to visit a friend in hospital
3 written to your parents
4 done your homework
5 said your prayers
6 paid your income tax

2 Peter has failed his exams. His father is telling him what he must do.

A Well Peter, you'll *have to* do better than that next time, won't you?
B *Have* I really *got to* do those exams again, Dad?
A Of course you *have*. You *must* try harder this time.
B And *must* I go back to school?
A No. You *needn't* do that. *You'd better* get a part-time job somewhere and go to evening classes.
B But Dad, I *should* be working full time at my age. I'm nearly seventeen.
A You *ought to* have worked harder, then you wouldn't have failed your exams. You'll *have to* take a job and study.
B What else *have I got to* do? Join the Army?
A Who knows? That might *have to* come later.

*(You can't get out of it is an expression meaning 'you've got to do it'.)

3 Talk to someone freely about the things you feel you **should/ought to** do (for example: take more exercise, be nicer to people, etc.) and the things you **have got to** do (pay bills, etc.). When you have finished talking **write down** in dialogue form the conversation you have had.

Permission

Here are some ways of asking
permission and of granting and
refusing it.

MAY I OPEN
THE WINDOW?

YES, OF
COURSE.

A May I . . . . . ?
     Can I . . . . . ?   *informal*

     Could I . . . . . ?
     Could I possibly . . . . . ?   *more polite*

     D'you mind if I . . . . . ?   *speaker intends to do*
                                    what he has asked

     Would you mind if I . . . . . ? (+Past Tense)

     Is it all right if I . . . . . ?   *formal and*
     Is it all right (for me) to . . . . . ?   *tentative*   *informal*
     I wonder if I could . . . . . ?
     D'you think I could . . . . . ?
       open/close the window
       ask you a question
       borrow your pen/umbrella (etc.)
       use the phone
       switch on/off the TV
       go now
       leave early
       just say a word
       look at your books

B (Yes) of course/certainly.
    (No,) I'm afraid not.
    No, I'm sorry, you can't.
    (No,) I'd rather you didn't.
    No, of course not.
    Yes, I do mind.
    No, that's all right.
    Yes, I would (mind).
    No, it isn't all right.
    No, I'm afraid not.
    If/As you wish/like.   *reluctant permission*

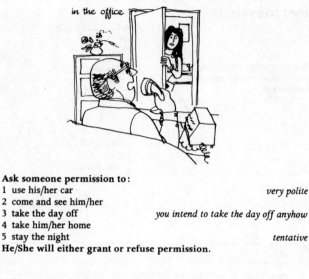

in the office

1 **Ask someone permission to:**
1 use his/her car   *very polite*
2 come and see him/her
3 take the day off   *you intend to take the day off anyhow*
4 take him/her home
5 stay the night   *tentative*
He/She will either grant or refuse permission.

2 Lucy Redington works as a secretary in a large London firm. Her boss is John Sutcliffe.

L R *May* I come in Mr Sutcliffe? (*Can/Could*)
J S I'd rather you didn't Miss Redington. I'm very busy just now.
L R *Can* I try later, then? (*Could/Could I possibly*)
J S Yes, of course.
  (an hour later)
L R *Is it all right for me to* come in now Mr Sutcliffe? (*Is it all right to/ Is it all right if I*)
J S Well . . . Mmm . . . I'm still pretty busy, but . . . all right, come in. What can I do for you?
L R *D'you mind if* I sit down? (*May/Would you mind if* (+*Past Tense*))
J S Not at all. Take a seat. Now, what can I do for you?
L R I want to leave the department. *D'you think I could* put in for a transfer? (*I wonder if I could/Could I possibly*)
J S Yes, but why should you want to do that?
L R *D'you mind if* I speak frankly? (*You don't mind if I . . . do you/ Would you mind if* (+*Past Tense*))
J S Not at all. Go ahead.
L R Well, you see; I don't like the office, I don't like the staff, and I'm afraid you and I don't get on. So, may I put in for a transfer?
J S Yes, I'd be delighted if you did.

3 **Ask permission** to do things. Someone will either **grant** or **refuse** you **permission.** When you have finished talking **write down** in dialogue form the conversation you have had.

that shared meaning rather than similarity of form is the criterion for inclusion at any particular point.

In the introduction, the author outlines the layout of each section:

Presentation and Practice:

A *Questions*   e.g. *may I . . . ? must I . . . ?*

B *Answers*   e.g. *(Yes) of course/certainly*

Exercises:

1. *Further practice* e.g. 'ask someone's permission to: (1) use his/her car (2) come and see him/her', etc.

2. *Dialogue*: a short dialogue — 12 lines or so — containing the appropriate forms and introduced by a brief statement of the setting in which the dialogue took place.

3. *Free practice* e.g. 'talk to someone freely about the things you feel you should/ought to do'.

The content of the two sections we have just reproduced follows this predetermined layout.

5.2. Activities

Unlike the three previous sets of materials, these are, we are told, 'not a course book' but 'a handbook for practice' which can 'be used in the classroom or by the student on his own for further study or reference' (de Freitas *op. cit.* v). Even so, the author does provide the teacher with 'detailed suggestions for classroom procedure' (*ibid*.) which he illustrates by referring to Unit 1 (merely, it should be noted, the first notion in alphabetical order; the units are not graded) on accusal and defence.

TO THE TEACHER

Each unit consists of a presentation and practice section followed by three exercises:

1 Further practice
2 Dialogue
3 Free practice

A unit takes about an hour to complete in the classroom. The use of a tape recorder is recommended wherever possible. For the presentation of these units, let us take as an example Unit 1: *Accusal and defence*.

Presentation and practice

(a) Ensure that the students know the vocabulary that features in the accusal section (Section A).

(b) Introduce the topic. Accuse students of things you know they haven't done (e.g. being late; not doing homework; missing class, etc.). Allow them to defend themselves as best they can. They may simply deny the accusations ineffectually, smile, or just look puzzled. Reassure them that what they have said is possible, but that they need to learn to defend themselves more effectively, in different ways and situations. Stimulate motivation by explaining that they must learn to stand their own ground without sounding unnecessarily rude, etc.

(c) Oral presentation and practice: The students respond either chorally, in groups, or individually.

TEACHER   You left the lights on.
CLASS   You left the lights on.
TEACHER   I don't think I did. (*polite*)
CLASS   I don't think I did.
TEACHER   Of course I didn't. (*assertive*)
CLASS   Of course I didn't.

Continue in the same way through the list of expressions denoting defence (Section B). The class should imitate as closely as possible the tone of voice used by the teacher (or tape) to indicate the particular mood. Meaning and mood can be conveyed by the teacher with the aid of gesture and facial expression. It is imperative that the learner should:

1   understand what he is saying
2   appreciate the link between tone and meaning
3   acquire the appropriate intonation

(The use of the recording is an obvious advantage for classwork and essential for the student working on his own.)

(d) Practice in pairs: The learners are now prepared to practise on their own, role-playing in pairs. The teacher monitors the class discreetly, interfering as little as possible. Only when there are genuine difficulties or gross mispronunciations should the teacher correct. The learners are free to practise in as relaxed and natural a fashion as possible. At this stage they begin to feel that they are conducting a normal dialogue and not merely going through a drill. Learners wishing to use variations or alternatives to those on the printed page are encouraged to do so.

Exercise 1: Further practice

This section is an extension of the Presentation and practice section. The students practise in pairs, or in groups, changing partners and roles. The teacher continues to guide them but only when necessary. This exercise is intended to take the learner one step closer to 'free' communication, so the less interference from the teacher the better.

Exercise 2: Dialogue

The language that the learners have been practising in varied contexts is now placed in a situation. The main object of this is to introduce variety into the learning process and also to relate the language to a realistic incident. It should not be thought that the situation is any more than one of innumerable settings that could be used to contextualize the language. The learner will understand that he might have to 'defend' himself in all sorts of unforseeable situations and that linguistic adjustments might be necessary.

To present the dialogue:
1 Teach new vocabulary, if any, in suitable contexts (e.g. fares; Oxford Circus.
2 Promote interest in topic: (e.g. D'you travel by bus? D'you like it? Are the fares high? Have you ever been given the wrong change? etc). Use visuals and other aids if necessary.
3 In the absence of the tape, role-play the dialogue – the students listening. Play it again, in short utterances – the students repeating in chorus or individually.
4 Explain the importance of intonation. If necessary, exaggerate these features for more effective mimicry.
5 The students are now ready to work in pairs, changing partners and roles whenever they wish, with the options in italics. In some dialogues no options are given. In others there are gaps for the students to fill in as they wish.

Exercise 3: Free practice
The 'freer' the practice in this last section the better. Learners should be encouraged to converse uninterruptedly, with little or no interference from the teacher.

The written dialogues are versions of their own conversations. These can be corrected at home by the teacher and returned to the learners for possible renderings in class later.

5.3. Theory of language
Although de Freitas makes no statement of allegiance to any particular linguistic theory, it is clear from his comments in the introduction to the materials and from the layout of the individual units that he is committed to a notional approach to language teaching. He tells us that the aims of the book are:
1. To focus the learner's attention on the spoken language.
2. To provide him with a handbook of important notional categories and their use.
3. To help him 'survive' wherever current English is required.

Later in the introduction he gives examples of students failing to express notions adequately – apology, cause, gratitide – and thus providing the motivation first for a series of 'speech workshops' and, ultimately, the collecting of materials worked up during them in the form of the book.

Since we have already discussed the theory of language which underlies notional syllabuses (in 7.5.) we shall not repeat what is said there but draw this discussion to a close with the statement that the content of these materials amply demonstrates an acceptance of the notional approach to language teaching and, hence, an acceptance of the theory of language which underlies it.

5.4. Theory of Learning

Although there is no clearly stated acceptance of any particular theory of learning, it is clear from the activities suggested by the author – particularly the extent to which he encourages pair work and role-play – that he does not see learning in stimulus-response terms. A cognitive orientation certainly comes through, e.g. 'The teacher monitors the class discreetly, interfering as little as possible. Only when there are genuine difficulties or gross mis-pronunciations should the teacher correct. The learners are free to practise in as relaxed and natural a fashion as possible . . . The teacher continues to guide them but only when necessary . . . the less interference from the teacher the better' (*op. cit.* vi).

The use of drills such as that reproduced in section 5.2. – pure 'mim-mem' – is reminiscent of behaviourism and the Michigan materials but, it should be recognized, these materials move on from drills almost immediately and into pair practice.

In short, the theory of learning implied by the materials appears to be essentially cognitive but with minor elements of earlier behaviourism showing through.

5.5 Summary

Survival English appears to be a clear example of a set of notional materials. The content is plainly notional – common meanings rather than common syntactic rules form the basis of selection – and the activities, for the most part, what one would expect: a reflection in part of the structuralist-behaviourist 'mim-mem' drill technique, in part of the aural-oral techniques pioneered by British and European language teachers in the decade before and after the Second World War (notably by Palmer) and techniques which demonstrate a sympathy with the reorientation of teaching towards the learner (most strikingly popularized by Curran and by Gattegno; see discussion in Chapter 3 Section 3.6.1.).

6. CONCLUSION

The four samples we have been discussing demonstrate a progression or change in emphasis over the quarter of a century beginning with the structuralist materials which were, as we saw, typified by their formal content, a content from which meaning and context (in the sociolinguistic sense of the term) were excluded, moving on through equally formal transformational and situational materials to our final example, the notional materials we have just looked at, in which the content – formal items acting as exponents it is true – was, by contrast, semantic rather than syntactic.

The four samples also demonstrate a shift of approach both in the change in theory of language – structuralist in the first and third, transformational in the second and functional in the fourth – and in the theory of learning espoused by the authors: plainly behaviourist in the first case, modified behaviourist in the second and third and eclectic, with leanings towards a cognitive theory of learning, in the last.

What is really striking is that the major change over the years spanned by these examples has been in the area of syllabus *content*; a change which has reflected clearly and relatively consistently the changes in linguistic theory over the same period (though, as in all applications of theoretical work, with a time-lag). Conversely, the *activities* promoted to help in the learning of the content have changed but little. We see to-day a greater feeling of freedom to experiment and to give the learner himself more control over the classroom activities and even over the design of the course itself but what has been lost since the days of the structuralists is the certainty that there is a one-to-one relationship between a particular linguistic theory and a particular theory of learning. It seems that we are now much more comfortable about the content of the syllabus — *what* we are to teach — but still floundering about seeking satisfying activities for *how* we are to teach.

To bring this book to a close, we might put our present situation in terms of the two key questions we asked right at the beginning. We now feel that we know what language is but we are still uncertain about the way we believe people learn languages and therefore we are also very unsure that we know how to help them learn.

Bibliography

Abercrombie, D. (1967) *Elements of General Phonetics* Edinburgh. Edinburgh University Press.

Alexander, L. G. (1978) *New Concept English* London. Longman.

Allen, E. D. & Valette, R. M. (1972) *Classroom Techniques: Foreign Languages and English as a Second Language.* Harcourt, Brace Jovanovich. New York 1972, 1977.

Allen, J. P. B. & Van Buren, P. (1971) *Chomsky: Selected Readings* Oxford University Press. London.

Allen, J. P. B. & Corder, S. P. eds. (1974) *The Edinburgh Course in Applied Linguistics*: vol. 3 *Techniques in Applied Linguistics* London. O.U.P.

Allen, J. P. B. & Davies, A. eds. (1977) *The Edinburgh Course in Applied Linguistics* vol. 4 *Testing and Experimental Methods* London. O.U.P.

Alyeshmerni, M. & Taubr, P. (1970) *Working with Aspects of Language* New York. Harcourt Brace.

Austin, J. L. (1962) *How to do things with words* Oxford, Oxford University Press.

Bach, E. & Harms R. eds. (1968) *Universals in Linguistic Theory* New York. Holt Rinehart.

Banathy, B. H. & Dale, L. L. (1972) *A Design for Foreign Language Curriculum* Lexington, Heath & Co.

Barthes, R. (1966) 'Introduction à l'Analyse Structural des Récits' in *Communications* vol. 8

Bates, M. & Dudley-Evans, A. (1977) *Nucleus: General Science* London. Longman.

Bell, R. T. (1973) 'The English of an Indian Immigrant: an Essay in Error Analysis' in *ITL* 22, 1973.

Bell, R. T. (1974) 'Error Analysis; a recent pseudo-procedure in Applied Linguistics'. Paper delivered at Colloquium on Cognitive Theories of Language Learning Louvain 1974 published in *ITL* special issue 23–24.

Bell, R. T. (1976) *Sociolinguistics: Goals, Approaches and Problems.* London. Batsford.

Bell, R. T. (1979a) 'Teaching Communication Skills: the Grammarian's Funeral?' in *Management Development* no. 24. Singapore. CSI & MSD.

Bell, R. T. (1979b) 'Teaching Communication Skills: some alternative approaches' in *RELC Journal* vol. 10 no. 20 Singapore.

Bell, R. T. (1979c) *The European Community: a Language Planning Simulation.* Singapore. Available from author.

Bell, R. T. (1980a) *Write it Right: a Reference Grammar for Written English.* Singapore. Eastern Universities Press.

Bell, R. T. (1980b) 'Notional Syllabuses: to grade or not to grade' in Richards, D. A. ed. 1980.

Bell, R. T. (1980c) 'Investigating Language-Training Needs in the Civil Service'. in *Management Development* no. 29. Singapore.

Berne, E. (1964) *Games People Play* New York. Grove Press.

Berry, M. (1977) *Introduction to Systemic Linguistics* London. Batsford.

Bhatnagar, R. P. & Bell, R. T. (1979) *Communication in English*. New Delhi. Orient Longman.

Bjorneberg, B. (1974) *A Follow-up study in Teaching Foreign Language Grammar.* Dept. of Educ. Res. Gothenburg.

Boydell, T. H. (1970) *A Guide to Job Analysis*. London. Bacie.

Bolinger, D. (1968) *Aspects of Language*. New York. Harcourt Brace.

Brethower, K. S. & Rummler, G. A. (1979) 'Evaluating Training' in *Indian Journal of Training & Development*. May 1979.

Bright, J. A. & McGregor, G. P. (1970) *Teaching English as a Second Language* London. Longman.

Brooks, N. H. (1960) *Language and Language Learning: Theory and Practice.* New York. Harcourt Brace & World.

Broughton, G. (1978) *Success with English*. Penguin. Harmondsworth.

Brown, G. (1977) *Listening to Spoken English*. London. Longman.

Byrne, D. (1976) *Teaching Oral English* London. Longman.

Candlin, C. N. et al (1978) 'Study Skills in English: Theoretical Issues and Practical Problems' in Mackay & Mountford eds. 1978.

Candlin, C. N. & Breen, M. P. (1979) 'Evaluating & Designing Language Teaching Materials' in *Practical Papers in English Language Education* vol. 2 Lancaster.

Chatman, S. (1969) 'Analysing Narrative Structure' in *Language & Style* vol. 2.

Chomsky, N. (1957) *Syntactic Structures* The Hague. Mouton.

Chomsky, N. (1959) 'A review of B. F. Skinner's *Verbal Behavior*' in *Language* 35.1.

Chomsky, N. (1965) *Aspects of the Theory of Syntax* Cambridge. Mass. MIT.

Chomsky, N. (1968) *Language & Mind* New York. Harcourt Brace Jovanovich. enlarged edition 1972.

Chomsky, N. (1969) 'Implications for Language Teaching' in Allen & Van Buren eds. 1969.

Christophersen, P. L. (1973) *Second Language Learning.* Harmondsworth, Penguin.

Cicourel, A. V. (1973) *Cognitive Sociology: Language and Meaning in Social Interaction* Harmondsworth. Penguin.

Commonwealth Office of Education (1965) *Situational English* revised edition of *English for Newcomers to Australia* 1956. London. Longman.

Corder, S. P. (1967) 'The Significance of Learners' Errors in *IRAL* vol. 4 1967. repr. in Richards, J. ed. 1974.

Corder, S. P. (1971) 'Idiosyncratic Dialects and Error Analysis in *IRAL vol.* 9. 1971. repr. in Richards, J. ed. 1974.

Corder, S. P. (1973) *Introducing Applied Linguistics* Harmondsworth. Penguin.

Council of Europe (1979) *A European unit/credit system for modern language learning by adults*. Strasbourg. Council of Europe.

Crewe, W. ed. (1977) *The English Language in Singapore*. Singapore. Eastern Universities Press.

Crystal, D. (1968) *What is Linguistics?* London. Edward Arnold.

Crystal, D. & Davy, D. (1969) *Investigating English Style*. London. Longman.

Curran, C. A. (1972) *Counseling-Learning: a Whole Person Model for Education* New York. Grune & Stratton.

Curran, C. A. (1976) *Counseling-Learning in Second Languages* Apple River. Apple River Press.

Davies, I. K. (1976) *Objectives in Curriculum Design* London. McGraw-Hill.

Derrick, J. et al (1968) *Scope: an introductory course for Immigrant Children*. London. Schools Council.

Diller, K. C. (1978) *The Language Teaching Controversy*. Rowley Mass. Newbury House.

Dulay, H. C. & Burt, M. K. (1974) 'You can't learn without goofing: An analysis of children's second language "errors"'. In Richards, J. ed. 1974.

Eckersley, C. E. (1963) *Essential English*. London. Longman.

van Ek, J. A. (1975) *Systems development in adult language learning: the Threshold Level*. Strasbourg. Council of Europe.

von Elek, T. & Oskarsson, M. (1975) *Comparative Method Experiments in Foreign Language Teaching*. Dep. Ed. Res. Gothenburg.

Fillmore, C. J. (1968) "The Case for Case" in Bach & Harms eds. 1968.

Firth, J. R. (1964) *Papers in Linguistics 1934–1951* London. Oxford Univ. Press.

Fishman, J. et al eds. (1968) *Language Problems of Developing Nations*. New York. Wiley.

Floyd, A. (1976) *Cognitive Styles* Part of *Educational Studies: Personality and Learning*. Block 5. (Course E201). Milton Keynes. Open University Press.

Frake, C. O. (1969) 'Notes on Queries in Ethnography' in Tyler (1969) 123–136.

de Freitas, J. F. (1978) *Survival English* London. Macmillan.

Fries, C. C. (1940) *American-English Grammar* New York. Appleton-Century.

Fries, C. C. (1952) *The Structure of English* Harcourt Brace. New York.

Fries, C. C. & Lado, R. (1943) *English Pattern Practice: establishing the patterns as habits*. Ann Arbor. Univ. Michigan Press.

Fries, C. C. (1947) *Teaching and Learning English as a Foreign Language*. Ann Arbor. Univ. of Michigan.

Fries, C. C. & Lado, R. (1954) *English Pronunciation: exercises in sound segments, intonation and rhythm*. Ann Arbor. Univ. Michigan Press.

Fries, C. C. & Lado, R. (1958) *English Sentence Patterns*. Ann Arbor. Univ. Michigan Press.

Fries, C. C. & Lado, R. (1964) *Vocabulary in Context* Ann Arbor. Univ. Michigan Press.

Gattegno, C. (1963) *Teaching Foreign Languages in Schools: the Silent Way*. New York. Educational Solutions Inc.

Getzels, J. W. & Thelen, H. A. (1972) 'A Conceptual Framework for the Study of the Classroom Group as a Social System' in Morrison & McIntyre eds. 1972.

Green, J. A. (1963) *Teacher-made Tests* New York. Harper Row.

Greenberg, J. H. (1957) *Essays in Linguistics* Chicago. Phoenix Books.

Greene, J. (1975) *Thinking and Language* London. Methuen.

Gregory, M. (1967) 'Aspects of varieties differentiation' in *Journal of Linguistics* vol. 3.

de Grève, M. et al eds (1973) *Modern Language Teaching to Adults:* Language for *Special Purposes.* Brussels AIMAV & Paris Didier.

Hajjaj, A. et al (1976) *English Syllabus for Secondary Schools.* Kuwait. Ministry of Education.

Halliday, M. A. K. (1973) *Explorations in the Functions of Language.* London. Edward Arnold.

Halliday, M. A. K. & Hasan, R. (1976) *Cohesion in English.* London. Lonman.

Harris, D. (1969) *Testing English as a Second Language.* New York. McGraw-Hill.

Harris, Z. S. (1952) 'Discourse Analysis: A Sample Text'. in *Language* vol. 28.

Hasan, R. (1968) *Grammatical cohesion in spoken and written English.* London. Longman.

Haycraft, J. (1978) *An Introduction to English Language Teaching.* London. Longman.

Heaton, J. B. (1975) *Writing English Language Tests.* London. Longman.

Herbert, A. J. *The Structure of Technical English.* London. Longman.

Hill, A. A. (1958) *Introduction to Linguistic Structures.* New York. Harcourt Brace & World.

Howatt, A. P. H. & Treacher, P. (1969) *Edinburgh English Course* Edinburgh. Edinburgh Univ. Press.

Howatt, A. (1974) 'Programmed Instruction' paper 8 of Allen & Corder eds 1974.

Hörmann, H. (1971) *Psycholinguistics: An Introduction to Research and Theory* Berlin. Springer.

Hymes, D. (1972) 'On Communicative Competence' in Pride & Holmes eds (1972).

Jackson, S. (1968) *A Teacher's Guide to Tests and Testing* London. Longman.

Jakobson, R. (1960) 'Closing statement: Linguistics or Poetics' in Sebeok ed 1960.

Jerrom, M. F. & Szkutnik, L. L. (1965) *Conversation exercises in everyday English* London. Longman.

Jespersen, O. (1904) *How to teach a foreign language* London. George Allen & Unwin.

Jespersen, O. (1966) *Essentials of English Grammar.* 1st published 1933. London. Allen & Unwin.

Joos, M. (1969) *The Five Clocks.* New York. Harcourt Brace.

Kirkham, S. (1835) *English Grammar* Rochester. New York.

Krohn, R. (1971) *English Sentence Structure* Ann Arbor. Univ. of Michigan Press.

Kuo, E. (1976) *A Sociolinguistic Profile of Singapore.* Singapore. Chopmen Enterprises.

Kurath, H. (1939) *Handbook of the Linguistic Geography of New England.* Providence Rhode Island. Brown Univ.

Labov, W. (1966) *The Social Stratification of English in New York City.* Washington. Center for Applied Linguistics.

Lado, R. (1957) *Linguistics across Cultures: Applied Linguistics for Language Teachers.* Ann Arbor. Univ. of Michigan.

Lado, R. (1961) *Language Testing: the Construction and Use of Foreign Language Tests.* London. Longman.

Leech, G. N. & Svartvik, J. (1975) *A Communicative Grammar of English.* London. Longman.

Lyons, J. (1970) *Chomsky* London. Fontana.

Mackay, R. & Mountford, A. J. eds. (1978) *English for Special Purposes: a Case Study Approach.* London. Longman.

Mackey, W. (1965) *Language Teaching Analysis.* London. Longman.

Marton, W. (1974) 'Syllabus Design and the Cognitive Approach to Foreign-Language Learning' in *ITL* vol. 25/26.

Mercer, N. & Edwards, D. (1979) *Communication and Context* Part of Language & Development (PE 232) Block 4. Milton Keynes. Open Univ. Press.

Miller, G. A. (1964) 'The Psycholinguists' Appendix to Osgood & Sebeok 1965.

Miller, G. A. (1967) *The Psychology of Communication* Harmondsworth. Penguin.

Ministry of Education (1967) *The Study of English in India* New Delhi. Government of India.

Morrison, A. & McIntyre, D. eds. (1972) *The Social Psychology of Teaching* Harmondsworth. Penguin.

Munby, J. (1978) *Communicative Syllabus Design* London. Cambridge Univ. Press.

Nemser, W. (1971) 'Approximative Systems of Foreign Language Learners' in *IRAL* 9 1971. repr. in Richards, J. ed. 1974.

Nesfield, J. C. (1898) *English Grammar Past and Present* Macmillan. London revised edn. 1924.

Oller, J. W. Jr. (1979) *Language Tests at School* London. Longman.

Osgood, C. E. & Sebeok, T. A. eds. (1965) *Psycholinguistics.* Bloomington. Indiana Univ. Press.

Oskarsson, M. (1977) *Approaches to self-assessment in foreign language learning* Strasbourg. Council of Europe.

Palmer, H. E. (1964) *The principles of language study.* Oxford. Oxford Univ. Press. 1st publ. 1921.

Palmer, H. E. (1940) *The Teaching of Oral English.* Longmans. London. 1940.

Palmer, H. E. (1965) *Curso Internacional de Ingles* Oxford U. P. Oxford 1965.

Perren, G. ed. (1971) *Science and Technology in a Second Language* London. CILT.

Piaget, J. (1971) *Structuralism* London. Routledge & Kegan Paul. trans. of *Le Structuralisme* Paris P.U.P. 1968.

Prator, C. H. (1968) 'The British Heresy in TESL' in Fishman, Ferguson & Das Gupta eds. (1968)

Pride, J. B. & Holmes, J. eds. (1972) *Sociolinguistics: selected readings* Harmondsworth. Penguin.

Quirk, R. et al (1972) *Grammar of Contemporary English.* London. Longman.

Richards, D. A. ed. (1981) *Advances in National Syllabus Design* Singapore. RELC.

Richards, J. C. ed. (1974) *Error Analysis: Perspectives on Second Language Acquisition* London. Longman.

Richards, J. C. & Tay, M. (1977) 'The *la* particle in Singapore English' in CREWE ed (1977).

Richards, J. C. (1980) 'Error Analysis' in *Annual Review of Applied Linguistics* Newbury House.

Richterich, R. (1973) 'Modèle pour la définition des besoins langagiers des adultes apprenant une langue vivante' in de Grève et al eds. 1973.

Roberts, P. (1962) *Corso d'inglese parlato* New York. Harcourt Brace.

Robinson, W. R. (1972) *Language and Social Behaviour* Harmondsworth. Penguin.

Roulet, E. (1972) *Linguistic Theory, Linguistic Description and Language Teaching* London. Longman.

Rutherford, W. E, (1965) *Modern English: a textbook for foreign students.* New York. Harcourt Brace.

de Saussure, F. (1915) *Cours de linguistique générale.* Paris. Payot.

Searle, J. (1969) *Speech Acts: an essay in the philosophy of language* London. Cambridge Univ. Press.

Sebeok, T. A. ed. (1960) *Style in Language* Cambridge Mass. MIT.

Selinker, L. (1972) 'Interlanguage' in *IRAL* 10 1972 repr. in Richards, J. C. ed. 1974.

Shannon, C. E. & Weaver, W. (1949) *The Mathematical Theory of Communication* Urbana. Univ. of Illinois Press.

Sinclair, J. Mc. H. & Coulthard, R. M. (1975) *Towards an Analysis of Discourse: the English used by Teachers & Pupils.* Oxford. Oxford U. P.

Skinner, B. F. (1957) *Verbal Behavior* New York Appleton-Century-Croft.

Spencer, J. (1973) 'Languages for Special Purposes; teaching rules or learning rules?' in De Grève et al eds. 1973.

Spolsky, B. ed. (1979) *Papers in Applied Linguistics: Advances in Testing: Series 1* Washington. Center for Applied Linguistics.

Stevick, E. W. (1976) *Memory, meaning and method: some psychological perspectives on language learning.* Rowley. Mass. Newbury House.

Strevens, P. (1977) *New Orientations in the Teaching of English* Oxford. Oxford Univ. Press.

Stringer, D. (1973) *Language Variation and English* Part of *Language & Learning* (E262) Block 1. Milton Keynes. Open Univ. Press.

Svartvik, J. ed. (1973) *Errata: Papers in Error Analysis.* Lund. CWK Gleerup.

Sweet, H. (1964) *The practical study of languages* Oxford. Oxford Univ. Press 1st publ. 1899.

Thomas, O. (1965) *Transformational Grammar and the Teacher of English* New York. Holt Rinehart.

Ticknor, G. (1832) *Lecture on the best methods of teaching living languages* Harvard.

Titone, R. (1968) *Teaching Foreign Languages: an historical sketch* Washington. Georgetown Univ. Press.

Todorov, K. (1966) 'Les Categories du Récit Litteraire' in *Communications* vol. 8.

Trim, J. L. M. (1977) *Report on some possible lines of development of an overall structure for a European unit/credit scheme for foreign language learning by adults.* Strasbourg. Council of Europe.

Tyler, S. A. ed (1969) *Cognitive Anthropology* New York. Holt Rinehart.

Valette, R. M. (1967) *Modern Language Testing: a Handbook* New York. Harcourt Brace & World.

Widdowson, H. G. (1971) 'The Teaching of Rhetoric to Students of Science and Technology' in Perren ed. 1971.

Widdowson, H. G. (1978) *Teaching Language as Communication.* Oxford. Oxford Univ. Press.

Wilkins, D. A. (1973) 'The Linguistic and Situational Content of the Common Core in a Unit/Credit System' in *Systems development in adult language learning* Strasbourg. Council of Europe.

Wilkins, D. A. (1976) *Notional Syllabuses* Oxford. Oxford Univ. Press.

General index

Structuralist linguistics (*cont.*)
   I.C. analysis 94, 102
   and language learning 95, 226f
   materials 97, 219–28
   and nature of language 92f, 226
   syllabus 56
Syllabus see also 'evaluation', 'grading',
    'programmes'
   a posteriori 53, 61f
   a priori 53, 57, 61f
   design of 41–46, 165–67
   grading of 50–53
   grammatical 53, 56f
   notional 55–57, 110, 146–51
   organization of 62–70
   responsibility for 28
   selection of items in 50–53
   sequencing of items in 50–53
   situational 54f, 57, 110, 143–46

Technique see 'materials'
Testing see also 'evaluation' and 'tests'
    33–40, 46–48, 164, 184–217
   criterion-referenced 190, 212
   discrete point 195
   effectiveness 35, 46–48, 169f, 186–90
   efficiency 35, 46–48, 169f, 186–90
   of input 33f, 39f
   integrative 195
   norm-referenced 190, 212
   of output 35, 46–48
   of skills 164
Tests see also 'evaluation' and 'testing'
    190–216
   aptitude 192, 201–4
   attainment 192f, 205
   aural comprehension 204f
   cloze 194, 207f
   content 192–96

Davies 192
diagnostic 193, 207f
Foreign Service Institute 196, 209–12
G.C.E. 193
as measuring instruments 190f
Michigan 192, 204f
objective 191
practicability 200f
private 197
procedure 191
proficiency 192, 212–16
prognostic 192
public 196
purpose 192f
reliability 197, 199f
self-assessment 212–16
TEOFL 192, 195
validity 197–99
Text 135–42
   defined 135
   and dialogue 135–42
Trainees see 'learners'
Training see also 'programmes' and
    'syllabus' 35, 37, 184–90
   adaptive system 186–90
   ballistic system 184
   defined 37
   guided system 184–86
Transformational-generative linguistics
    see also 'grammar' 90, 99–110,
    180f, 228–34
   and applied linguistics 100
   and description of language 100–04
   and error 106, 180f
   and language learning 104–07, 233
   materials 107–09, 228–34
   and nature of language 100, 105, 232f
   and structuralism 104f

Index of personal names

Abercrombie, 119
Aesop, 80
Alexander, 78, 193
Allen, 199, 201, 216
Alyeshmerni, 91
Austin, 113, 121, 132, 148, 151

Banathy, 56, 71
Barthes, 135
Bates, 70
Bell, 23, 31, 38, 42, 46, 61, 76, 119,
    124, 127, 132, 147, 150, 182, 196,
    212
Berlitz, 80
Berne, 46, 63, 135
Berry, 117
Bhatnager, 150, 193, 207, 208
Bowen, 107, 232–34
Boydell, 37, 56, 159, 160, 266
Brethower, 35, 184, 190
Bright, 31
Brooks, 96
Broughton, 78
Brown, 139
Byrne, 44, 56

Candlin, 44, 71, 218
Chatman, 135
Chomsky, 24, 30, 99, 101, 105, 113,
    115, 116, 154
Christophersen, 31
Cicourel, 23
Comenius, 80
Corder, 31, 62, 172, 173, 181
Crystal, 31, 119, 128
Curran, 63, 64, 65, 66, 67, 256

Davies, 41, 56
Derrick, 70
Dulay, 171
Diller, 71, 76, 87

Eckersley, 78
van Ek, 152
Einstein, 100

Fillmore, 117

Firth, 116, 248
Frake, 23
de Freitas, 150, 248, 253
Fries, 92, 97f, 105, 110f, 176, 182,
    219, 225
Floyd, 111

Gattegno, 63, 256
Getzels, 152
Green, 197
Greenberg, 20, 23
Greene, 110
Gregory, 119

Hajjaj, 70
Halliday, 116, 117, 131, 152
Harris, 56, 191, 216
Harris, 99
Hasan, 134, 152
Heaton, 193, 200, 216
Herbert, 131
Hill, 134
Howatt, 68–70, 201
Hörmann, 79
Hull, 96
Hymes, 77, 125

Jackson, 216
Jakobson, 120
Jespersen, 87, 88, 91, 135, 139
Joos, 118

Kirkham, 81f
Krohn, 219, 225
Kuo, 128
Kurath, 118

Labov, 77
Lado, 97f, 111, 176, 177, 182, 216, 219
Leech, 147, 194
Locke, 80
Lyons, 110

Mackey, 44, 60, 71
McGregor, 31
Mercer, 132
Miller, 59, 105